THE EVOLUTION OF SELF PSYCHOLOGY

Progress in Self Psychology
Volume 7

Progress in Self Psychology

Editor, Arnold Goldberg, M.D.

THE EVOLUTION OF SELF PSYCHOLOGY

Progress in Self Psychology
Volume 7

Arnold Goldberg
editor

THE ANALYTIC PRESS

1991   Hillsdale, NJ   London

Copyright © 1991 by The Analytic Press
365 Broadway
Hillsdale, NJ 07642

ISBN 0-88163-130-2
ISSN 0893-5483

Printed in the United States of America
10 9 8 7 6 5 4 3 2 1

Acknowledgment

The preparation of this book was financed in part by funds from the Harry and Hazel Cohen Research Fund. Ms. Chris Susman provided secretarial and editorial assistance.

Contents

Contributors

Howard A. Bacal, M.D., Training and Supervising Analyst, Toronto Institute of Psychoanalysis; Coauthor (with K.M. Newman), *Theories of Object Relations: Bridges to Self Psychology* (1990, Columbia University Press).

Michael F. Basch, M.D., Professor of Psychiatry, Rush Medical College; Training Analyst, Institute for Psychoanalysis, Chicago.

Bernard Brandchaft, M.D., Training and Supervising Analyst, Los Angeles Psychoanalytic Institute; coauthor (with R. Stolorow and G. E. Atwood) of *Psychoanalytic Treatment: An Intersubjective Approach* (1987, The Analytic Press).

James L. Fosshage, Ph.D., Core Faculty, Institute for the Psychoanalytic Study of Subjectivity; Faculty Member and Supervisor, Postdoctoral Program in Psychoanalysis, New York University.

Robert Galatzer-Levy, M.D., Faculty, Institute for Psychoanalysis, Chicago; Lecturer in Psychiatry, University of Chicago.

Raanan Kulka, M.A., Training and Supervising Analyst, Israel Institute of Psychoanalysis; Clinical Director, Milgo-Institute of Psychoanalytic Psychotherapy for Children and Adolescents, Jerusalem.

Frank M. Lachmann, Ph.D., Core-faculty, Institute for the Psychoanalytic Study of Subjectivity, New York City; Training Analyst, Senior Supervisor, Postgraduate Center for Mental Health, New York City.

Jule P. Miller, Jr., M.D., Training and Supervising Analyst and Past Director, St. Louis Psychoanalytic Institute.

Hyman L. Muslin, M.D., Professor of Psychiatry, University of Illinois College of Medicine, Chicago.

Anna Ornstein, M.D., Professor of Child Psychiatry, University of Cincinnati College of Medicine; private practice of psychoanalysis.

Paul H. Ornstein, M.D., Professor of Psychiatry, University of Cincinnati College of Medicine; Co-Director, International Center for the Study of Psychoanalytic Self Psychology, Department of Psychiatry.

Karen Peoples, Ph.D., Associate Professor and Clinical Supervisor, Doctoral Psychology Department, California Institute of Integral Studies; private practice, clinical psychology, San Francisco, CA.

Estelle Shane, Ph.D., Founding President, Center for Early Education and College of Developmental Studies, Los Angeles; Assistant Clinical Professor, Department of Psychiatry, UCLA.

Morton Shane, M.D., Director of Education, Training and Supervising Analyst in Adult and Child, Los Angeles Psychoanalytic Society and Institute; Associate Clinical Professor, Department of Psychiatry, UCLA.

Peter Thomson, M.D., Assistant Professor of Psychiatry, University of Toronto; Training and Supervising Analyst, Toronto Institute for Psychoanalysis.

Paul Tolpin, M.D., Senior Attending, Michael Reese Hospital, Chicago; Training and Supervising Analyst, Institute for Psychoanalysis, Chicago.

Rachel Wahba, L.C.S.W., Clinical Supervisor, Operation Concern, Pacific Presbyterian Medical Center, San Francisco; private practice.

Deborah Weinstein, M.A., M.F.C.C., Clinical Faculty, Langley Porter Neuropsychiatric Institute, San Francisco; private practice.

Ernest S. Wolf, M.D., Faculty, Training and Supervising Analyst, Institute for Psychoanalysis, Chicago; Assistant Professor of Psychiatry, Northwestern University Medical School, Chicago.

Introduction: Self Psychology Searches for Its Self

Robert M. Galatzer-Levy

Self psychology is no longer a unity. Like other revolutions in thought, self psychology's essence was at first embodied in the person of its creator. For long periods, metaphysics remained Aristotelian, physics Newtonian, Communism Marxist, evolution Darwinian, and psychoanalysis, Freudian. In other fields, no matter how well based the deviation or consistent with the founder's teaching, deviation from the received image of the master's theory meant leaving the discipline. This does not seem to be self psychology's fate, at least up to the present. As this volume illustrates, Kohut's death did not halt the development of self psychology. Instead, self psychologists have created diverse points of view that amplify, extend, and correct Kohut's work.

Some of the reasons for this rapid evolution are apparent. First, Kohut's ideas were not thoroughly worked through and were clearly changing when he died, so they entreat further development rather than dogmatic adherence. Second, as Wolf demonstrates, Kohut's thinking is part of a new, increasingly egalitarian world view in which received truth can never play the central role. Third, Kohut and many of those he attracted to himself were iconoclasts whose creativity involved the reaction against venerated points of view; orthodoxy would never satisfy them. Finally, self psychology's contribution to understanding idealization means that many self psychologists have thought about and, to varying extents, worked through the meaning of idealization of a leader, and so these self psychologists are more likely to have freed themselves of the limiting effects of this idealization.

As welcome as the free spirit of self psychology is, this same free spirit leaves us perplexed about the nature of the field. Each of the authors represented in this volume in some sense addresses the question of the essence of self psychology. What are the implicit theories of knowledge that inform self psychology? What are the data of the field? What are selfobject and objects and how are they related? How do formulations from other psychoanalytic perspectives relate to those of self psychology? To what clinical and extra-clinical situations is self psychology applicable? What is the self that preoccupies us so?

WHAT ARE THE IMPLICIT THEORIES OF KNOWLEDGE THAT INFORM SELF PSYCHOLOGY?

Kohut's interest in epistemology was limited to ensuring that the empathic point of view on observation not be labeled "unscientific." His remarks on the topic (e.g., Kohut, 1977), were confined to observations that respectable scientists, such as physicists, have discarded the epistemological views of the 19th century, so that psychoanalysts need not feel bound to these archaic views. Analysts, like Schafer (1970, 1975) and Klein (1976), presented thorough critiques of mechanistic views of the mind, but these mechanistic formulations continued to play an important role in Kohut's thinking, all be it in some new forms, like the bipolar self. Although Goldberg (1988) and Stolorow, Brandchaft, and Atwood (1987) presented sophisticated visions of the nature of knowledge, especially knowledge about human psychology, the main impact of these views generates questions of the admissability of various kinds of data to the discourse of self psychology. Self psychology largely continues in a mode of naive realism about entities like self, selfobject, and mind despite careful commentary that suggests more sophisticated positions.

WHAT ARE THE DATA OF SELF PSYCHOLOGY?

Many self psychologists regard Kohut's (1957) *Introspection, Empathy and Psychoanalysis* as the seminal paper of the field. Once the psychoanalyst uses empathy as his principle means for understanding other people, many of the findings of self psychology—the primacy of the self, the role of selfobject functions, the various means by which the self is protected—follow from its systematic application. The empathic point of view virtually ensures close attention to clinical experience, since this viewpoint assumes that information derived by means other than vicarious introspection (which is best achieved in the clinical situation), has no place in psychoanalysis. Kohut's position was either a major step forward or a major step backward, depending upon the analyst's opinion of the importance of drives and related concepts derived from biology.

In the three decades since the publication of *Introspection, Empathy and Psychoanalysis* problems as well as rewards of the empathic position have become evident. Archaic biological and mechanistic theories are automatically expunged from psychoanalytic thinking when this point of view is consistently adopted. Interestingly, newer, and more promising points of view, extrinsic to psychoanalysis, were also excluded. Basch (1976, 1990), for example, observed that ideas derived from infant observation and theories about information and cybernetics address matters central to self psychology. Although Kohut's equation of a discipline with its prevailing mode of observation has proved inordinately fruitful in the development of self psychology and possesses an undeniably logical force, many students of human psychology find that discarding promising ideas derived from other sources is too high a price to pay for methodological purity.

In the realm of clinical data, the empathic point of view opposed an emerging trend in psychoanalysis, using countertransference as a central source of information about patients (Racker, 1968; Blum, 1986; Tyson, 1986; Boyer, 1989). Kohut (1971) viewed countertransference in a very traditional fashion, that is, as interference with the empathic comprehension of the patient caused by inadequately analyzed elements in the analyst's personality. The analyst's wishes to avoid blaming the patient for his own negative responses to the patient and the intricate but sometimes virtually telephatic mechanisms of countertransference suggested by Kleinians all discouraged self psychologists from exploring this rich source of data. Thompson's discussion (this volume) illustrates how the data of countertransference can be used from an intersubjective perspective and raises the question of the status of this data within self psychology.

Like transference, empathic observations are not limited to the psychoanalytic setting; empathic observations are a daily fact of life. The traditional psychoanalytic setting does, however, provide extraordinary opportunities for prolonged immersion in the psychological life of another person. When do the conditions of observation become so problematic that we no longer find the data reliable? In this volume, Miller and his discussants study the relationship between psychotherapy and psychoanalysis and Weinstein's data regarding exhibitionism in group psychotherapy implicitly address this question. Less directly, Muslin's reexamination of Hamlet's psychology raises many old questions as to the meaning of psychological data derived from the study of fictional characters: Does it inform us about the author's psychology? Does it tell us about the reader? Are the findings from fictional characters properly extended to include real people? (Trosman, 1985). How are we to determine if data collected outside of the psychoanalytic situation is too superficial, too unrealistic, or too distorted by extrinsic factors to be useful in formulating psychological ideas? How severely do we limit our psychological thinking by excluding data from these other sources?

Self psychologists do not, at this time, share a point of view as to exactly what constitutes adequate and appropriate data within the field. Our several implicit and explicit positions about the data of self psychology are a major challenge to the field.

What is the Nature of Selfobjects and Objects?

Psychoanalysts often debate about definitions although their real concerns are psychological. Like Tweedledom, we can choose the meanings of words as we please, provided that we are willing to state clearly what we mean by the words. In the course of clinical psychoanalyses, Kohut discovered, as others had discovered long before the invention of psychoanalysis, that the experience of other people can serve as an aspect, or support of, an endangered self. He systematically described some of the ways that the analyst selfobject functions and posited a "cradle to grave" line of selfobject functioning based on reconstructions from analyses, informal observations, and various cultural experiences. Kohut's formulation of the selfobject concept proved inordinately useful in work with a wide range of patients, and the concept is the basis of the popularity of this theories among clinicians.

However, selfobjects are abstractions. They are neither the entities that serve selfobject functions nor the full experience of those entities, but rather the aspect of those experiences that contribute to the self. What at first appears to be a rather theoretical discussion in Basch and Ornstein's chapter about the selfobject concept and its relations to the psychoanalytic concept of object is, in fact, an attempt to address a problem that has plagued thinkers for millennia: Why are people so important to one another? If the self is forever vulnerable to disruption and enfeeblement in the absence of adequate selfobjects, our attitudes toward others must be profoundly shaped by this fact. This is true even if the forms of selfobject function change across the course of life. Alternatively, less intense selfobject needs may open the way for people to have other psychological meanings and functions. Possibly, some people evolve so that selfobject function need no longer be provided by their relations with other people. These seem to me to be empirical issues. We need to use specific terms when making empirical studies, but the question of what we mean to each other cannot be resolved by discussing the analyst's language.

One reason for wanting to be precise about psychoanalytic terms like *object* is that if self psychology shares a common ground with other psychoanalytic perspectives that have studied a group of phenomena, then self psychology can freely borrow from these studies. However, if similar terms disguise profound differences of meaning, a dangerous confusion of tongues can result.

How Do Formulations From Other Psychoanalytic Perspectives Relate to Self Psychology?

For more than 70 years, psychoanalysts using very different perspectives than self psychology have worked with patients who we would think of as suffering from disorders of the self. Melanie Klein and her students, as well as a wide range of object relations theorists whose ideas derive in varying measure from Klein's, describe many of the clinical phenomena so readily observable in these patients. Yet the basic notion held by these analysts of what these patients are trying to do is often radically at odds with a self psychology point of view. Even on this deeper level, integration of the various viewpoints is often possible. For example, the vicissitudes of destructiveness described by Klein can be understood as attempted solutions to the problems generated by chronic, narcissistic rage.

Some of the authors in this volume, such as Bacal and Wahba, see a fruitful cross fertilization between object relations theories and self psychology. Wahba, in particular, working on a clinical level, demonstrates how a Kleinian sensitivity to issues of envy can fruitfully combine with an understand of selfobject transferences to reveal an important clinical configuration. Others, like Ornstein, see the two viewpoints as so alien, both in theory and practice, that integrative attempts only serve to muddy the waters.

How and whether self psychologists should use other psychoanalytic perspectives in clinical and theoretical work seems to me to be one of the major strategic questions in the development of our field. The same question naturally applies to the use of ideas from other investigative fields.

TO WHAT CLINICAL SITUATIONS IS SELF PSYCHOLOGY APPLICABLE?

Self psychology's origins and success come from the inadequacy of older psychoanalytic concepts in the understanding and treatment of people with disorders of the self. Just as Freud generalized his findings about the psychology of hysterics to all of mankind, Kohut developed a general psychology of the self from his study of disorders of the self. Although self psychology is an attractive, general, explanatory framework for human psychology, just as Freudian theory was, its findings have only been tested in depth in the psychoanalysis of relatively well put together people. Broader application, no matter how attractive and exciting, requires careful scrutiny. In this volume, Peoples presents an engaging proposal about the effects of incest on the developing self; Weinstein reports a fascinating experience of the vicissitudes of mirroring within a group; Muslin applies self psychology concepts to understanding Hamlet. Miller, Tolpin and Fosshage each address the sameness and differences of analysis and psychotherapy from a self-psychological perspective. All of these efforts are most welcome; some of them certainly expand the range of self psychology.

Psychoanalysts were the objects of well deserved criticism when they applied insights from the analytic situation to the larger world without carefully investigating the problems inherent in this move. Self psychology can learn from that experience. We should not avoid widening the scope of self psychology, but we should do so only after careful exploration as to whether such insights are appropriate.

WHERE'S THE SELF?

This seventh volume of *Progress in Self Psychology* continues a long, paradoxical tradition. The volume contains virtually no discussion of the self. Basch reiterates Stern's (1985, 1989) description of early aspects of the self, but even here the core concepts remain unaddressed.[1] Kohut's protestation that the self is an "experience near" concept is a fancy way of saying "you know what I mean."

---

[1]Stern's formulations, which are less firmly based in observational data than his writings suggest, refer to disparate psychological functions that share the common feature of being closely related to what we call the self in the mature individual. But the precise relationship of these functions and experiences to what we think of as the self remains unclear. The situation is similar to Erikson's concepts of identity, which as Kohut (1971) observed, is not only different from the self but falls within a different conceptual framework. Though identity is an important support of the self, it is distinct from the self.

One solution to the problem of the self is to abandon it. As Wolf (1988) observed, self psychology is really selfobject psychology. The great contributions of self psychology have been to the understanding of selfobject function. Perhaps we do not need a clear conceptualization of the self to enable us to realize good selfobject psychology. We may be in the position of a botanist, whose interest in the sun lies only in the extent to which it produces light and heat here on earth. Though he recognizes that all life evolves from the sun, he has no need to concern himself with astrosphysics to explain the phenomena in his particular field of interest.

Since the concept of self and the essential nature of the self seems to have eluded the greatest thinkers of all ages, it is hardly an embarrassment that we self psychologists have not achieved more. Still I believe that an elucidation of the concept of self is central to our ongoing search.

CONCLUSION

At this point in the evolution of self psychology, the borders of the field of self psychology are indistinct and the field's central concepts need conceptual and empirical clarification. The current volume reflects the complexities of a growing field. As Wolf observes in this volume, self psychology reflects a shift in outlook as much as a specific concept. This exploratory, egalitarian, and relativistic position reflects the spirit of the age (see also Galatzer-Levy and Cohler, 1990; Cohler and Galatzer-Levy, in press). The search for the self continues along a diversity of paths, many of them very different from those anticipated or approved by Kohut. "Kohut's legacy" may be, as he wished, that self psychology is not Kohutian.

REFERENCES

Basch, M. F. (1976), The concept of affect: a re-examination. *J. Amer. Psychoanal. Assn.*, 24:759–777.

Basch, M. (1990), *Understanding Psychotherapy*. New York: Basic Books.

Blum, H. P. (1986), Countertransference and the theory of technique: Discussion. *J. Amer. Psychoanal. Assn.*, 34, 309–328.

Boyer, L. B. (1989), Countertransference and technique in working with the regressed patient: Further remarks. *Internat. J. Psycho-Anal.*, 70:701–714.

Cohler, B., & Galatzer-Levy, R. (in press), *American Psychological Association Centenary* volume.

Galatzer-Levy, R. & Cohler, B. (1990), The developmental psychology of the self. *The Annual of Psychoanalysis*, 18:1–43. Hillsdale, NJ: The Analytic Press.

Goldberg, A. (1988), *A Fresh Look at Psychoanalysis*. Hillsdale, NJ: The Analytic Press.

Klein, G. (1976), *Psychoanalytic Theory: An Exploration of Essentials*. New York: International Universities Press.

Kohut, H. (1957), Introspection, empathy, and psychoanalysis: An examination of the relationship between mode of observation and theory. In: *The Search for the Self, Vol. 1*, ed. P. Ornstein. New York: International Universities Press, pp. 205–232.

_____ (1971), *The Analysis of the Self*. New York: International Universities Press.

_____ (1977), *The Restoration of the Self*. New York: International Universities Press.

Racker, H. (1968), *Transference and Counter-Transference*. New York: International Universities Press.

Schafer, R. (1970), The psychoanalytic vision of reality. *Internat. J. Psycho-Anal.*, 51:279–297.

_____ (1975), *Psychoanalysis without psychodynamics. Internat. J. Psycho-Anal.*, 56:41–55.

Stern, D. (1985), *The Interpersonal World of the Infant*. New York: Basic Books.

_____ (1989), Developmental prerequisites for the sense of a narrated self. In: *Psychoanalysis: Toward the Second Century*, ed. A. Cooper, O' Kernberg & E. Person. New Haven, CT: Yale University Press, pp. 168–180.

Stolorow, R., Brandchaft, B., & Atwood, G. (1987), *Psychoanalytic Treatment: An Intersubjective Approach*. Hillsdale, NJ: The Analytic Press.

Trosman, H. (1985), *Freud and the Imaginative World*. Hillsdale, NJ: The Analytic Press.

Tyson, R. L. (1986), Countertransference evolution in theory and practice. *J. Amer. Psychoanal. Assn.*, 34:251–274.

Wolf, E. (1988), *Treating the Self: Elements of Clinical Self Psychology*. New York: Guilford Press.

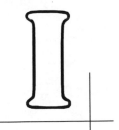

Theory

Chapter 1

Are Selfobjects the Only Objects? Implications for Psychoanalytic Technique

Michael Franz Basch

Are there objects other than selfobjects? Since the word "object" in psychoanalysis is not only a vestige of the biologically disproven instinct theory advanced by Freud (see Basch 1975, 1984) but has also been equated with "person," the question must be modified. When we use the term selfobject, we are referring to a hypothesis about normal development made by Heinz Kohut, an extrapolation back to infancy from observations made by him in the analyses of adults. Kohut (1971) noted that in the analysis of Miss F, and later in that of other patients, he was treated, not as an individual in his own right, but dealt with as if he were no more than an extension of the patient; the patient expected him to understand, anticipate, and meet her needs, and then to disappear until his services were again required. When Kohut taught himself to accept the patient's demands as not being evasions and focused on understanding the meaning of what she was trying to tell him rather than insisting that she meet his preconceived expectations of what should happen in an analysis, Miss F was able to mature. Using this and similar patient experiences, Kohut drew the following conclusions: The vulnerable infant frequently requires the help of caregivers to meet his physical and psychological needs. Through the caregiver's intercession, the infant eventually learns to perform for himself the functions that previously he could not carry out—this process Kohut called *transmuting internalization.* Transmuting internalization leads to the formation of *psychic structure* and to the expansion and strengthening of the

3

cohesive self. Ultimately, this process eventuates in healthy, normal maturity, by which Kohut meant, (adhering to the biologist C.D. King's, (1945) definition), functioning according to design.

Significant failure to meet an infant's or a child's needs, *empathic failure*, creates faults in psychic structure that later manifest themselves, (as they did in Miss F), in an inappropriate infantile demanding that represents a chronically damaged and continuously threatened self, a self in need of experiences that might correct the damage done by inadequate and/or insufficient empathic responsiveness in early development.

Because the infant is not yet able to differentiate self and other conceptually, Kohut hypothesized that although to the objective observer the parent was an individual, an "object" in the traditional language of Freud's dual instinct theory of motivation, to the infant the parent was part of his undifferentiated self experience. Hence, Kohut, who at that time still adhered to the instinct theory, coined the term *selfobject*. However, although Kohut initially referred to selfobject in the traditional sense as being a person invested by the infant with narcissistic libido, he altered this in *The Restoration of the Self* (1977), after which he used selfobject to refer to a postulated, intrapsychic experience. He also concluded that maturity and selfobject experiences are not mutually exclusive; this led to a distinction between archaic and mature selfobject experiences. All people, when stress of one sort or another threatens to fragment, devitalize, or in other ways disorganize the self, need selfobject experiences to heal themselves. This need is not a pathological one unless it is for archaic rather than mature or age-appropriate selfobject experiences. Therefore, the question we should ask is: Are there other object experiences besides selfobject experiences? That is, are there situations in which infants, children, and adults are not in a state where selfobject experiences are needed to maintain the structure of the self? My answer to that is "Yes,"—when the individual is functioning, as Kohut defined functioning, as a center of independent initiative or a cohesive self.

Since, unfortunately, we are still mired in the terminology of Freud's instinct theory, I suggest that, in keeping with the usage of selfobject or selfobject experience to refer to a situation in which an endangered self is strengthened by the intervention of another, we use the word "object" or the term object experience to refer to a situation in which a cohesive self is expressing itself affectively—for instance, distress, affection, anger, fear, shame, love, hate, and so on, signaling an attempt to effect a certain outcome or solve a particular problem without the self structure being endangered; neither the use of selfobject or object referring to instinctual discharge, but only referring to the structural state of the self system (Basch, 1988).

There are those who, like Wolf (1988), think of the selfobject experience as any experience that either maintains the cohesiveness of the self, strengthens the self, or is otherwise related to the self. In that case, of course, there are no other experiences other than selfobject experiences because one cannot imagine anything happening to an individual, at least on the psychological level, that is not related to the self system. However, such a definition vitiates Kohut's seminal idea of a particular sort of experience that makes up for an inadequacy in the self structure; and, furthermore, undermines the concept of a cohesive self as a center of initiative—a concept which seems to imply at least a contrast between the well functioning self and the self in need of support.

Anna Ornstein (personal communication), favoring Wolf's position, suggests that the learning experience is a selfobject experience leading to transmuting internalization, though the self of the learner may not be endangered. I would disagree with that interpretation. Insofar as the self system of the infant (or a child or adult) is operating cohesively in an age-appropriate manner, learning takes place in the context of an object experience. In other words, transmuting internalization and selfobject experience should not be equated. Transmuting internalization is the broader concept and can be used to describe what may happen when an endangered self benefits from a selfobject experience, as well as what may occur when a cohesive self engages an object experience. By the same token, learning or transmuting internalization need not necessarily accompany either state. (This is what happens in psychopathology, where, prior to effective therapy, the potential for anxiety precludes growth through transmuting internalization.)

To understand the practical implications of both the selfobject concept and the functioning of a cohesive self, it is necessary to take a look at normal development and the forces behind it; neither Freud nor Kohut did this. Freud had no choice; he had to try to construct a theory of normal development from his study of psychoneurotic patients because no viable theory of brain functioning and brain development existed at the time. Kohut, believing that psychoanalysis was best served by concepts generated from clinical observation, made a deliberate choice to ignore the burgeoning field of normal infant studies and what was being learned about the functioning and developing brain. As a result, though Kohut's concept of the selfobject need of an endangered self is very much in keeping with what infant research has also discovered. However, many of his other conclusions regarding development are contradicted by what brain science and observation of, and experiments with, infants and children have to teach us. One of the most significant errors Kohut made in his conclusions regarding development is his concept of a virtual self; that is, the idea that a cohesive self is not present at the beginning of life and comes into play only somewhere around the second year. Till then, according to Kohut, the self of the infant exists only in the mind of the mother who sees her baby as a person. The implication here is that before the second year, there is no cohesive self system, no sense of self, the baby being perforce merged with the mother throughout that time. Were that so, then indeed all experiences of the infant would be selfobject experiences; without the mother's constant intercession, there would be only fragmentation and, by force of circumstances, infancy would resemble nothing more than a borderline state. However, that is not the case.

Stern (1985) cites his own and others' evidence to demonstrate that a sense of self is present from birth, if not before, and that after the second month, what Kohut termed a cohesive self is present. This evidence has some interesting and important implications for the treatment process; it affects our way of thinking about selfobject transferences, and about the process of transmuting internalization, that is, what is learned when and how. Stern talks about various stages in the development of the sense of self: emergent, core, subjective, verbal, and, though not in his 1985 book but added later, the sense of a narrative self (Zeanah, Anders, Seifer, and Stern, 1989).

SENSE OF AN EMERGENT SELF (0-2 MONTHS)

The infant's orientation, with his caregivers' help, to the environment into which he has been thrust gives him his first sense of self. It is the very activity of extracting meaningful information from a multitude of stimuli and experiencing the dependable rhythms that make up his existence that allows a sense of self to emerge. So it is throughout life; the process of orientation is the foundation of maintaining one's sense of oneself as a cohesive entity.

The trained and skilled observer can identify evidence of a cohesive self in infants of this early age. Fajardo (1991) describes a well-functioning, premature infant at 32 weeks postconception: Darla

> easily established rhythmic behaviors such as sucking and rapid eye movement patterns, and her startles during a lengthy quiet sleep period were also rhythmic . . . Darla was a good example of an infant who had a remarkable capacity for self-soothing. Even at this young

age she was able to accomplish some successful hand-to-mouth movements. Particularly notable were her lengthy awake states, as she lay calmly and intently surveying her surroundings. She seemed to be able to experience a cause–effect relationship between her eye movements and her visual sensations. This seemed to be a pleasurable experience, one which she prolonged and repeated on other occasions [p. 116].

Fajardo goes on to speculate that "characteristic of Darla's emerging self is her experience that organizational processes come about reliably and spontaneously, and that there is a steadiness about the relatedness of one experience to another" (pp. 13–14).

As described, we realize that this baby and others like her are functioning as centers of initiative, as age-appropriate, cohesive selves. They are not blobs or tabulae rasae waiting to be programmed by the parent, but are seeking and utilizing stimulation to generally make sense out of the world. No doubt, such self-starting activity is performed against the background of the parents' empathic immersion in the child's needs. When that immersion is missing, or when for reasons, such as prematurity or illness, the infant cannot use the parents' attempts at meeting its needs, then—and Fajardo describes such cases—the cohesive self is not able to form and function, and the potential for pathology is present; but, as will be discussed, in these cases the selfobject experience deficits and the consequences of such will be quite different from those deficits Kohut found in narcissistic personality disorders and, therefore, the therapeutic intervention needed will also differ.

SENSE OF A CORE SELF (2-7 MONTHS)

At this point, the baby learns to experience itself as an invariant center of activity and perception. Everything in the environment changes, sometimes only in minor ways, at other times dramatically, but what remains steady for the infant is the sense of itself as an attentive observer, as an initiator of action, and as a locus for bodily sensation. Now the infant begins to organize and generalize experience into practical action schemas, which it then repeats when seemingly similar conditions of experience arise. In this way, the infant encodes rules for behavior that greatly increase his or her effectiveness; and, the more effective, the stronger the infant's cohesive self. Failure to achieve efficacy or competence arouses the affect of distress and the need for selfobject experiences that will set the learning process back on the right track. It is in the latter case that learning and the subsequent formation of psychic structure takes place as Kohut suggested through optimal frustration.

However, that is not the only way in which psychic structure forms. As Lachmann and Beebe (1988) described, there are at least four roads to structure formation. The fundamental process is that of ongoing mutual and self regulation, that is, mother and infant form a system in which the responses to one another regulate and maintain the relationship, while at the same time the infant is also regulating his own self. There are three ancillary forms of structure formation that are particular variants of the basic process: frustration and gratification (which was so important for Freud); rupture and repair (Kohut's optimal frustration); and the structure-forming effects of heightened affective moments (Pine). This is why it is incorrect to speak, as Kohut did, of the cohesive self as an independent center of initiative; the effects of mutual regulation are always in evidence in self functioning, even when the infant is not in the company of its mother. It would be much more accurate, based on the previous description of the core self, to speak of the cohesive self as an invariant center of initiative, or what later gives rise (when conceptual thinking becomes possible) to the sense of identity, or what Federn (1952) called the "Ich-gefühl."

SENSE OF A SUBJECTIVE SELF (7-9 MONTHS)

In this phase, the infant seems to become aware of the other in the sense of needing affective validation—what Stern calls *affect attunement*—for his activities and state of being. The infant expects the mother to participate with him or her in some way, conveying that experience is being mutually shared and the infant's self state understood. Failure in this phase may result in the problems that lead to narcissistic personality disorders, and it is this type of empathic failure with which Kohut made us familiar.

SENSE OF A VERBAL (PRIVATE) SELF (15-18 MONTHS)

Infancy ends and childhood begins when reflection and evocative recall become a possibility. The infant lives in the present, he accommodates to the immediate situation, and assimilates what he learns from experience into patterns of expectation with which he meets the next event. The unique capacity of human beings for unlimited reflection, made possible by symbolic representation of events, makes possible evocative recall and fantasy and the concepts of past and future. Words are especially powerful symbols that can be used to recreate the past and to plan for the future. An inner reality or private world can be created that may enhance actual experience, falsify it through fantasy, or forecast a reality that has not yet been experienced and may never be experienced. It is the presence of a manipulable intrapsychic reality that makes us human beings, and it is with the onset of this phase of development that what Freud called the "primary process" makes its appearance. Obviously, "primary" is a misnomer, as this fantasy-distorted record of experience comes quite late in the development of the self.

Sense of a Narrative (Consensually Validatable) Self (36 Months)

Not discussed by Stern in his 1985 book, but added later by him (Zeanah et al., 1989), the sense of a narrative self is the contribution made to the self when one either privately thinks over, or shares with others, the scripts and working models for orientation and action that one has developed. It is a way of rethinking and then validating or dismissing the solutions for problems or other plans for action one is considering.

According to Stern, each phase of development does not end when the next one comes on line; rather, each phase continues its development and plays a part in the ongoing maturation of the individual. Practically speaking, what this means is that, in evaluating a patient and thinking about a treatment plan, we can approach the situation from a developmental point of view.

The self, as I have explicated elsewhere (Basch, 1988), is a collective noun that subsumes the hierarchy of information processing feedback cycles that adapt us to our environment while assimilating the environment to our needs. The self is one aspect of the ordering function of the brain. So, to use Kohut's definition, when we speak of the self, or the cohesive self, as a center of initiative, what we are talking about operationally is, to use Fajardo's (1991) apt description, the capacity to become organized and to be reorganized after disruption. This is one instance of what Waddington (1966) called the self-righting principle in biology. As we evaluate a patient, it is very helpful to see how he or she is functioning in each of the domains described by Stern; that is, (a) How has each of these domains matured; (b) What evidence is there for arrests in any one of them; and (c) How readily has the patient dealt with disruptions at any point in this hierarchy.

To illustrate, let me cite the example of a patient, Ms. R, whose treatment I described elsewhere (Basch, 1988, pp. 239ff.). Ms. R. came to therapy with the complaint that though she was successful by the world's standards, she felt unhappy and inwardly dissatisfied — as she summed it up for me, "Outside, hooey! Inside, phooey!"

When I first see a patient, I know that sufficiently detailed insight into what is wrong with that patient will remain an enigma for a period of time. What is available to be studied in depth is what is right with the patient, that is, in what domains of development and in what sectors the patient functions as a cohesive self; is engaged in object experiences and not overcome by selfobject needs and the defenses against those needs.

I should explain what I mean by sectors, a term also used by Kohut. Just as the chronology of development is more than a linear progression from the simple to the more complex, the categories of action in which development is played out are not all of a piece either, nor do they necessarily mature in lock step. So we have the sector of psychosexual development, the aspect of development that Freud did so much to explicate; the sector of attachment, identified by Bowlby (1969) and the focus of Kohut's practical contribution; and the sectors of autonomy and creativity, which are not as well worked out as psychosexual development and attachment.

As my patient, Ms. R., told me about herself, not only her history but the manner in which she related to me, showed me that, in the domain of the emergent self, she functioned in cohesive fashion. Although the rhythm of her life had been disrupted by several divorces and a number of career changes, she recovered well and did not get disoriented. By the same token, her ability to adjust and to learn the rules for functioning in new situations and turning them to her advantage told me that the domain of the core self was, for the most part, intact. One exception to this, in the sector of creativity, was her defensive withdrawal when a manuscript she had submitted to a publisher was summarily rejected. But it was in the domain of the subjective self and in the sector of attachment that she experienced her most serious difficulties. Her longing for approval; her conviction, as it came out very quickly in her relationship to me, that she would not be accepted or understood; and her opportunistic but unsatisfying marriages, all indicated to me that in the domain of the subjective self, Ms. R was functioning only with difficulty. The domains of the verbal or private self and the domain of the narrative self, although undoubtedly affected by the problems of the subjective stage, were essentially intact. She had a rich fantasy life and was able to tell me about her inner world. Indeed, it seemed to me, that the private self and the narrative self had played a great part in defending against the deficit apparent in the domain of the subjective self experience.

Accordingly, I approached the patient as much from her strengths as from her pathology. Kohut (1984) spoke of three kinds of selfobject transferences: the alter-ego or kinship transference, the idealizing transference, and the mirror transference. It has been my experience that the nature of the transference is a function of, and an indicator of, the patient's development, and that the transferences do not exist in isolation but form a developmental sequence. It is during emergent self-development that the basis for kinship is laid down. The later, unspoken conviction that one belongs to humanity generally, and to one's particular cultural subgroups specifically, is the outcome of orienting oneself to the rhythm of life without undue stress, strain, or obstacles—baby Darla provides an example of that. If the process of emergent self-development is seriously impaired, an archaic emergent self may be in evidence in later years (an example of this will be given).

If the capacity for kinship is relatively unimpaired, the next step, the potentiality for idealization, is made possible. Idealization will come on line during the development of the domain of the core self. It is at this time that the infant lays down the rules for accommodation, allowing him or her to develop scripts for behavior in various situations. Given the relative helplessness of the infant, both to carry out many planned actions by itself or to soothe itself when in distress in the increasingly complex world that it is creating for itself. The assistance of the mother or other caregivers is often required. It is in these situations, repeated innumerable times every day, that the infant has the experience of being helped by a greater power that can be called upon when needed. This help and assistance forms the background for the later healthy idealizations that are part of a cohesive self. Finally, during the stage of the subjective self, and building on the groundwork laid down by the capacity for kinship and idealization, the affective validation of one's subjective experience becomes part of self-formation. When these basic needs fail to get appropriate satisfaction, a deficit manifested by selfobject needs, typical of the mirror transference, will evolve in the therapy of an adult so affected.

The infant who has had a reasonable evolution of the self through the first three stages of development enters the domain of the private or verbal self with a security that will prepare the child to cope with the idiosyncratic and fantasy distorted aspects of his or her private world; provided, however, that the parents can be reasonably empathic with that child's sexualized assertiveness in the psychosexual sector. This is what Kohut (1977) meant when he said that everyone has an oedipal phase, but not necessarily an oedipal conflict. Further strengthening of the cohesive self continues as the stage of the narrative self permits the child to increasingly establish the difference between the freedom and uses of his private world and the accommodation necessary to meet the constraints of the environment in which he or she functions. Psychoneuroses develop in relatively rare cases where we see patients who have entered the domain of the verbal or private self essentially undamaged, but have then been traumatized by their parents' inability to respond with equanimity to the child's oedipal development. However, more often than not in our patient population, deficits and resulting shame about needs that have been traumatically frustrated in the first three domains significantly impair the development of the private self and, as described by Kohut (1977), draw oedipal development into the already existing problems.

What this progressive evolution of the selfobject transferences implies, and what I have found to be born out in practice, is that when there is no capacity for kinship, as there often is not in borderline patients who feel alienated from everything and everyone, it is futile to hope that the patient will respond to one's well-meant attempts to hold out the possibility of affect attunement (mirroring) in the domain of the subjective sense of self in the hope that this will aid them in their recovery. Similarly, the absence of the capacity for idealization necessitates that the domain of the sense of a core self be tended to before other steps are taken. In other words, the selfobject transferences do not exist side by side or in isolation; each is part of a hierarchy of self development and it is the whole to which we as therapists need to pay attention.

So, having established that Ms. R gave evidence of taking for granted our kinship, and that by clearly indicating to me by the fulsome and somewhat uncomfortable investment she had made in me that her need to idealize was in good order, I made the decision to work with her in the area of the subjective self and affect attunement—what Kohut called "mirroring." By showing her that I understood and did not disapprove of her need to be understood, I laid the groundwork that later permitted her to bring into the transference the vulnerable aspects of herself so that these aspects could be interpretatively dealt with.

Ms. R is officially classified as a narcissistic personality disorder, but, as Kohut correctly taught us, the term narcissistic disorder should be replaced with the term selfobject disorder. It is the latter term that carries with it some implications for how one should deal with the patient. I would like to carry this further to its logical conclusion.

Because, as Kohut pointed out, oedipal conflicts are also a form of selfobject disorder, the term selfobject disorder does not say enough.

I would suggest that we combine the term selfobject disorder with a reference to the developmental stage, and when possible to the sector of character development where we believe the patient's damage resides.

When we free ourselves of phenomeonological labels and base our diagnoses on both the patient's capacity for object relatedness and his or her selfobject needs, some interesting things happen. Take Miss F in Kohut's (1971) *Analysis of the Self,* for example. Phenomenologically speaking, she was certainly grandiose and had a very strong sense of entitlement; so did my patient, Ms. R, but there the similarity stops. Because Miss F had severe damage in the domain of the emergent sense of self, the basic rhythm of life eluded her. She could not tolerate anything being other than what she imagined a particular thing needed to be. Similarly, her inability to use her analyst as a source of strength and comfort indicated a deficit in her core self, as did her need to lay down the rules for her treatment. Therefore, Miss F in terms of standard classification should be thought of as a borderline personality, and not a narcissistic personality disorder. And indeed, the years of empathic immersion that Kohut said were required by patients such as Miss F before the mirror transference proper could develop are not, in my experience, needed by patients with narcissistic personality disorder. Indeed, these patients, as do psychoneurotic patients, come to therapy more or less transference ready and, as was the case with Ms. R it is usually possible to work within the transference from the beginning of therapy.

However, there was more to Miss F than her pathology. She was not just functioning on the basis of an endangered self. We may assume she kept her appointments, left the session when it was time to do so, paid her bills, probably got out of bed in the morning, brushed her teeth, and shopped for groceries. For all we know, she had a responsible job and related to people at work in a coherent and productive manner.

It is through the patient's cohesive self that we gain the leverage that will let us deal with their selfobject needs; what is right with the patient is as important to assess and understand as what is wrong with the patient. Patients are not just sick; there are more often than not large areas of development that, though not problem free, are being dealt with adequately. The question then becomes why this or that aspect of a person's life is not being dealt with on the level of object experiences—it is that investigation that usually leads us to the selfobject need and the flawed aspect of psychic structure that requires attention.

CONCLUSION

Freud and Kohut each used the lens of psychopathology to see some basic truths about normal development; Freud, the unconscious nature of thought and the transference of patterns of expectation from the past to the present situation, and Kohut, the selfobject needs of the endangered self system. However, as important as these discoveries are, neither alone nor together do they give us a sufficient understanding of normal development to provide the template with which to orient ourselves to the problems presented to us by a wide variety of patients, or even the problems presented in the in-depth treatment of any one patient.

What Freud equated with normal development was a description of the vicissitudes of the transference as it unfolded in the treatment of psychoneurotic patients; similarly, Kohut's bipolar self describes the transference of patients with narcissistic personality disorder. The danger of equating development with what unfolds in a psychoanalysis is the skewed and limited view that then becomes the basis for one's theorizing. Freud's equation of normal development with what he discovered about the pathology of the psychosexual sphere of development in psychoneurotic patients led to treating every person as if he or she were suffering from a psychoneurosis. Kohut was the first to systematically demonstrate that patients with narcissistic personality disorders could be treated successfully only if one took a very different view of the patients' development. His great contribution to the practice of analysis and psychotherapy was to free us from the unnecessary constraints of the instinct theory. However, he then repeated Freud's error, pathomorphism, and formulated a theory of development and a theory of the self, on the basis of his findings with this one group of patients. As a result, we now find that many people who style themselves "self psychologists" are repeating history and dealing with all patients as if they were narcissistic character disorders, under the mistaken impression that affect attunement is the equivalent of empathy. It is not. Empathic understanding (Kohut called it vicarious introspection), or finding one's way into the operation of another person's psychic structure involves more than identifying the feelings of that person. Therapeutic empathy, or, to use Bacal's (1985) felicitous term, optimal responsiveness, requires that one understand those feelings against the background of the patient's development, and that one's interventions address both the domain of self-development and the category of action involved. Only an understanding of a viable theory of normal human development, one that takes into consideration object experiences as well as selfobject needs, can prepare us to find our way into another's psychic structure.

REFERENCES

Bacal, H. A. (1985), Optimal responsiveness and the therapeutic process. In: *Progress in Self Psychology, Vol. 1,* ed. A. Goldberg. New York: Guilford Press, pp. 202–227.

Basch, M. F. (1975), Toward a theory that encompasses depression: A revision of existing causal hypotheses in psychoanalysis. In: *Depression and Human Existence,* ed. E. J. Anthony & T. Benedek. Boston, MA: Little, Brown, pp. 485–534.

_____ (1984), Selfobjects and selfobject transference: Theoretical implications. In: *Kohut's Legacy,* ed. P. E. Stepansky & A. Goldberg. Hillsdale, NJ: The Analytic Press, pp. 21–41.

_____ (1988), *Understanding Psychotherapy: The Science Behind the Art.* New York: Basic Books.

Bowlby, J. (1969), *Attachment: Attachment and Loss,* Vol. I. New York: Basic Books.

Fajardo, B. (1991), Analyzability and resilience in development. The *Annual of Psychoanalysis,* Vol. 19. Hillsdale, NJ: The Analytic Press, pp. 107–126.

Federn, P. (1952), *Ego Psychology and the Psychoses,* ed. E. Weiss. New York: Basic Books.

King, C. D. (1945), The meaning of normal. *Yale J. Biol. Med.,* 17:493–501.

Kohut, H. (1971), *The Analysis of the Self.* New York: International Universities Press.

_____ (1977), *The Restoration of the Self.* New York: International Universities Press.

– – – (1984), *How Does Analysis Cure?* ed. A. Goldberg & P. Stepansky, Chicago: University of Chicago Press.

Lachmann, F. & Beebe, B. (1988), On the formation of psychic structure in infancy. Unpublished manuscript.

Stern, D. (1985), *The Interpersonal World of the Infant.* New York: Basic Books.

Waddington, C. H. (1966), *Principles of Development and Differentiation.* New York: Macmillan.

Wolf, E. (1988), *Treating the Self.* New York: Guilford Press.

Zeanah, C. H., Anders, T. F., Seifer, R. & Stern, D. (1989), Implications of research on infant development for psychodynamic theory and practice. *J. Amer. Acad. Child & Adolesc. Psychiat.,* 5:657–668.

Chapter 2

Why Self Psychology Is Not an Object Relations Theory: Clinical and Theoretical Considerations

Paul H. Ornstein

There are many creative and fruitful ways to survey the entire field of psychoanalysis and account for similarities and differences in its various paradigms. One such recent, informative, and challenging study by Greenberg and Mitchell (1983) encompassed the field in terms of its basic models: (1) the drive structure model; (2) the relational structure model; and (3) the mixed model. Greenberg and Mitchell's approach led them to examine the essential features of each psychoanalytic model and the model's clinical implications. They also made an in-depth comparison and contrast of all significant parameters of each basic model. By focusing on the main characteristics of each model, they were able to capture fundamental similarities and differences in the major competing theories.

It is possible, in a broad, historical–conceptual study such as theirs, to choose the parameters for examination so as to register the similarities and differences in the various models with sufficient objectivity. There may, however, be an unrecognized tendency or an explicit, goal-directed strategy to accentuate the similarities or the differences, depending on what one wishes to illustrate.

An important question remains: How does one decide whether the similarities or the differences are of greater significance or of over-riding importance? In other words, there may be many similarities and only few differences—and yet, these few differences may sharply divide and render incompatible two models that also appear to have many similarities. The structural image of two similar chemical

17

compounds comes to mind, where the different location of one single element in the molecule of one of the compounds is of greater significance than the sameness and identical location of all other elements—the one difference outweighs all other similarities. In self psychology, that one element of decisive difference is the concept of the selfobject with its far-reaching clinical, theoretical, and developmental implications.[1] I shall follow my story line leading up to this centrality of the selfobject concept.

In our clinical work, we do need guiding principles in order to detect what line of interpretive approach is compatible or incompatible with another and what line of interpretive approach will help implement our therapeutic goals. These are, therefore, practical, clinical, questions and not just esoteric, theoretical concerns.

I find the recognition of similarities in the various forms of psychoanalysis fascinating and deeply reassuring. The similarities are to me, at times, more intriguing than the differences, because I take the latter for granted on account of the differing observational methods, theoretical premises, and treatment techniques from which they may originate. But I am always surprised by apparent similarities that grow out of a different methodological and theoretical soil. Such similarities, if they turn out to be substantive, call attention to some hitherto unrecognized factor(s) that might be of importance. Focusing on the differences, however, may sharpen our grasp of each model and its clinical consequences and may also highlight intrinsic incompatibilities.

The difficulty in sorting-out what is truly novel in the various psychoanalytic models partly stems from the fact that, in his 1914 paper, "On Narcissism," Freud already presented the outlines of his forthcoming ego psychology, the beginnings of an object relations theory, and the rudiments of a self psychology. He could have advanced in any of the other two directions also, had he not been locked into his drive theory as one of the factors that propelled him in the direction of a drive-based ego psychology. That move thwarted the emergence of an object relations theory for some time, and it also delayed the emergence of a self psychology within psychoanalysis.

With or without drive theory, psychoanalysis has long defied a generally acceptable classification. Does it belong to the natural

---

[1]Another way to phrase the question about similarities and differences somewhat whimsically and not quite accurately is this: When do similarities add up to "sameness" and wipe out the differences as being fundamentally significant? And when do similarities simply remain similarities without creating sameness, hence leaving the differences untouched and overriding?

sciences? Is it a hermeneutic discipline — a part of the humanities? Or, should it be thought of as a pure psychology — an "empirical science sui generis" and, as such, a part of psychology? Can it be viewed as more than any one of these at the same time? (See Goldberg, 1988, pp. 3–18, for a cogent discussion of these philosophical issues.) Whatever our answers to these unsettled questions, they have far reaching, and not yet fully explored, implications for psychoanalytic theory and practice. The issue goes back again as far as 1914, when Freud himself claimed that psychoanalysis was and ought to remain a pure psychology — but he did not always adhere to his own maxim.

So, perhaps it was not drive theory alone that stood in the way, because others had been able to overcome this particular obstacle and move toward an object relations theory as clinical practice compelled them to do. Rather, it may have been Freud's conviction that only a biologically anchored psychoanalysis could be scientific that made him adhere to his drive theory — which favored the pursuit of ego psychology over the other two possible routes, object relations theory and self psychology. This stance of Freud's is somewhat surprising in the face of his previously mentioned claim that psychoanalysis was and ought to remain a "pure psychology." Kohut solved this issue more definitively than did Freud because he progressively viewed psychoanalysis, consistently and unambigiously, as a pure psychology. With this view in mind, Kohut was determined to reformulate the method, concepts, and theories of psychoanalysis accordingly. In 1959, in his methodologic treatise on "Introspection, Empathy and Psychoanalysis," this was Kohut's scientific agenda. This was long before he had any inkling of his internally evolving self psychology. At that point, he already spoke of psychoanalysis as a pure psychology, in the sense of it being clearly and sharply differentiated from sociology on the one hand, and from biology on the other, and he wanted to cleanse the field from its sociologic and biologic infiltrations. In other words, he argued against sociologizing and biologizing psychoanalysis. Although biology, psychology, and sociology all address the human condition, they are, he claimed, distinctly different (neighboring) fields because of the particular mental operation required for their study. We can understand an aspect of external or internal reality on the basis of the particular operation we perform to learn about it. This operationalism is at the bottom of all of Kohut's work. It is this orientation that aided him in his vision of a pure psychology, and it is this orientation that aided him later in translating his vision into a formulation of his version of the psychoanalysis of the self as a pure psychology (see also Kohut, 1982). Without recognizing the centrality of the empathic observational mode as something specific to his approach, his theoretical and clinical formulations cannot be fully appreciated.[2]

SELF PSYCHOLOGY AND ITS RELATION TO OBJECT RELATIONS THEORY

If we now accept Kohut's claim tentatively and consider the empirical science of psychoanalysis a pure psychology, the question arises: Where does self psychology fit in relation to the other major current paradigms of psychoanalysis, ego psychology and object relations theory, and their correlated treatment techniques? And what kind of a psychology is self psychology, and why should it not simply be considered a variant of object relations theory as some claim it to be? Or, could self psychology be compatible with and fully encompassed by an (expanded) ego psychology as others claim it to be?

Self psychology's kinship to other theories and approaches in psychoanalysis is well established. How could it be otherwise when the territory all these theories cover is the same—the inner life of man—and when their conceptual roots are so thoroughly intertwined? In a broad sense, the ancestors of all approaches go back to Freud's (1914) paper "On Narcissism." Thus, although self psychology and the need for it did not emerge anew from Kohut's inner world alone, neither did he draw specifically on the works of the British object relations theorists (as this is so often taken for granted and responded to with considerable indignation because his assumed debt to them is thought to have remained unacknowledged). What did emerge from Kohut's own inner world undoubtedly became amalgamated with prior analytic knowledge and experience and led to his thoroughly transformed version of psychoanalysis.

This long assumed and often claimed direct relationship between self psychology and object relations theory, however, has received little public attention from self psychologists thus far. The recent contributions of Bacal (1987) and Brandchaft (1986) have filled a gap in this regard and point toward further necessary work. Their first-hand acquaintance with, and in-depth understanding of, both object relations theory and self psychology gives Bacal and Brandchaft a unique

---

[2]Of course every analyst is empathic and inevitably utilizes empathy. But the prolonged, systematic, empathic immersion in the patient's subjective experiences—especially their transferences—is a sine qua non for the self psychologically informed analyst. Because the theoretical concepts of self psychology also derive from this observational mode, these concepts, therefore, enhance entry into the patient's inner world. There are undoubtedly psychoanalytic concepts that do not enhance this entry and perhaps make it even more difficult.

vantage point for their observations. Their contributions thus far have enriched our perspective.

Both Bacal and Brandchaft carefully delineate what they consider to be the similarities and differences between the various British object relations theories and self psychology (see also Sutherland, 1980). They have fully recognized the unique features of self psychology, even where they stressed the similarities between Kohut's work and those of the British. Bacal helps us focus on the similarities in order to show what we may learn from them. He concludes that many of the British object relations theorists (some more so than others) had made significant steps toward the discovery of self psychology, even if they never quite achieved a systematic formulation of it. As I see it, none of their contributions could have been designated as self psychology because none of these theorists achieved that overriding transformation sufficiently—and that is what makes them different in spite of the many similarities. We can only agree with Bacal that a close study of their works would benefit self psychology. Brandchaft frames his intent of comparison with a different emphasis. He, too, registers the considerable overlap between Kohut's contributions and the many observations and contributions of the British analysts. But he asks that we focus on the unique features of Kohut's work in order to challenge ourselves to demonstrate what self psychology has to offer that goes beyond what the British object relations theorists had discovered and were then able to disseminate among their own colleagues and in the United States, before Kohut.[3] He asserts that, from the current vantage point of the influence of self psychology, many of the writings of the British object relations theorists can now be read with greater appreciation and understood in greater depth than before. This is how Brandchaft (1986) warns us against premature integration of different theories:

> . . . the prospects that the innovations begun by Kohut may have a wider impact [than works of the British object relations theorists' had, except for M. Klein] depends upon whether his work will be found to have added something sufficiently unique and significant as to prove more enduring. If in fact, Heinz Kohut has made it possible for us to see and understand more of human experience and the psychoanalytic

---

[3]The clear impression that the British object relations theories were neglected or even disregarded by American ego psychology and became more acceptable (and even somewhat fashionable) as a way to diminish the suddenly more "threatening" influence of Kohut's emerging theories and their correlated, clinical approach on the American psychoanalytic scene, would deserve a thorough study and documentation.

process than before, it is important that this growing body of work follow its trajectory toward the realization of its own potential [p. 246].

There are undoubtedly subtle differences in Bacal's and Brand-chaft's approaches to their tasks as well as in their conclusions; both would merit extensive and detailed further consideration. But what is important from my perspective is that it did not occur to either Bacal or to Brandchaft to characterize Kohut's self psychology as a variant of object relations theory, in spite of the many similarities they astutely discovered. I consider that point significant. I assume they both concluded that, in spite of the many similarities between the various object relations theories and self psychology, the differences were, in the end, fundamentally more significant than the similarities. Because neither Bacal nor Brandchaft state explicitly what makes self psychology not an object relations theory (quite apart from the issues of priority and originality), and because neither of them spells out what the irreducible differences in these two theories are, it is my purpose to state these differences explicitly in order to raise them for discussion.

What exactly separates self psychology from the object relations theories? Kohut himself amply demonstrated what separates self psychology from ego psychology and some of the object relations theories; his arguments are well known and need not be recounted. Some of the crucial variables can be found in the methodological realm, others in the clinical realm, and still others in the conceptual-theoretical realm, especially in regard to respective views of the transference and respective developmental theories. To stress one single point: All of the crucial variables of self psychology together, the tightly connected ensemble of them, their logical and inseparable interrelatedness, make for an irreducible difference. Each and every one of these variables is well known and so is their necessary and inevitable connectedness, but I hope that by offering my particular emphasis I shall evoke ideas, assents, or dissents.

METHOD AND STRUCTURE OF PSYCHOANALYTIC SELF PSYCHOLOGY

This idea of the ensemble of the variables is of overriding importance. We look at the total picture first, the whole gestalt, before we attempt to give meaning to the details. In relationship to the patient's inner experiences, it is this totality within which the meaning of single experiences can be discerned. And so it is with our theories. We need to account for the theoretical position that single clinical observations and concepts have within a particular theoretical system. It is only then that we can assess the general importance and validity of a particular observation or concept. Take the concept of mirroring for instance: The term and some of the meaning of the concept had been around before; but, did it in any prior contexts have the same far-reaching developmental, clinical, and theoretical position that it has in self psychology? The answer is clearly no, Lacan and Winnicott (among others) notwithstanding. This examination may profitably be repeated with each major concept, with the same result.

There are three interrelated elements in method and concepts that give self psychology its distinctive structure and correlated clinical approach: (1) the idea that prolonged introspection and empathy are the central data gathering tools of psychoanalysis; and (2) simultaneously, the field itself is delineated as encompassing the introspective-empathically graspable subjective experiences of the patient; and (3) as a result of the systematic and sustained empathic immersion[4] in the patient's subjective experiences, the analyst's position in the analytic situation is viewed exclusively from the patient's vantage point; that is, the perspective from which the patient experiences the analyst.

And crucial to this last component, a not-further-reducible difference between self psychology and other approaches, is the notion of the self as not delimited by the physical boundaries of the person. The self is an open system, open to include others; or, it may include itself in the self of others. The idea that hampered other approaches and presumably precluded an encompassing self psychology prior to Kohut—no matter how many steps toward it some of the British object relations theorists may otherwise have made—had to do with their essential adherence to the idea that the boundaries of the self stop where our skin does—that our self is locked up inside our bodies. The transference was therefore seen as being played out between two well-delimited selves, each of whom could be the recipient of projections in the transference–countertransference experience.

Kohut's redefined method of psychoanalysis spawned the clinical observations of the selfobject transferences, and the working through of these transferences gave rise to the core concept of the selfobject. This redefined method gave Kohut an entirely new view and unified

---

[4]Frequently disregarded is that "sustained empathic immersion" is significantly different from what is often viewed as an empathic perception of a single affect or even of complex affect-states. The clinical–theoretical consequences of this sustained immersion then remains unrecognized and contributes to the blurring of many of the distinctive features of self psychology and its correlated clinical approach.

conception of health, illness, and cure. I am calling your attention to these well known facts in order to underline the remarkable unity and harmony Kohut was able to establish between his method of observation, his clinical findings and theories and his therapeutic approach and theory of cure. Kohut did not "cut and paste" his theories; they are essentially of one cloth, which is what makes comparisons in relation to the separate parts of this total edifice so difficult. (When I say total, I do not mean complete or perfect; I only mean the way the various layers of the theory are woven together; the way the method of observation determines the nature of the findings and thereby unifies the theories and the treatment approaches that evolve from them.)

Object and Selfobject—Do We Need Both in Self Psychology?

The selfobject concept as the centerpiece of psychoanalytic self psychology determines, defines, and separates this theoretical system from all other components of other theoretical systems. We may certainly view self psychology as a "blood relative" of all other psychoanalytic systems, but we can not view self psychology and object relations theory as identical twins that have been reared far apart.

There is not a single significant concept in self psychology that does not derive from, or directly relate to, the concept of the selfobject and the observational method that defines it. Kohut spoke of two kinds of selfobject experiences: Those of structure building and those of structure maintaining. He defined the selfobject at various times as intrapsychically structured experiences, whose function it is to build up the nuclear self; or as the intrapsychically structured experiences, whose function it is to maintain the strength, cohesion, harmony, and vitality of a reasonably well-structuralized self throughout life.[5] And he brought these two different functions together when he said that we needed selfobjects from birth to death. From then on, the concept object lost its theoretical position in self psychology and the concept of the mature selfobject took the object's place. But not entirely, and that is still our theoretical problem. The selfobject concept since then has clearly encompassed various needs, functions, capacities, or experiences: (1) it refers to the quality of the experience the self has of the other and, as a consequence, to the quality of experience the self

---

[5]I believe it is implied in this second function of mature selfobjects that they also make possible or enhance the unfolding or actualization of the innate life-program of the nuclear self.

has of itself; (2) the selfobject concept refers to the phase-appropriate needs of the self from the other—needs that are conceived of here as the specific emotional nutrients for the development of the nuclear self and beyond (such as when we speak of the oedipal selfobjects; adolescent selfobjects; mature selfobjects, and the like); and (3) it calls attention to the fact that in psychoanalysis we always have to view the object from the emotional position or vantage point of the self (hence the term selfobject). For all these reasons and, in order to spark debate, I suggest we drop the term object from our vocabulary and speak in theoretical contexts only of the archaic and mature selfobjects (and the various other, to be specifically delineated, forms), the only others that have a methodologically and theoretically justified position so far in self psychology.

I raised this question about the usefulness and validity of the concept object some years ago, when discussing Stolorow's paper, "Self Psychology—A Structural Psychology" (Ornstein, 1980, p. 347), which is relevant in the present context. "I fully subscribe [I said] to Stolorow's (1980) assessment that the concept of a selfobject radically alters our understanding of the meaning of patient's experiences in the analytic situation." I then proposed that "we [should] now state explicitly that this assessment not only applies to the archaic selfobject, but is equally valid regarding those on more advanced developmental levels (i. e., to all of a patient's experiences in analysis), a view that is then even more radical than Stolorow envisioned." I (Ornstein, 1980) elaborated on this radical view briefly (but only in a footnote:

> The question [is] . . . what we mean now in self psychology when we speak of a self as a well-demarcated and firmly consolidated structure with its own independent center of initiative and what we mean by the recognition of the well-demarcated separateness and well consolidated, independent center of initiative, in the other. Does the latter qualify as a "true object" or a "love- or hate-object" to be contrasted with a selfobject? Suffice it to say that to whatever extent the separateness and independence of the other is recognized (perceptually, or cognitively, which is not the issue here), from the vantage point of self-experience—and therefore also from the vantage point of the empathic observer—the other is always a selfobject—archaic or mature. This view is the result of placing self-experience consistently at the center of psychoanalytic inquiry and asking how a person experiences the other rather than taking the position of the external observer and speaking of "whole object" or "part-object." [p. 347, see also Schwaber, 1978, p. 215 in this connection].

In other words, in addition to defining the archaic and mature selfobject on the basis of their specific functions, (dependent on the

needs and/or wishes of the self in a state of proneness to enfeeblement and fragmentation on the one hand, and with a reasonably
firmly established cohesion and vitality on the other), I also offered,
tentatively, a definition based on the observational perspective of the
analyst, further underscoring the inseparable connection between
observational method and theoretical concepts.

I am fully aware of the fact that Kohut retained the concept of the
object in a pragmatic-clinical sense and defined it (Kohut, 1984) as the
recipient or target of our desires and love as well as of our aggression
and anger. This is a makeshift definition, good until we can come up
with a theoretically sound one. The problem with the definition
becomes clearer when we recall one of Kohut's key observations
regarding the precipitating circumstances that trigger a severe self-
disorder, that "the archaic selfobject-need [that arises in the patient at
such clinical moments] did not proceed from the loss of the love
object but from the loss of a more mature selfobject experience" [i. e.,
such outbreak of self-disorder is a regression from a capacity for more
mature to more archaic levels] (Kohut, 1984, p. 197).

The reverse situation also appears to be true. Kohut, in his clinical
studies, observed the emergence of object love at the end of successful analyses of patients with narcissistic personality disorders as
a function or capacity of the restored, now cohesive and vital self.
Later he equated "mature selfobject resonance with mature relationship with the love object" (Kohut, 1984, p. 219), attesting to the fact
that the self's ability to enjoy love and lust and engage in assertive
acts are functions of a cohesive, strong, and harmoniously organized
self. Does this not express the idea that the concept of the mature
selfobject has replaced the concept of the love object in self psychology? For me it has, since 1977. Furthermore, the previously quoted
statement also expresses Kohut's idea that, in a reasonably healthy
individual, there is no sharp dichotomy between a mature selfobject
and a love object—these are experientially thoroughly intertwined,
and almost unrecognizable as qualitatively different. The sharp
dichotomy, the recognition of different qualities of selfobject and love
object, as observed clinically, is already a mark of some form of
self-pathology. It was the need to account for this pathology and its
origins that necessitated (in the early phase of Kohut's theorizing) his
most fruitful assumption of a separate (but not independent) line of
development for narcissism and object love. But since *The Restoration
of the Self* (Kohut, 1977) we have begun to move decisively beyond
narcissism, to the psychology of the self. Without narcissism (and the
rest of libido theory), we now have to reconceptualize the origin(s)
and developmental vicissitudes of love—which we have not yet done

systematically. We do not have a self-psychological conception of love, and surely cannot use Freud's derivation of it from the sexual drive. Until we find a theoretical position for love in our system, we cannot define the theoretical position of that other whom we love. If love is a capacity of a healthy self, can love not be fully amalgamated with other needs and wishes in relation to that other whom we now describe in our conceptualizations as a mature selfobject? What do we really need the concept of an object for? What clinical facts necessitate the retention of an object, or the elaboration of an equivalent that is not a tainted substitute, which would also be indiginous to the psychology of the self?

It should be obvious from the foregoing that we have a problem with retaining the term object (instinctual object or love object) in our theoretical vocabulary, even if we redefine it, as many have. First, there is the elaborate set of accumulated associations connected with object; second, the original theoretical definition includes the assumption of a simultaneous libidinal and aggressive cathexis of the other, for that other to be viewed psychoanalytically as an instinctual object and later, as a love object. We also speak of whole object and part object with important theoretical connotations that preclude their having a place in our current conceptual system. As a consequence, the use of the term object (in any of its variants) now injects much confusion into our discourse, especially because it clashes with the concept of the mature selfobject, whose qualities and organization include its own center of initiative as well as the recognition of a separate center of initiative in the other.

Why Self Psychology is a Structural Psychology and Not an Object Relations Theory

How does all this relate to why self psychology is not an object relations theory? Many have called it a "selfobject theory" because its central clinical focus is on selfobjects, their vicissitudes, and functions; this is its most distinguishing feature. On account of this feature alone, it could not be appropriately considered an object relations theory, especially if we agree that the object has no theoretical position in self psychology.[6] In fact, all forms of psycho-

---

[6]A comprehensive historical-conceptual analysis of the concept "object" can be found in Compton (1986). It appears from that careful, highly sophisticated, in-depth assessment that the theoretical position of the "object" is quite ambiguous even within traditional psychoanalysis. I derive from Compton's work further justification for my claim that self psychology does not need and cannot profitably use the concept "object" side by side with the concept "mature selfobject."

analysis deal essentially with relationships and "linkages" (Goldberg, 1988) in their clinical endeavors. The same logic that gave id psychology its name (retrospectively); ego psychology its name (concurrent with its development); and the various object relations theories their name, also gave self psychology, at a certain point in its evolution, its name. In each instance, the designation stressed the most distinguishing basic features of the particular model or paradigm, especially in contrast to what other forms of psychoanalysis had emphasized before. The generic term psychoanalysis first covered id psychology and remained relevant even after the advent of ego psychology. Those who wished to stress that they had embraced the new formulations, for quite some time referred to this new development as ego psychology until it became synonymous with an updated psychoanalysis. History has repeated itself, except subsequent developments have not supplanted ego psychology as decisively (as yet) as it has supplanted id psychology.

Id psychology focused on the object as an appendage to the drives, primarily as a facilitator and recipient of drive-discharge and as a provider of satisfaction. Id psychology received its name for the primacy of drives, even though it dealt with relationships, however inadequately, from our current vantage point. Ego psychology received its name from the shift from drives to ego, even though this advance in psychoanalysis retained the drives in a central position and included a subordinated object relations theory and a rudimentary self psychology under its umbrella. Object relations theory received its name from the fact that with or without bypassing the drive theory, it placed the relations to objects into a primary position; this was also coupled with a redefinition of the object and its relation to the drives in some of these theories. (See, for instance, the drive as "object-seeking" and not "pleasure seeking" in Fairbairn, 1954.) Object relations theories had to introduce their own definition of the object. These theories did not make the necessary next step, however, of putting the self at the center of the psychological universe and viewing the other exclusively from the self's vantage point. Neither did these theories introduce the conception of a self whose boundaries did not coincide with the surface of the skin. This latter characteristic is one major reason why self psychology is not adequately characterized by viewing it as an object relations theory. If we add to this the fact that self psychology focuses on subjective experience (or self-experience), which includes the experiencing of the other as a selfobject; and if we then recognize the structure building and structure maintaining functions of the other, which leads us to a central concern with the structural integrity of the self (the focus on self-states), we shall immediately recognize how we have moved beyond relationships per se to those self structures on whose integrity, or deficiency, the nature and quality of all relationships depend. It is in this sense that self psychology is more accurately defined as a structural psychology, and it deserves this designation under the ever broadening umbrella of psychoanalysis.

REFERENCES

Bacal, H. A. (1987), British object-relations theorists and self psychology: some critical reflections. *Internat. J. Psycho–Anal.*, 68:81–98.

Brandchaft, B. (1986), British object-relations theory and self psychology. In: *Progress in Self Psychology, Vol. 2*, ed. A. Goldberg. New York: Guilford Press, pp. 287–296.

Compton, A. (1986), The beginnings of the object concept in psychoanalysis. In: *Psychoanalysis: The Science of Mental Conflict*. Hillsdale, NJ: The Analytic Press, pp. 177–189.

Fairbairn, W. R. D. (1954), *An Object-Relations Theory of the Personality*. New York: Basic Books.

Freud, S. (1914), On narcissism: An introduction. *Standard Edition*, 14:73–102. London: Hogarth Press, 1957.

Greenberg, J. R. & Mitchell, S. A. (1983), *Object Relations in Psychoanalytic Theory*. Cambridge, MA.: Harvard University Press.

Goldberg, A. (1988), *A Fresh Look at Psychoanalysis: The View from Self Psychology*. Hillsdale, NJ: The Analytic Press.

Kohut, H. (1959), Introspection, empathy and psychoanalysis: An examination of the relationship between mode of observation and theory. In: *The Search for the Self*, Vol. 1, ed. P. H. Ornstein. New York: International Universities Press, 1978, pp. 205–232.

Kohut, H. (1977), *The Restoration of the Self*. New York: International Universities Press.

Kohut, H. (1982), Introspection, empathy and the semicircle of mental health. In: *The Search for the Self*, Vol. 1, ed. P. H. Ornstein. Madison, CT.: International Universities Press, pp. 537–567.

Kohut, H. (1984), *How Does Analysis Cure?* ed. A. Goldberg & P. Stepansky. Chicago: University of Chicago Press.

Ornstein, P. H. (1980), Discussion of papers by Drs. Goldberg, Stolorow, and Wallerstein. In: *Reflections on Self Psychology*. ed. J. D. Lichtenberg & S. Kaplan. Hillsdale, NJ: The Analytic Press, pp. 339–384.

Schwaber, E. (1978), Self psychology and the concept of psychopathology: A case presentation. In: *Advances in Self Psychology*, ed. A. Goldberg. New York: International Universities Press, 1980, pp. 215–242.

Stolorow, R. (1980), Self psychology: A structural psychology. In: *Reflections on Self Psychology*, ed. J. D. Lichtenberg & S. Kaplan. Hillsdale, NJ: The Analytic Press, pp. 287–296.

Sutherland, J. D. (1980), The British object-relations theorists: Balint, Winnicott, Fairbairn, Guntrip. *J. Amer. Psychoanal. Assn.*, 28:829–860.

Chapter 3

Commentaries

SELFOBJECT OR SELF-REGULATING OTHER
Morton Shane

Basch and Ornstein have taken provocative, opposing views on the question of whether it is useful to conceptualize object experiences other than selfobject experiences in self psychological theory. Basch answers clearly in the affirmative; Ornstein answers clearly in the negative; and each argues his position most effectively.

Basch asserts that an object experience refers to a situation in which a cohesive self expresses itself affectively with the affect itself, (i.e., the distress, the affection, the anger, the fear, shame, love, hate, or whatever), signaling an attempt to bring about a certain outcome or to solve a certain problem without the self being in danger of losing its cohesiveness. This is distinctly different from a selfobject experience wherein the self is threatened, and wherein a particular function is required to make up for an inadequacy in the self structure. The difference, then, between the object experience and the selfobject experience relates exclusively to the self-state of the individual, whether the self-state is cohesive or shaky. In this way, Basch distinguishes himself from those who would define a selfobject as anything that relates to the self, for by that definition there would indeed be no other experience; the selfobject experience would include everything. Basch contends that such a definition serves to vitiate Kohut's central contribution; namely, that selfobjects are required to make up for inadequacies in self structure.

First, Basch develops a basis for distinguishing among the variety of self-states requiring selfobject experience. Using Stern's hierarchically developing domains of the self, he first defines the nature of the sense of self available to the infant in each domain. Second, Basch delineates what is required of the caretaker to respond effectively to the infant, inferring that there are object as well as selfobject experiences in each domain of the self throughout life. In this regard, Basch identifies the deficits and arrests in development consequent to failures in the interactive infant–mother system in terms of specific pathology, moving from the borderline personality, stemming from selfobject failure in the domain of the emergent self; to the depressive-hypochondriacal character stemming from selfobject failure in the domain of the core self; to the narcissistic personality disorder stemming from selfobject failure in the domain of the subjective self; to, finally, neurotic pathology stemming from selfobject failure in the domain of the verbal and then the narrative selves. And third, Basch identifies the response that is appropriately and effectively empathic for each domain of the sense of self wherein selfobject function is required. He argues that it is not sufficient to respond to all patients, or even to problems presented in the in-depth treatment of any one patient, with a universally applied palliative of affect attunement; rather, what is necessary is to assess the specific arrest or vulnerability in the sense of self, and respond in a manner that meets the domain-specific selfobject need. It is only this more specific response that is truly empathic.

Thus, Basch not only retains the concept of object but also fractionates the concept of selfobject in order to achieve a more accurate definition of pathology and a more accurate definition of the empathic response that will ameliorate pathology. These understandings are based upon infant observation and studies of brain functioning; together, these studies provide a viable theory of human development upon which to base an understanding of normalcy and pathology. He thus distinguishes himself from both Freud, who had no such viable theory available, and from Kohut, who deliberately chose to ignore it, being confident that the psychoanalytic method informed by empathic introspective emersion into the subject world of the patient would yield the best insights into normal and pathological, psychological development. In effect, then, Kohut, like Ornstein, views the reconstructed, clinical infant as a better source of data than the real, observed infant; whereas in contrast, Basch derives a good deal of inspiration from that real, observed infant discerned from research studies.

Taking a very different position from that put forward by Basch, Ornstein presents his own internally consistent arguments for dropping the object concept entirely, replacing the object concept with the mature selfobject, the only "other," he argues, that has thus far been methodologically and theoretically justified in self psychology. Ornstein comes to this position by fully accepting Kohut's methodological approach (contrary to Basch); that is, that prolonged introspection and empathy are the central data gathering tools of psychoanalysis; that the subjective world of the patient delineates the field; and that the analyst's position in the analytic situation is to be viewed exclusively from the patient's vantage point. It was by implementing this unique and creative transformation of analytic technique that Kohut was able to discover the selfobject transferences (and, I would add, the concomitant countertransferences), and to work them through with his patients. And it was via this experience that that centerpiece of psychoanalytic self psychology, the selfobject concept, was formulated. Ornstein makes the point that once Kohut came to delineate the developmental movement from archaic to mature selfobject function, the object concept was, perhaps, no longer useful or necessary to describe the nature of the mature individual's interactions with the other. The mature self-selfobject matrix, or system, might suffice, but not entirely, as Ornstein states, adding that the object concept still remains a theoretical problem.

By following Ornstein's carefully articulated, consistent, and historically informative line of reasoning, two explanatory features of his theoretical position regarding the object concept become clear: First, he contends that pieces of self psychology are not sufficient in and of themselves to explain the entire selfobject system, and not sufficient either to compare it constructively to a theoretical system that includes the object concept, such as object relations theory; just as pieces of the patient are not sufficient in and of themselves to explain the whole person from a self psychological perspective. It does violence to the theory in its entirety to attempt to understand it as anything other than a crucially connected set of variables creating a unique ensemble. Self psychology's ensemble does not need, nor does it have room for, the object concept. Second, Ornstein argues that this view of self psychology, consistent as it is with Kohut's approach, represents a self-contained unit, or system, not requiring input from any source other than the consulting room where the object is not germane. Here, the selfobject reigns supreme. Typically, the analyst serves at first an archaic selfobject function; and then, following structure building through transmuting internalization, the analyst serves a mature selfobject function. Object becomes an unnecessary construct.

Though I was impressed and enlightened by Ornstein's discussion, and I now understand considerably better the rationale for excluding the object as a concept in self psychology, I remain nevertheless convinced by Basch's approach, which maintains in self-psychological theory a distinction between a self-state that requires support and a self-state that is cohesive. Not only does Basch's perspective expand the theory to take in a wider range of pathology, but it permits an understanding of normal development consistent with, and promising to remain consistent with, current research. This position is more in line with my own predilection to refine, expand, and broaden psychoanalytic constructs, and to keep them current with the data generated by the larger community of scientists. In fact, I would take what Basch says even further, applying, more extensively, infant observation and Stern's model to this redefinition of psychoanalytic terminology. That is, I would employ the term "other" to unpack and particularize not only the selfobject concept, but the *object* concept as well, with qualifying descriptors to convey more exactly just what the self's relationship with that other is. This would only be taking Basch a little further than he takes himself when he fractionates the concept of selfobject in order to achieve a more accurate definition of pathology and a more accurate definition of the empathic response that will ameliorate pathology. Thus we could speak of the human, rhythmic, resonant other postulated by Basch, the other that is required to provide for the needs expressed by the sense of the emergent self; we could speak of the self-regulating other conceptualized by Stern, which Stern has equated to a selfobject, to provide for the needs expressed by the core self; we could speak of a self-attuning other, a self-affirming other, and a hedonic, intimacy-sharing other connected to the needs of the subjective self; and we could even utilize a fantasy-distorted other related to the verbal or narrative selves. In such descriptions, we would have to include the state of self, whether it is cohesive or in need of support, to specifically indicate whether there is an object function or a selfobject function that is required of the other, because I agree with Basch that such distinctions are necessary to preserve the essence and meaning of the selfobject concept, Ornstein's centerpiece of self psychology. Were we to follow this expanded description of the self and other, perhaps we could drop both object and selfobject from our lexicon (in this regard, see Horowitz, 1988). I may be accused here of ignoring one of Ornstein's most important points: namely, that by particularizing the selfobject concept and equating it with the other, I am in danger of losing what Ornstein perceives as the essential nature of the selfobject: that it is part of the self. Ornstein contends that the self in self psychology does not end with the skin; a self that does end with the skin is the self delineated in object relations theory. But I would counter that infant observation, and inferences from it, lead to the conclusion that the human being is hard-wired to easily, almost immediately from birth on, make this distinction, and, by and large, keep it, leaving aside the magical moments of merger described by Pine (1985). Thus, the self does end with the skin, that is, the subjective perception of the physical self, but the self experience most certainly does not, and it is this that is at the heart of the selfobject concept. In normal development, the appreciation of the other as not part of the self experience is a function of the slow, incremental process of decentering, a process that remains invisible in the reconstructed version of the infant and child, but is clearly visible and demonstrable in the observed infant and child.

Change or evolution of any concept in psychoanalysis is extremely hard won, which is why Ornstein writes of dropping the object concept as a sure-fire way to spark a debate. So it is not without trepidation that I support further particularizing of the selfobject term, and making other a psychoanalytic concept in its own right toward the end of, eventually, doing without both the object and selfobject terminology. But I do so with a confidence born of my experience with self psychology that, in identification, affection, and respect for Heinz Kohut, has revealed a capacity to be unusually responsive to new developments and new data generated from within or from without the field. The very concept of the *selfobject* has undergone a metamorphosis so that, in keeping with infant observation, it no longer connotes a developmental stage of undifferentiation between self and other. This capacity for change inherent in self psychological theory, its identification with the ambivalently iconoclastic Kohut, together with its relative youthfulness, permits self psychology to lead the field, thoughtfully selecting and integrating what is useful, and cheerfully discarding what is outmoded and inaccurate. In this way, to paraphrase Adlai Stevenson, another hero of mine, self psychology can bring all of psychoanalysis kicking and screaming into the 21st century.

REFERENCES

Horowitz, M. (1988), *Introduction to Psychodynamics*. New York: Basic Books.
Pine, F. (1985), *Developmental Theory and Clinical Process*. New Haven, CT: Yale
    University Press.

NOTES ON THE RELATIONSHIP BETWEEN OBJECT
RELATIONS THEORY AND SELF PSYCHOLOGY
Howard A. Bacal

Does an object relations theory exist in self psychology? Is self
psychology a distinct theoretical system? One might also, with equal
intellectual legitimacy, ask the question, "Does a self psychological
perspective exist in theories of object relations?" I have addressed
these questions at length elsewhere (Bacal, 1987, 1990; Bacal &
Newman, 1990); now, the rich presentations of Drs. Ornstein and
Basch provide opportunities for further discussion.

One tends to think about object relations theory as focusing on the
relationship between the self and others, and the self's experience of
the relationship is usually given only passing notice. However,
anyone familiar with Kohut's work who attended the recent conference in Edinburgh honoring the work of Fairbairn, might have
wondered from time to time whether he had wandered into a
European conference on the psychology of the self. The position
paper delivered by Sutherland at that conference, which identified
the essence of Fairbairn's work, strikingly demonstrated how self
psychological his work was, although almost everyone there simply
recognized it as a fundamental theory of object relations. I wonder
how many people at our conferences on self psychology hear views
that they unquestioningly recognize as quintessentially self psychological but that are, in effect, inherent in the work of Fairbairn and
other object relations theorists?

In fact, a number of object relations theorists tacitly (though
inconsistently) recognized various aspects of what self psychology
later conceptualized as the selfobject and selfobject relationships, and
regarded them as centrally significant: Suttie, in his emphasis on the
importance of companionship and the responsiveness of the object;
Fairbairn, in his assertion that pleasure seeking is not a primary
motivator, but that one is essentially moved by the need to establish

relationships with objects from whom one may derive support; Balint, in his understanding of human interaction as largely determined by the attempt to reestablish safe relationships with objects as a response to the disruption of a harmonious primitive relatedness in infancy; Bowlby, as the attachment to significant others by an affectional bond that provides a sense of security; and Winnicott, in his emphasis on the importance of a "good-enough" mother and her provision of a holding environment for healthy psychological development. In America, anticipation of the nature of the selfobject and the selfobject relationship was less specific, although Sullivan and Mahler made pioneering contributions to the focus on the early mother–child ties in shaping the child's internal world.

Whereas self psychology focuses on self experience and apparently ignores object relationships, the selfobject and self-selfobject relationships (the pivotal concepts of self psychology), imply the experience of a particular kind of relationship as the determinant of self-experience and the vehicle for self-development. From this perspective, the term, object relation[1] would designate the generic, overall concept and the idea of selfobject relation would be a specific example of the concept.

Object relations theory and self Psychology are, in my view, both misnomers—misnomers of omission. What is missing in theories of object relations is the recognition that object relations are also psychologies of the self: the experience of the relationship is significant because of its effect on the sense of self and its development. What is missing in self psychology theory is the explicit recognition that it is not only, or even mainly, the self of the patient that self psychology must study in order to learn about the self, but rather the experience of the relationship that affirms, sustains, disrupts or restores the sense of self. This relationship, I believe, is *tacitly* recognized in the *practice* of all self psychologists.

And yet, Ornstein is right. Self psychology is distinct from both classical analytic theory and object-relations theory. Although several of the object-relations theorists, especially Fairbairn, imply the centrality and ultimate importance of self-experience and self-development in relationships, it is only in the work of Harry Guntrip, who was Fairbairn's best known expositor, that it is clearly and

---

[1]The frequently heard criticism that the concept, *object relation* is not psychoanalytic because it denotes an interactional rather than an intrapsychic perspective is vitiated by the fact that object-relations theorists themselves define the term, *object relationship* as the experience by the individual of his relationship with his object (explicitly distinguishing it from the idea of the relationship between the subject and the object, which is an interpersonal relationship (Rycroft, 1972, p. 101).

explicitly recognized as such. Several of the object-relations theorists appreciate the importance of what we now call the selfobject experience. Some of them (such as Balint, Winnicott, and Bowlby), even accord it a central position in the experience of the infant, and one of them (Bowlby), acknowledges the validity of this viewpoint throughout the life cycle. None of these theorists, however, placed selfobject experience consistently at the center of their clinical thinking, with its fresh implications for viewing transference and the analyst's responses to it; not only because some of them persisted in maintaining that the central motivating factor that linked self and object was instinctual, but because all of them retained a moralistic view on so-called narcissism.

In my view, there are five major related characteristics that distinguish self psychology from classical psychoanalysis: (1) the removal of instinctual motivation as a central factor in development and pathogenesis; (2) the shift from a one-body to a multi-body psychology; (3) the placement of the self and its subjective experience consistently at the center of consideration; (4) the specification of a central, significant form of relationship between the self and the other (the selfobject relationship) that constitutes, in effect, the fifth distinguishing characteristic of self psychology: (5) a transformation of the traditional perspectives on narcissism.[2] The first two are variously shared by certain object-relations theories. The latter three are unique to self psychology, and have led to the elaboration of clinical theory in which the new concept of *selfobject transferences* has become central. With this concept, Kohut, in effect, "de-moralized" narcissism and created a fresh climate in the psychoanalytic situation that tacitly invites the patient to establish, or reestablish, as the case may be, a sense of entitlement to the analyst as a figure who provides functions that sustain a sense of self and enhance self-development.

Ornstein reminds us of Kohut's assertion that our methodology and the psychological nature of our field are indissolubly related. I agree; but this is not one of the distinctive marks of self psychology theory. It is applicable to the elaboration of any psychological theory whose proponents are willing to listen. But no one, not even Kohut, ever listened to patients without some theory (without hypotheses). One of Kohut's basic hypotheses was that the patient really does

---

[2]The traditional perspectives on narcissism have essentially been that it constitutes a fixation at the stage of primary identification (undifferentiation between self and object), or that it represents a defense against anxieties associated with object-instinctual strivings. Self psychology regards narcissism as a self defect or self distortion resulting from a significant failure of selfobjects and the mounting of defenses against the anxieties associated with the expression of selfobject needs.

know more about himself than we do, and that we will discover this if we can but listen to him[3], that is, to his "subjectivity." (It is largely for this reason, I believe, that Kohut regarded his article, "Introspection, Empathy and Psychoanalysis" (Kohut, 1959), which anticipated this perspective, as his most important paper. Whether the application of even this hypothesis is always the most therapeutic for the patient deserves our continuing investigation, but this is another issue. Apart from this, though, problems inevitably arise in listening openly when we begin to conceptualize what we have learned; that is, we make theories and apply them in our attempt to understand the next patient. Self psychologists are, however, considerably freer to listen receptively to their patients than other theorists, because of their consistent regard for the validity of their patients' subjective experience. My own view is that, when other theorists listen consistently in the way Kohut did, they begin to hear what Kohut heard, and more. Schwaber is a particularly strong proponent of this view, and the listening perspective she advocates—which is, in effect, Kohut's—must regularly inform her of her patients' experiencing her as a most attentive selfobject.

There is an issue that both Ornstein and Basch address in their papers. If we can agree that we know about the self of another through our empathic perception of the self's experience of the relationship—assisted, as Basch (1988) pointed out by our extra-clinical knowledge of the patient—an interesting question remains: Are we always describing this experience accurately by using the selfobject concept?

One of the great problems in communicating clearly with our object relations colleagues is that we have not evolved a common language; indeed, as Basch's chapter demonstrates, we are also still attempting to evolve and clarify our own language so that we may communicate clearly with one another. For instance, what Sutherland, Fairbairn and a number of other object relations theorists tacitly but centrally identify as an object relation, some self psychologists would regard as a selfobject relation, which they maintain is not really a relationship with an object, but a particular kind of experience, in relation to which the object is incidental. One might call this the issue of specificity. Self psychology theory has, in effect, focused on the

---

[3]"If there is one lesson that I have learned during my life as an analyst, it is the lesson that what my patients tell me is likely to be true—that many times when I believed that I was right and my patients were wrong, it turned out, though often only after a prolonged search, that *my* rightness was superficial whereas *their* rightness was profound" (Kohut, 1984, pp. 93–94).

experience of selfobject function, and has lost sight of the object that provides that function, and of the importance of the relationship with that object for the patient. In practice, self psychologists are well aware of the enormous importance to the patient of the specific object that is experienced as providing reliable selfobject function—for example, the patient's mother, father, friend, or the analyst—as well as the significance of the relationship with the specific selfobject. Thus, I would add to Stolorow's caveat—that the selfobject should be conceived of as a dimension of experiencing an object (Stolorow, 1986, p. 274)—that this experience is also embodied in a significant object. In adding this idea to self psychology theory, we should acknowledge our debt to Bowlby, who emphasized the centrality of the psychological significance of a particular other in his attachment theory, a major object relations theory.

We return now to the question, "Are we accurately designating the nature of significant objects?" Basch would have us use the word, "selfobject", or the term, selfobject experience, to refer to a situation in which an endangered self is strengthened by the intervention of another, and that we use the word, "object" or the term, object experience, to refer to a situation in which a cohesive, nonendangered self is expressing itself affectively. This is a nice distinction and, at first glance, seems eminently workable. However, some self psychologists, notably Wolf, would be reluctant to be this exact. They would point out that the selfobject experience[4] is necessary for life, and we need it like we need oxygen, not because life or self is endangered, but because both (the selfobject experience and oxygen) fuel our life. For example, a student who learns from his violin teacher could be said, according to Basch, to be having an object-experience or object-relationship with his teacher—that is, the experience of being taught. However, to the extent that the student depends upon the teacher for his self-esteem, the student also has a selfobject experience or selfobject relationship with his teacher. Although this experience renders the student's self stronger (if you like, more "cohesive"), his self may not have been endangered.

Should those who acknowledge us and affect even our cohesive sense of self be designated as objects, as Basch would have it, or as selfobjects? I like Goldberg's example (personal communication 1978) of a selfobject experience: that one feels good about oneself when seeing the nodding head of at least one member of the audience when

---

[4]The definition of *selfobject experience* that I am employing here is the experience of an object that provides functions in a relationship that evoke, maintain, or otherwise positively affects the sense of self.

one is speaking. But this experience may or may not be needed to maintain the cohesion of the speaker's self, or even his self-esteem. If not one person nodded, the speaker may or may not experience a drop in self-esteem, depending on the cohesion or strength of his self. That is, a selfobject experience occurs on a continuum—from the self-enhancing use of available selfobjects toward the requirement of selfobject responsiveness for maintaining self-esteem or the intactness of the self.

While Kohut (1977) conveyed that selfobject experience makes up for an inadequacy in self structure, he also understood selfobject experience to be intrinsic to normality:

> The primary psychological configuration . . . is the experience of the relation between the self and the empathic selfobject [p. 122, italics added] . . . The psychologically healthy adult continues to need the mirroring of the self by self-objects . . . and . . . continues to need targets for his idealization. No implication of immaturity or psychopathology must, therefore, be derived from the fact that another person is used as a self-object—self-object relations occur on all developmental levels and in psychological health as well as in psychological illness . . . the difference between health and disease is seen here to be relative [p. 188].

That is, when Kohut asserted that the self needs selfobject responsiveness from birth to death, he was underscoring the psychological legitimacy of this need. The need for selfobjects does not disappear; the need's urgency and intensity decreases and becomes more phase-appropriate and situation-appropriate as the self becomes stronger. Yet, I welcome Basch's recommendation that we distinguish more sharply between the experience of the immature and poorly functioning self and the experience of the mature and well-functioning self. I welcome this as a guide to the choice of an optimal therapeutic response for the patient. Basch's practical application of Stern's schema of development affirms my view that our task as therapists should not be rigidly determined by an adherence to a prescribed model of intervention. If our interventions are intelligibly guided by our knowledge of which domains of development and in what sectors the patient is functioning more or less cohesively, the mode of responsiveness that is therapeutically optimal for a particular patient will vary accordingly. For example, Miss F, for a long time, could only make use of Kohut's echo of her own views. He did not interpret that she needed echoing; he echoed her. To do otherwise, for her, simply did not work. However, we must also recognize that, except in extreme instances, such as in the case of Miss F, experiences of cohesiveness and noncohesiveness tend to be relative and fluctuating, and require other responses, such as the sequence of understanding (that is, recognition) followed by explanation (that is, interpretation).

A further value in distinguishing between self-cohesiveness and nonself-cohesiveness is in the study of the mature self. When one feels noncohesive, selfobject experiences are necessary, but when one feels more solid and vigorous, one feels not only less needy of selfobject responsiveness but feels the inclination, which Suttie long ago recognized as natural to the healthy self (Bacal & Newman, 1990), to share, to give—spontaneously: "[T]he child wakes up to life with the germ of parenthood, the impulse to 'give' and to 'respond' already in it. This impulse, with the need 'to get' attention and recognition, etc., [already] motivates the free 'give and take' of fellowship" (Suttie, 1935, p. 58). The latter constitute experiences that I would view as mature, regardless of the age of the individual. I doubt, however, that self-esteem regulation is absent from these experiences; rather, they are likely replete with this selfobject experience.

In citing evidence from infant research that indicates we should abandon the concept of the virtual self, Basch raises the question as to whether we always need selfobjects. Yet, the appearance of a self-sense early on, even in the normal newborn, or even earlier, does not preclude the possibility that this self-sense is evoked and maintained by the availability and responsiveness of the maternal surround. Self-cohesiveness does not occur in a vacuum. To me that means that, while there may not be any sense of undifferentiation as an absence of boundary between the infant and the mothering figure, one cannot speak of the state of an infant's self without at the same time taking into consideration, as both Winnicott and Kohut did, the quality of the caregiving by the caregiver. In other words, there is no self without selfobjects; the healthy self state depends on the experience, conscious or unconscious, of the self-selfobject tie.

In my view, the selfs of our patients are sustained by an unconscious knowledge that selfobjects are available. What is the nature of this knowledge? I submit that it constitutes the sense of a linkage, often an unconscious one, with the selfobject. In other words, the cohesive self—the self that does not apparently need selfobject experiences to maintain its self structure—the self state, in effect, that Basch would have us regard as object-related—is one in which unconscious (as well as preconscious and conscious) relationships with selfobjects are strong. This is a kind of paradox, but one that does not need to be resolved. It is comparable and similar to Winnicott's idea that the capacity to be alone is tantamount to being alone in the presence of someone. The relatively cohesive self does not need selfobjects as much and as often, because it has them; they are, as it were, more or less strongly linked with his or her self, and these linkages are responsible for what we call a strong self. Threats to self-cohesion and self-strength are, in effect, due to threats to these linkages, and the self then cannot maintain its strength and sometimes not even its integrity, and it may weaken and fragment. People like Miss F do not harbor these linkages and therefore cannot transfer such an inner experience onto the therapist. In other words, Miss F's grandiose and entitled behavior thinly concealed a self which, having virtually no inner links with selfobjects, was weak and felt constantly endangered, and she therefore needed to control the conditions for her treatment in order to maintain her precarious cohesiveness.

Are there objects other than selfobjects? How, for example, should we regard "bad" objects? Whereas they may be selfobjects that have failed, can they be regarded as selfobjects during the time they are experienced as failing to provide a selfobject function? And, of course, there are certainly bad objects that have never been selfobjects at all. They do not evoke the sense of self; they distort it, or negate it, or fragment it, and so forth. We must also recognize that there are psychologically nonsignificant objects. Objects may be experienced as quite neutral, and then they are also not selfobjects. We do not have a name for these objects. To cite a commonplace illustration[5]: A gasoline station attendant, whose inability to provide fuel because the pumps are empty, has no affect on the customer's sense of self at that moment, and he will simply shrug his shoulders and drive on to another gas station. At another moment, of course, when his self-state renders him vulnerable to selfobject failure, he might experience the gas-station attendant as having a significant effect on his sense of self, and react quite strongly.

And what are we to call sexual objects and experiences with them? They may or may not be just objects, in Basch's sense. They are, in fact, usually imbued with selfobject characteristics, even when they are experienced by the cohesive self: Good sexual experience, especially with significant others, that is, selfobjects, can feel deeply self-vitalizing and self-enriching. In other circumstances, they are sought to provide immediate sensual experiences that produce some sense of intactness or aliveness in a self that has become fragmented

---

[5]I am grateful to Dr. Ernest Wolf for this example.

or deadened as a result of self–selfobject rupture. The same may be claimed for mood-enhancing substances (Lichtenberg, 1991), even though the substances are not good for us.

I agree with Ornstein that self psychology does embody a unique ensemble of connected variables. I would submit, however, that self psychology is such a near blood relative to certain theories of object relations that it may legitimately be regarded as the heir apparent of these theories. Thus, although I would concur with his view that the study of object relations theories is useful because we can now understand these theories in greater depth than before from the current vantage point of self psychology, there is more to be gained than this understanding. Although the son may now be able to understand his forefathers better because he has found himself, he will also now be able to understand more about himself by learning from his forefathers. In studying the work of certain object relations theorists, self psychologists can benefit significantly from the experience and original thinking of some remarkably like minds.

REFERENCES

Bacal, H. A. (1987), British object-relations theorists and self psychology: Some critical reflections. *Internat. J. Psycho-Anal.* 68:81–98.

_____ (1990). Does an object relations theory exist in self psychology? *Psychoanal. Inq.* 10:197–220.

Bacal, H. A. & Newman, K. M. (1990), *Theories of Object Relations: Bridges to Self Psychology.* New York: Columbia University Press.

Basch, M. F. (1988), Further thoughts on empathic understanding. Presented at the 11th Annual Self Psychology Conference, Washington, DC.

Kohut, H. (1959), Introspection, empathy and psychoanalysis: An examination of the relationship between mode of observation and theory. In: *The Search for the Self, Selected Writings of Heinz Kohut: 1950–1978,* Vol. 1, ed. P. Ornstein. New York: International Universities Press, pp. 205–232.

_____ (1977), *The Restoration of the Self.* New York: International Universities Press.

_____ (1984), *How Does Analysis Cure?* ed. A. Goldberg & P. Stepansky. Chicago: University of Chicago Press.

Lichtenberg, J. (1991), What is a Selfobject? *Psychoanal. Dial.*

Rycroft, C. (1972), *A Critical Dictionary of Psychoanalysis.* New York: Penguin.

Stolorow, R. (1986), On experiencing an object: A multidimensional perspective. In: *Progress in Self Psychology,* Vol. 2, ed. A. Goldberg. New York: Guilford Press, pp. 273–279.

Suttie, I. D. (1935), *The Origins of Love and Hate.* London: Free Association Books.

Chapter 4

Can Psychotherapy Substitute for Psychoanalysis?

Jule P. Miller, Jr.

Shortly after becoming a candidate, I read several papers published in the *Journal of the American Psychoanalytic Association* (1954) dealing with the question of the similarities and differences between psychoanalysis and psychotherapy. I remember well my reaction. The papers that I read, by Gill, Rangell, and Stone, each found grounds for sharply separating psychoanalysis from psychotherapy—for making a qualitative distinction between the two. I read the papers rather hastily and remember thinking that the authors were twisting themselves into pretzels intellectually in an attempt to establish a spurious position. It seemed clear to me that there was a continuum from the less intense forms of psychotherapy to the most rigorous psychoanalysis, and I felt that the authors were "reaching" in an artificial way in their attempts to establish a qualitative difference. I thought that perhaps they were doing so for reasons of empire building or establishment of guild solidarity.

After many years of experience doing both analysis and therapy, I continue to believe that they are on a continuum and that there is no sharp dividing line either in theory, technique, goals, or results between psychotherapy and psychoanalysis.

However, in preparation for this chapter, I reread the contributions of Rangell and Gill and found them valuable. I believe my original judgments were too harsh, perhaps colored by my youth. After rereading the contributions, I do not believe that they were written for empire building motives, but were sincere attempts to fashion a distinct identity for a field that both authors deeply valued.

It may be of interest to review these early contributions. They illuminate the analytic atmosphere of the times, and raise issues that are still being considered today. For example, in his 1954 paper, Rangell sketches out the respective roles of the analyst and therapist in the way in which they work. He states:

> Let us consider that the mental apparatus exerts around it a field of magnetic energy. In psychoanalysis, the therapist takes up his position at the periphery of this magnetic field of his patient, not too far away, so that he is useless and might just as well not be there, nor too close, so that he is within the field interacting with it with his own magnetic field (he can err equally in both directions). Immune from repulsion or attraction (at least optimally, within the limits set by his own unconscious), he sits at the margin, like a referee in a tennis match, so that he can say to the patient, "this is what you are now doing, here is impulse, here defense, here resistance, here compromise formation, here symptom" . . . In psychotherapy, in contrast, the therapist does not sit consistently in that seat, though he may sit there momentarily. He is, rather, generally on the court with his patient, interacting with him, the two magnetic fields interlocked, with the therapist's own values, opinions, desires and needs more or less actively operative [pp. 741–742].

I doubt that Rangell would describe the two processes in quite that way today. Reading his 1954 description serves to remind us of the differences, for most analysts, between then and now. Today, especially from a self psychologically informed position, we emphasize the intersubjective context of both psychoanalysis and psychotherapy, and the ever-present, fluctuating, mutual influence of patient and analyst on each other. Today we realize that the magnetic fields of both patient and analyst are always in contact and interacting, a realization that has led to new therapeutic leverage in both analysis and therapy.

In his 1954 paper, Rangell described controversy among the members of the American. He wrote:

> The Committee on Evaluation of Psychoanalytic Therapy, [was] set up within the American Psychoanalytic Association in 1947. In the years of its work since then, this Committee was never able to pass the initial and vexatious point of trying to arrive at some modicum of agreement as to exactly what constitutes psychoanalysis, psychoanalytic psychotherapy, and possibly transitional forms. In its last report about half a

year ago, . . . the Committee not only failed to arrive at any acceptable formulations in this regard, but was forced to conclude, incredibly enough, "that a strong resistance to any investigation of this problem existed among the members of the American Psychoanalytic Association" [pp. 734–735].

Rangell noted, however, that, according to the results of a questionnaire, in the view of the majority of the members of the association, "the two disciplines, at far ends of a spectrum, are qualitatively different from each other, though there is a borderland of cases between them" (p. 737). Rangell indicated his own ambivalence by saying, in relation to the issue of a qualitative difference that, "day is different from night, though there is dusk; and black from white, though there is gray . . ." (p. 737). Of course, one can look at such metaphors in two ways—as illustrating a qualitative difference between the two extremes or, as emphasizing the infinite number of gradations between them, shading from one end of the continuum to the other.

To clarify his position, Rangell (1954) gave a definition of psychoanalysis. He stated:

psychoanalysis is a method of therapy *whereby* conditions are brought about favorable for the development of a transference neurosis, in which the past is restored in the present, *in order that*, through a systematic interpretative attack on the resistances which oppose it, there occurs a resolution of that neurosis (transference *and* infantile) *to the end* of bringing about structural changes in the mental apparatus of the patient to make the latter capable of optimum adaptation to life [pp. 739–740].

He adds, "I submit that the items in above definition are *sine qua nons* and nonexpendable, and that no nonexpendable issue or condition has been omitted from it" (pp. 739–740).

In Gill's 1954 contribution, he also, offered a definition. He wrote: "psychoanalysis is that technique, which employed by a neutral analyst, results in the development of a regressive transference neurosis and the ultimate resolution of this neurosis by techniques of interpretation alone . . ." (p. 775). Both of these definitions are carefully constructed and valuable.

Good definitions of analysis are not frequent. Kohut gave us two more recent definitions, each on a different conceptual level. In *The Analysis of the Self* Kohut (1971) described analysis as requiring the inclusion of the central area of the patient's pathology in a stable transference configuration that can then be successfully worked through. If a patient is not analyzable (borderline or psychotic), as Kohut originally believed, transference configurations may be established that include aspects of the pathology, but these configurations cannot successfully include the core of the patient's psychopathology (pp. 30–32). A less clinical but more general definition of analysis is given in *The Restoration of the Self* (1977). Kohut states, "the essence of psychoanalysis lies in the scientific observer's protracted and empathic immersion into the observed, for the purpose of data gathering and explanation" (p. 302).

Freud's major statements of what constitutes analysis are well known and are given in several places. He usually includes the idea that therapy based on the concepts of unconscious motivation, resistance, and transference may be considered psychoanalytic.

Two items are of particular interest in regard to each of these aforementioned definitions. None of the five definitions makes any reference as to the number of times per week that the patient is seen, nor to the position of the patient (whether or not the patient is on the couch). Rangell, Gill, and Kohut considered these auxiliary issues, and not part of the essentials to be included in a definition of analysis. In my opinion, intensive, dynamic psychotherapy may be conducted in such a way as to fully satisfy the criteria of each of these definitions.

To return to Gill's paper, I believe that he realized that a great deal went on in analysis in addition to interpretation; he simply specified interpretation as the only valid technique for resolving the transference neurosis. If one wished, one could apply such a specification with equal force to psychotherapy. In explicating his view, Gill stated:

> the transference must be resolved by techniques of interpretation alone. *"By techniques of interpretation alone"* means *"and not by any other techniques of interpersonal behavior."* This is not meant to deny that unceasing processes of affective nonverbal communication go on between analyst and patient but that the goal of analysis is not to rest until these affective nonverbal interchanges have been converted into explicit verbalizations and have been encompassed by interpretation [p. 780].

I believe this last statement is an example of the idealization of analysis that characterizes the papers of the period. Of course there are unceasing processes of active, nonverbal communication, but, as most analysts realize today, it is out of the question to imagine that each and every one of these nonverbal communications can be explicitly verbalized and encompassed by interpretation. By the time the analyst cleared up a fair sized segment of material in this manner, innumerable additional unexamined affective interchanges between analyst and patient accumulated. Therefore, analyst and patient can explicate only some of the affective interchanges between them; most must remain unexamined.

Gill's (1954) ambivalence about making a qualitative distinction is strong. He stated:

> I feel that if I have not been clear or if I have been misunderstood, it will be said that I first demonstrated that psychotherapy cannot possibly do what psychoanalysis can and then said that it does in fact do so. Rather than that, I have tried to say that techniques and results in psychoanalysis and intensive, relatively non-directive psychotherapy are not the polar opposites which they are often declared to be, and that a more positive and detailed description of changes both in psychoanalysis and in psychotherapy . . . will help to make this clear [pp. 795-796].

In the years since I read these papers, I have heard and read many discussions of the relationship of psychoanalysis to psychotherapy. Most analysts have continued to maintain that there is a sharp, qualitative line separating the two procedures. Among the various claims that have been made are:

> Analysis promotes the transference neurosis whereas psychotherapy either avoids it or cannot promote it adequately.
>
> In analysis the transference neurosis is resolved or eliminated by interpretation, whereas in psychotherapy the transference persists and is handled by manipulation.
>
> Analysis leads to changes in the central core structures of the personality and therefore to enduring improvement, whereas psychotherapy is able to change only the derivative structures, and sometimes those only partially, and therefore the changes are incomplete and relapse more likely to occur.
>
> Suggestion is operative in psychotherapy, often as the central agent, and continues to color the results of the treatment. Suggestion also operates in analysis, but its effects are removed by interpretation of the suggestive influences.
>
> Parameters, non-interpretive interventions, are frequent in psychotherapy and remain unanalyzed, whereas they are minimal in psychoanalysis and then are removed by interpretation of the parameter.

Other differences have been adduced, but the aforementioned are the principal ones that stay in my mind. I believe that each of these distinctions is fallacious. If one is considering intensive uncovering psychotherapy with ambitious goals, the differences, in regard to any of these dimensions, is at most one of degree, and the two forms of treatment may blend imperceptibly into each other. In general, I believe that the creation of such lists of dichotomies resulted from an idealization of analysis and an underestimation of the possibilities of psychotherapy. Idealization of analysis is nowadays less pronounced, and psychotherapy has become more sophisticated and its potential more widely respected.

The frequently made comments about employing interpretation to remove the effects of parameters, to remove the effects of suggestion, or to eliminate or resolve the transference neurosis are, in my opinion, untenable. One cannot undo or remove anything that has occurred in analysis or psychotherapy by interpretation or by any other means. Recall the stanza of the Rubáiyát of Omar Khayyám:

> The Moving Finger writes; and, having writ,
> Moves on: nor all your Piety nor Wit
> Shall lure it back to cancel half a Line,
> Nor all your Tears wash out a Word of it.

By appropriate interpretation, exploration, and other techniques we may modify, ameliorate, or diminish the effects of our interventions; we may be able to change the patient's feelings about our interventions, often in such a way as to further the progress of treatment. But those feelings cannot be completely removed or abolished to leave some type of retrospectively pure surface behind. Follow up studies of analysis, for example, show that powerful transference formations are never eradicated but persist with surprising intensity. If a successful analysis depended upon removing the transference neurosis by interpretation, there would be, according to the best available empirical data, no successful analyses.

In a recent article in *Psychoanalytic Inquiry*, Rangell (1989) commented on his original paper. He noted that in 1979, 25 years after the publication of their original papers, Gill, Stone and he reviewed their positions at a symposium in Atlanta and brought them up to date in the light of their accumulated experience. He stated,

We all agreed that the area between the two [psychoanalysis and psychotherapy] were less definitive than we had thought, that analytic goals could be achieved on each side of the technical border. Gill (1979), however, now held that since the two approaches were mainly a continuum there was no qualitative differences between the two, I felt, along with Stone, that while there is an overlap, as indeed we had stated earlier, there is also still a difference. Now as then there is day and night, although there is also dusk [p. 58].

Rangell (1989) expressed a greater recognition of the similarities between analysis and therapy, and a richer appreciation of the power of psychotherapy. For instance, Rangell described several cases that were treated in psychotherapy by him in a somewhat irregular manner. These were patients that he saw in his second home in Carmel, California. He saw the patients sometimes for several sessions on alternate weekends; at other times he might not see them for three or four weeks. Despite this limitation, he noted a number of instances of remarkable improvement. For example, one patient "extended her life creatively and socially in a manner and to a degree which would have been considered successful in psychoanalysis" (p. 61). Another case, a woman who was seen about once a month, changed profoundly. Rangell wrote, "A change in sexual and gender identity was achieved which would have been a proud result in a more typical and longer if not more definitive analytic exposure. Her clothes, appearance, demeanor and attitudes changed, which coincided with her interest now in the upbringing of her little girl" (p. 62). Rangell noted in this article that he also treats patients in psychotherapy, one to three times per week in his practice in Los Angeles. He stated "Structural changes here too are achieved by many" (pp. 60–61). I believe his frank observations are very helpful. Rangell is clear that these exceptional results have been attained with patients who had unusual abilities to utilize the psychotherapeutic process. I had similar results, as I believe many analysts had who practice both therapy and analysis.

I am describing aspects of Rangell's thirty-five year span of writing on this issue because he is a valued contributor to our field and, in addition, the developments and changes in his view of the relationship of psychotherapy to analysis parallel that of many present day analysts.

There are some patients who are particularly able to utilize psychotherapy. If such patients are seen two or three times a week, they may achieve a depth of openness and contact with the therapist and a degree of therapeutic progress that are fully the equal of those that are attained in many analyses. Once in a while, one sees a patient, with a genius for being a patient, who may accomplish analytic goals, usually over a prolonged period of time, in once-a-week psychotherapy.

Similar considerations apply concerning the longevity of results. I had occasion, over many years, to follow patients treated by me and by colleagues. Very salutary results achieved in psychotherapy tend to be long lasting, comparable to the stability of improvement achieved in many analyses.

Patients who were analyzed in their youth will sometimes present themselves for a period of psychotherapy. Usually these patients benefited substantially from their previous psychoanalyses, but residual problems, or problems brought to the surface over the intervening years, led to their seeking additional treatment. Often, these mature patients prefer psychotherapy to the commitment of undertaking another analysis and they tend, as a group, to be capable of rapid and deep changes.

I believe that there is a single most important factor common to all psychotherapies, and that it is helpful to keep an overview of this factor in mind. Schematically stated, I believe that the central underlying process in psychotherapy is the formation and maintenance of a self–selfobject bond between patient and analyst. This bond enhances the patient's self-functioning. As it is maintained over time, the effects of this bond are internalized and lead to lasting improvements in the functioning of the patient's personality. From the quality of this improvement, one may infer that both structural growth and a reduction of intrapsychic conflict have occurred.

The therapist's optimal responsiveness to the patient, based on his empathic understanding of the patient, powerfully enhances the core therapeutic process. The therapist's responsiveness helps the patient feel secure enough to form a deeper bond. The therapist's responsiveness to disruption of the self–selfobject bond is vital in restoring the bond when the inevitable disruptions do occur. The understanding and repair of ruptures in the self–selfobject bond is, in my opinion, one of the most important technical operations in therapy. The emphasis on empathic understanding and optimal responsiveness by self psychologically informed therapists furthers their ability to maintain the self–selfobject bond, and accounts for much of the increased therapeutic effectiveness of self psychological work.

How does this descriptive process compare to the major underlying process in psychoanalysis? In my opinion, there is no substantial difference. The most essential underlying process is the same in both psychotherapy and psychoanalysis. I believe, as did Kohut (1984), that therapy conducted by members of other analytic schools, if successful, is effective because of the same core process—the formation of a self–selfobject bond, its maintenance, and internalization. Since therapy involves a human being working with another human being, all therapists experience, and respond to, a degree of mutual empathic contact with their patients. Significant aspects of this contact may be outside of the therapist's awareness, and non-verbal. Even if the therapist specifically disavows any role for empathic understanding, it cannot be entirely circumvented, and is, in my opinion, an essential part of any therapeutic progress that may be achieved by that therapist.

The view that this core process is essential for genuine progress in any form of dynamic therapy helps to explain important clinical data. For example, the observation that therapists from different schools, who rely on widely differing understanding of their patients and often make very different interpretations, may each achieve substantial therapeutic results. It helps to explain, also, the observation that profound changes may occur in some patients where interpretation is used sparingly, and insight is minimal, whereas few changes may occur in other patients despite systematic interpretation and, seemingly, extensive insight into relevant dynamics. These clinical data may be understood when we realize that the theory a therapist believes is less important than the core therapeutic process itself; the content of interpretations is less important than the formation of the self–selfobject bond, its maintenance, and internalization.

Psychoanalytic lore holds that a famous old-time analyst, I believe it was Hanns Sachs, once said that the deepest analysis is comparable to scratching the surface of a continent with a stick. When I heard this, as a young candidate, I found the comparison puzzling and disheartening. Now I find it overdrawn, but more understandable. We initiate powerful changes in psychotherapy and in psychoanalysis, yet even in the most complete treatment, much remains unchanged. Of equal importance, we understand only partially what we have initiated, and we understood only partially the way in which we have effected changes. In my opinion, there is much room in these areas of understanding for careful study and observation.

Having discussed work with gifted patients, we consider the average situation. If one compares a typical analysis with a typical twice-weekly psychotherapy, the self–selfobject bond that is formed in the analysis will usually be deeper, and the explication and understanding of the bond will usually be more extensive, and the internalizations more complete, leading to deeper and more far-reaching improvement. However, although these differences may be important, they are only differences of degree. A significant transference formation usually develops in both forms of therapy; this formation is typically more apparent in analysis than in therapy, although at times it may not be very visible in either. The more intense the psychotherapy and the more it is conducted in an analytic fashion, the less the difference between the two modalities.

Some of the emphasis on making a distinction in the earlier literature may center around how psychotherapy was formerly practiced. In his 1954 article, Gill made the point that most psychotherapy done by analysts tended to be brief, with very limited goals, and was actively conducted. He hypothesized that, perhaps if therapy were done in a less active fashion, more comparable to the way in which one conducts analysis, and if it could go on for a longer period of time, the results might well be termed intermediate, between brief supportive forms of psychotherapy and true psychoanalysis. Today, in contrast to the time when Gill wrote, we have a number of therapists engaging in very long-term, intensive, uncovering psychotherapy, (sometimes with the patient on the couch). These therapists have ambitious goals for the outcome of the psychotherapy.

How is such treatment distinguished from psychoanalysis? In regard to this particular form of intensive psychotherapy, there are probably no intrinsic differences between this form and psychoanalysis. Distinctions may be made on historical or territorial grounds; for example, sometimes the distinction is based on whether the treatment is being conducted by a psychotherapist or by a psychoanalyst, or, on the kind of credentials that the therapist possesses. Certainly, the skill of the therapist and the "fit" between therapist and patient is very important. But the aforementioned do not amount to general and intrinsic differences between the two procedures – perhaps, in this particular instance, better designated as one procedure with two names. And there is no guarantee that any particular form of training or credentials will produce the most skillful therapist or analyst for a given patient.

To return now to the topic: "Can Psychotherapy Substitute for Psychoanalysis?" (The question, as I am asking it, refers to patients who would be considered suitable for psychoanalysis.) The answer to the question is yes, if properly conducted. For maximum improvement, patients need to regress to the level of their most central psychopathology. Some patients, who are gifted as patients, may achieve the necessary depth of regression relatively easily because their defenses are pliable and the important issues are relatively accessible. With such patients, several-times-a-week psychotherapy over a prolonged period of time may be fully satisfactory. Most patients are not particularly gifted as patients, however; they are more rigidly constructed, their defenses are more impermeable, and they may need the maximum frequency of meetings, the use of auxiliary techniques (such as the couch, etc.), in order to experience an optimum level of regression. In other words, they will do best in an analysis, or its equivalent. It is the less accessible patients, with ingrained psychopathology, who require either an analysis or a form of intensive psychotherapy that closely approximates it, to obtain the best therapeutic results.

I recall one patient, a young woman, who consulted me years ago for help in adjusting to a business educational program. This was accomplished by once-a-week psychotherapy. Then she said that she wished to marry, which she had been unable to do. She also wished to be able to have a child. We increased the frequency of our meetings from once a week to twice a week, and then she began to use the couch. However, after a considerable period of time, the therapeutic work became flat and stagnant. We discussed this stagnation, and I suggested that she try coming four times a week, and we would convert her treatment to analysis. She was interested in this, although somewhat skeptical, saying that she felt that she had been wasting her time at twice a week. I replied that I thought it might be harder for her to waste her time at four times a week. Laughingly, she agreed to give it a try. To the surprise of both of us, within two months, she was in the midst of a florid, explicit, transference neurosis. The rest of the analysis, which went on for several years, was difficult but rewarding.

I believe that many analysts have similar experiences. Some patients may do very well at twice a week; others require more intensive work in order to make maximum progress. Similarly, some patients can work satisfactorily face-to-face, whereas others find their optimum level of regression more easily if they are using the couch.

Some therapists are not comfortable facilitating or working with deep regressions, and this may lead to difficulties. I believe it is unfortunate when a patient, who could profit from an intensive experience, is maintained instead in a less intense form of psychotherapy. Such patients may improve, the improvement may be considerable, yet it still may be substantially less than would have been possible for them. I believe one should either work with such patients intensively so that they may achieve maximum benefits, or, if the therapist is not comfortable doing intensive work, he or she should refer the patient.

For reasons of brevity, I have written of the patient largely as if he or she existed in isolation. For example, I have written of patients with an unusual gift for being patients, and of more average and rigidly defended patients. Of course, no patient exists in isolation; it is always the unique pairing of patient and therapist, and their interaction, that are determinative. A gifted patient working with one therapist might be much less gifted if working with another therapist.

This leads me to a related issue. I believe that self psychologically oriented therapists are, in general, more effective therapeutically than therapists with other orientations. In making referrals, I try to choose a self psychological therapist or analyst, depending on the intensity of treatment that I believe is required. A problem arises when a patient needs intensive work and a self psychologically informed therapist is available, but the only analysts available are of other orientations. To me, this is a dilemma. If I know the analyst to be particularly sensitive and aware of selfobject issues, I may refer to him or her. However, if the analyst seems rigid, or insensitive to selfobject issues, especially to the effects of narcissistic injury, I am inclined to choose a self psychologically informed therapist, even though he or she may not work at more than moderate intensity. In these instances, and they are not uncommon, the benefits of a self psychological orientation seem to be more important than the frequency of the sessions.

To obtain the greatest depth of therapeutic effect in patients with longstanding problems, the variables of both frequency of sessions and duration of treatment must be considered. In the large majority of such patients, progress is slow, and treatment, whether analysis or therapy, must often be protracted. At present, it appears that, with most such patients, treatment must also be frequent, in terms of the number of sessions per week, if one is to achieve profound change, whether or not the treatment is designated as therapy or analysis. Years of effort have not yielded a way to reduce the duration of treatment with most chronic patients and still attain maximum results. Two related areas of speculation, however, have led me to wonder whether or not the frequency of sessions might be, at least more often, successfully varied. The first has to do with the expectations and "set" of the therapist; the second with the way in which treatment is conducted.

As to the first speculation, it is an oversimplification to believe that frequency of sessions or use of the couch are important only because of an intrinsic effect that these factors have on the patient. The analyst is affected as well by the frequency of interviews and position of the patient. Perhaps more important, the expectations both patient and analyst have for the results of treatment are affected by these variables. For example, attitudes such as, "this is only therapy," or, "this is psychoanalysis!," whether held by the analyst or the patient, may powerfully affect the outcome of treatment.

Many of the patients I have followed, who have made extensive gains in twice-weekly therapy, have been patients whom I followed in supervision or consultation. The patients were usually treated by nonmedical therapists who were well trained but were not analysts. Part of the success of these therapists was possible, I believe, because they were not hindered by a conviction that analysis was necessary to achieve genuine and profound change in their patients. When I do psychotherapy myself, my exposure during analytic training to the idea that only analysis can be maximally effective, may be a limitation on my work. I believe that, because of this bias, I have subtly limited what some of my psychotherapy patients could achieve. (This may have been a factor in the stagnant period of twice-weekly couch therapy described in the case vignette.) I believe I have seen a similar limitation in the work of analytic colleagues. Certain patients, however, because of particular features of their history, enabled me to circumvent this bias. Thus freed, I was able to facilitate the achievement of deep and lasting structural change in twice-weekly psychotherapy with these particular patients.

On reflection, I believe similar issues may have influenced Rangell's work as well. Perhaps working in his summer house, under circumstances where he could not conduct a traditional analysis, freed Rangell from a bias similar to mine, a bias to the effect that a patient must be in analysis for profound changes to occur. Thus freed, he may have been open to the full potential of his patients and thereby able to achieve outstanding therapeutic results.

Secondly, perhaps our traditional emphasis on the frequency of interviews in order to produce an optimal level of regression is an artifact of the way in which analysis has often been conducted. Childhood trauma may be duplicated and repeated in analysis if the analyst does not maintain a consistently empathic stance. This leads to retraumatization of the patient, a dislocating experience, and, as a consequence, to increased resistance to therapy. Perhaps such iatrogenically promoted resistance has required us to try to force regression by means of a high frequency of sessions. Perhaps psychotherapy conducted sensitively, from a self psychological point of view may, by reducing iatrogenically heightened resistance, more often lead to an optimal level of regression with sessions of lesser frequency. Perhaps the occasional outstanding results with psychotherapy reported by various analysts may, through a self psychological approach, be attained more often. Such an approach could well act synergistically with changes in the "set" of the analyst, leading to exciting prospects for more effective therapeutic results. These are, of course, empirical questions to be decided by observation of self psychologically informed treatments of varying frequency.

I want to conclude with some thoughts about self psychology and therapy. The self psychological point of view has made our therapeutic work more effective. I believe the results are more favorable in part because we come closer to addressing the essential psychopathology and, in part, because we take more care to avoid inflicting narcissistic injury on our patients and are more alert to detect it and to attempt to repair it when it does occur. I was tempted to say that, because of self psychology, psychotherapy of moderate intensity has become relatively more potent in relation to analysis than it was in the past; that self psychology has narrowed the power gap between them. However, the self psychological perspective has also substantially enhanced the therapeutic results of analysis, and the full extent of this enhancement may not yet be apparent. Therefore, I believe that the clinical power of both dynamic psychotherapy and psychoanalysis has been increased, both to an extent that is not yet fully ascertained, and it will therefore remain for further observation to determine if one mode of treatment has profitted more than the other from the self psychological perspective.

REFERENCES

Gill, M. M. (1954), Psychoanalysis and exploratory therapy. *J. Amer. Psychoanal. Assn.*, 2:771–797.

Kohut, H. (1971), *The Analysis of the Self*. New York: International Universities Press.

———— (1977), *The Restoration of the Self*. New York: International Universities Press.

———— (1984), *How Does Analysis Cure?*, ed. A. Goldberg & P. Stepansky. Chicago: University of Chicago Press.

Rangell, L. (1954), Similarities and differences between psychoanalysis and dynamic psychotherapy. *J. Amer. Psychoanal. Assn.*, 2:734–744.

———— (1989). Structural and interstructural change in psychoanalytic treatment. *Psychoanal. Inq.*, 9:45–63.

Chapter 5

Commentaries

ANALYTIC PSYCHOTHERAPY AND PSYCHOANALYSIS:
A CONTINUUM?
Paul H. Tolpin

In his chapter Jule Miller tackles a rather difficult issue with a mix of thoughtfulness, candor, and awareness of complexities that is both stimulating and satisfying.

The title of the chapter, "Can Psychotherapy Substitute for Psychoanalysis," is instantly alerting, posing an unexpected question about the value of the two modalities with the use of the surprise word "substitute." Miller does not ask how psychotherapy and psychoanalysis are similar or how they differ, or when one can be used to greater advantage; rather he asks, in effect, whether psychoanalysis is replaceable by psychotherapy. My "mind-jerk" reaction to the title, the word, the question, was a mix of curiosity and distress. First of all, "substitute"—was it really the appropriate word? If so, in how large a sense was it meant? And psychotherapy—how was it to be defined? And what's more, how was psychoanalysis to be defined?

Of course, I had given some thought to the general issue any number of times before but from a different perspective: Namely, when is psychotherapy indicated and when is psychoanalysis indicated?—not in terms of practicality but in a clinically relevant sense. Reading further, it became clear that Miller had chosen his words

59

carefully. He was considering a specific issue and a specific kind of psychotherapy. Only long-term, intensive, dynamic psychotherapy, the aim of which was the mobilization and the adequate resolution of moderate to moderately severe psychological problems, was included. And Miller added an additional requirement: that both modalities, psychotherapy and psychoanalysis, were to be guided by self psychological theory.

As you read, Miller concluded his exploration of whether psychotherapy can indeed substitute for psychoanalysis with the statement, "Yes, in many cases." Miller holds that there is a continuum between intensive, long-term psychotherapy and psychoanalysis. According to him, there is "no sharp dividing line either in theory, technique, goals or results between psychotherapy and psychoanalysis." He believes that, at most, there is a quantitative difference between the two, based on the degree or depth of the selfobject bond formed in the therapeutic endeavor. However, he adds that in analysis, "the explication and understanding of [the selfobject bond] will usually be more extensive and the internalizations more complete [and will lead to] deeper and more far-reaching improvements." For him, analysis is really "one procedure with two names." Intensive psychotherapy and psychoanalysis are qualitatively the same, if done by competent therapists and, if the selfobject bond is sufficiently deep and its disruptions, empathically understood, and repaired through optimal responsiveness.

As I read Miller's chapter, I felt pulled first in one direction and then in another. At one moment, Miller's arguments seemed quite convincing and at another moment, I found myself balking. How to resolve this? I turned to an old standby—my own clinical experience.

Although I have not had the same kind of experience Miller describes about various types of patients, I have had cases that, without considering the work as strictly analytic, had surprisingly good outcomes. I considered them to be intensive, psychoanalytically-informed psychotherapy, but not psychoanalysis.

One such case, that of a well-functioning, 23-year-old single male, very bright and psychologically gifted, from a stable, upper-middle-class family (although his parents were divorced when he was 18 years old), was seen in treatment twice a week, face to face for about a five-year period. (The decision about this period of treatment arose from a mix of realistic and personal issues. His schedule did not permit more frequent sessions, but he also did not want them for reasons I shall mention shortly.) His main complaints were his fear of involvements with women, moodiness, difficulty concentrating on his graduate studies, and general unhappiness. Together with a generally positive feeling about me, a very intense, rather specific transference reaction developed almost immediately. This transference reaction rarely arose in the same manner after the first two years of treatment; it manifested as a periodic, sudden, deep distrust of my interest in him. Any assumed sign of my lack of interest triggered feelings of terrible humiliation and rage. Such breaks in the selfobject bond, recognized by a perceived look on my face of weariness, distractedness, or self-absorbtion, evoked an explosive reaction such as, "If you do that once more, I'm getting out of here!" And later in the hour, "You did it again. I can't take it!" After a time, he would calm down when I would say in effect that though I wasn't aware of the feeling he ascribed to me, I had apparently done something that made him feel I had lost touch with him.

Although these reactions were explored, they did not seem to be tied to any clearly defined transference issue. But it did appear to me that the reactions arose at a time when greater feelings of openness on his part were beginning to surface, and that he was fearful of revealing them to himself or to me; he expected injury. This complex seemed to be related sometimes to mother, sometimes to father, both of whom in some way had, indeed, injured him.

After that earlier treatment period, the reaction significantly diminished, and the therapeutic work centered predominantly on his fear of involvements with women. In time, he began to feel secure enough to begin sexual relations with several, and to fall in love with one. To relate it very briefly, much of the therapeutic work then focused on his reactions to various people in his life, and on how those reactions related to the presence of the past in the present. More specifically, his reactions occurred in relation to his back-and-forth, deepening affection for, and need to withdraw from, his girlfriend. Within the framework of a generally positive transference, his predominant feelings were that I was a reliably supportive mentor who could help him by encouragement and advice, and that I could help him to recognize the present-day sources of his "irrational sensitivities," as he called them, with me in the transference, and with others as well. In fact, I was able to help him to recommence his arrested development without fear of reprisal or abandonment from those elements within himself that reproduced internalized dangers from the past. However, and this is a crucial "however," there was a problem he spoke about in the first few months of treatment that we had never dealt with. Commenting one day about the couch in my office, he said, "If I were to lie down on it, I'd curl up into a kind of ball and cry so hard I couldn't stop. I'd like to do that but I won't." Actually, he never cried during treatment except perhaps for rare times when I could see some sudden moistening of his eyes. But there were never any tears. He could not go that far in my presence, though he told me that sometimes he did cry when he was alone watching what he derisively called sentimental movies or television advertisements. His fear of using the couch seemed to be related to his fear of exploring the depths of sadness, emptiness, and reactive anger he both did and did not want to reexperience. Despite that, much was meaningfully explored and understood, and we both considered his therapy quite successful so far as his overcoming a considerable degree of inhibition in his development. As I said earlier, he terminated treatment after five years, having discovered a great deal about himself, having dealt with, modifying, and overcoming many serious problems. He was living with the woman with whom he had fallen in love (and later married), and who seemed to be a very good choice for him. He felt far more secure and satisfied with himself and with how his life was going. He had changed from a vulnerable person in delicate balance to a man reasonably positive about himself and his relationships with others and with his work. He occasionally experienced revivals of the tearful, angry periods brought on by the old feelings of failure and inadequacy, which he linked to childhood experiences of being unloved. His wife-to-be was usually an effective antidote to these relapses. He said that was one of the reasons he had chosen her: he knew she would never leave him. Was this good psychotherapy or incomplete analysis? Or a combination of both?

Part of Miller's definition of all psychotherapies is the formation of a self–selfobject bond between patient and analyst that enhances self-functioning and promotes structural growth. Internalized, it leads to lasting improvements in the functioning of the patient's personality. According to Miller, much of the effectiveness of the therapeutic or analytic work results from the breaks in, and repair of, the self–selfobject bond by empathic understanding and optimal responsiveness. He says that this is the same process that goes on in psychoanalysis, with no substantial difference.

I would like to retain and include the preceding definition and expand on it in my definition of psychoanalysis. The essential features of psychoanalysis are that the goals of the therapist are to facilitate the development of a therapeutic atmosphere in which the patient can emotionally relive, recognize, and be able in some manner or degree to modulate the effects of the *most primary levels* of the origin of his pathology. For some patients, these levels may have little organized structure, but ultimately, whatever the primary level or levels of difficulty are, they should be revived, experienced and dealt with in the analytic work. Secondary levels of organization, such as defensive, compensatory, or characterological structures must, of course, also be recognized and worked with in terms of their adaptive and maladaptive effects. And their origins in, or relationship to, the maintenance of a cohesive, nuclear self should be explored. In my experience, a sustained intensity of engagement with the analyst is required to form the essential bond that permits the mobilization of the depths of the patient's personality. In my experience, this most often requires sessions at least three and more likely four times per week for the patient to maintain a base level of openness to, and contact with, his depths. This analytic process goes on for a fairly long period of time, three-to-five years or more, and with whatever auxiliary measures are needed to facilitate and maintain its development and unfolding.

My work with the young man I described would not be considered an analysis, but rather selfpsychoanalytically informed psychotherapy. The earliest origins of his pathology, the source of his stifled tears, were dealt with very little, if at all. Treatment was aimed at and limited to the mobilization, and further unfolding of, a kind of arrested development, within an understanding, supportive, and encouraging atmosphere.

So, do I agree with Miller's thesis that psychotherapy can substitute for psychoanalysis? As I define the terms, the answer depends on what one's goals are or can be because of both internal and external circumstances.[1] If they are less, or different from, what I have suggested psychoanalytic goals must be, the answer is that yes, psychotherapy can or should be substituted for psychoanalysis. If the goals are to reach, and to be able to explore the essential depths of the personality, I would say no, psychotherapy cannot be substituted for psychoanalysis. My experience with most patients has been that the quantitative difference at some point becomes a qualitative one, and that true, in-depth engagement requires both an analytic goal and adequate frequency of sessions. I would contend that except for

---

[1]After he read my comments, Arnold Goldberg informed me of an article he had written on this subject. I was not aware of his paper, but our differentiation of psychoanalysis from psychotherapy is very similar.

In addition, I recently rediscovered that in his article, "Summarizing Reflections" in *Advances in Self Psychology*, Kohut (1980) had much to say on the subject similar to what I believed I had arrived at on my own. At the time I wrote these comments, I had no recollection of having heard or read them before. In fact, the crucial idea of different goals in psychoanalysis and psychotherapy was a sudden, pleasurable inspiration, a last-minute, clarifying addition to the last draft of my paper. However, external evidence, (underlining in my copy of *Advances*) make it clear that indeed I had read them before.

a rare patient and analyst combination, the selfobject bonds do not become sufficiently deep and/or sustained for the core of the patient's neurosis to become adequately engaged and worked through without the preceding time and goal requirements having been met. Of course these requirements do not in themselves lead to a true analytic process; but that is another story.

But I must also qualify what I've just said. Different or less does not necessarily mean insufficient. The kind of indepthness I have described may not be suitable, or possible for, every patient and the results may sometimes be as good in a practical sense; in that case, less is enough no matter what the treatment is called. And I must add further that such a brief discussion of a very complex subject is too constraining. It is only the beginning of what must be an extended dialogue between therapists with different experiences and with differing opinions. Dr. Miller's paper is an excellent starting point for such an endeavor.

REFERENCES

Goldberg, A. (1980–81), Self psychology and the distinctiveness of psychotherapy. *Internat. J. of Psychoanal. Psychother.* 8:66–70.

Kohut, H. (1980), Summarizing reflections. In: *Advances in Self Psychology*, ed. A. Goldberg. New York: International Universities Press, pp. 531–536.

BEYOND THE BASIC RULE
James L. Fosshage

By releasing ourselves from the shackles of our limited vision of psychoanalytic treatment, we are able to recognize the complexity of the interactional field and the broad range of interventions that, heretofore, have too often been relegated to that poor step child of psychoanalysis, psychoanalytic psychotherapy. By questioning some of the traditional assumptions in psychoanalysis, Dr. Miller attempts to expand the horizons of psychoanalytic treatment beyond the bounds of the basic rule. He depicts how psychoanalytic treatment actually occurs, not how it is said to occur.

In psychoanalysis, interpretation became the primary sanctioned form of the analyst's intervention (i.e., action) and served as the "banner to distinguish psychoanalysis" (Friedman, 1978, p. 536) from psychotherapy. Because interpretation, as Goldberg (1990) suggests, is "probably much more rare an event than it is a common one," the analyst is officially granted an extremely narrow range of action. A host of interactions occur that are not included in our theory of psychoanalytic technique. Many of these Goldberg (1990) places "under the umbrella of ordinary human intercourse." What do we do with all of those actions that do not conform to the basic rule? One common solution is to exclude from psychoanalysis proper those actions that do not conform to the basic rule, whether it be noninterpretive remarks or, for some self psychologists, interventions from an external vantage point. These actions are regarded either as momentary parameters or, if they are more frequent, as indicative of a somewhat demoted process where such actions are allowed, namely, in psychoanalytic psychotherapy (probably rendering some of our most effective actions to psychotherapy). This solution belies how psychoanalysis is actually practiced.

In addressing the essentially post-Freudian (Lipton, 1980) distinction between psychoanalysis and psychoanalytic psychotherapy, Miller lists and explores five criteria that have been used to differentiate the two processes, all of which he assesses, with considerable clinical evidence, to be "fallacious." These five criteria are essentially what Gill (1984) called "intrinsic criteria," that is, criteria related to the techniques and goals of analysis in contrast to "extrinsic criteria." The intrinsic criteria are: the centrality of transference, neutrality, the induction of regressive transference, neutrality, the induction of regressive transference neurosis, and the resolution of the transference neurosis by interpretation alone or mainly by interpretation. The extrinsic criteria are: frequency of sessions, the couch, a relatively well-integrated patient, and a well-trained analyst. I wish to focus briefly on several of these intrinsic criteria for further consideration, and then to address Miller's overall position regarding the distinction between psychoanalysis and psychoanalytic psychotherapy.

The analysis of transference is commonly seen as the central task in psychoanalysis, although opinion widely diverges as to the nature of transference and, correspondingly, to the task of how to effectuate its analysis; for example, promoting or not promoting the transference, exclusiveness of transferential focus, management of extratransferential material, personal disclosure, and timing of interpretations. It is often claimed, as Miller notes, that the transference or transference neurosis is promoted in analysis, whereas it is avoided in psychotherapy, and is resolved via interpretation in psychoanalysis, whereas it is manipulated into a so-called transference cure in psychotherapy. Although suggestion is seen as a primary mode of technical intervention for psychotherapy, interpretation is the predominant mode for psychoanalysis and, in addition, is used to overcome the "contaminant" of suggestion.

The recent reconceptualization of transference by Wachtel (1980), Gill (1982), Hoffman (1983), Stolorow and Lachmann (1984), and Fosshage (1990) as an organizing activity profoundly undermines these claims. Organizing principles or schemas operate ubiquitously and, therefore, are ever present in both psychoanalysis and psychotherapy. Because transference is ubiquitous, a psychoanalytic goal of promotion is untenable. Any of the analyst's actions will evoke the patient's organizing activity. Some of the analyst's actions will evoke more problematic and invariant schemas, while others will serve as the basis for the establishment of new schemas. Promotion would entail an analyst purposefully behaving to evoke a particular schema, an event that would tend to recapitulate thematic experiences and reinforce the particular schema. The transference also cannot be "controlled" or "titrated," a recommended procedure for psychotherapy. Whether it be psychoanalytic psychotherapy or psychoanalysis, the principle goal, if transference is ubiquitous, must be to affect the transference. The principle procedure for addressing the transference in psychoanalysis is interpretation, namely, the illumination, understanding, and explanation of the transference. Although interpretation occurs in psychoanalytic psychotherapy, it is claimed that the transference in psychotherapy is often addressed through suggestion, support, and manipulation. These assumed differences will be discussed.

As Miller notes, psychoanalysis is often said to promote a regressive transference neurosis, whereas psychotherapy either avoids the transference or is not sufficiently intense to create it. Despite considerable disagreement as to how transference differs from transference neurosis, those who make the distinction commonly hold that the difference is quantitative. The transference neurosis is usually seen as entailing a patient's more comprehensive, intense, and persistent involvement with the analyst. As Gill (1984) suggested, the traditional procedures of abstinence and avoidance of early analysis of transference often iatrogenically induce a more intense transference. (Paradoxically, these procedures could be viewed as a form of manipulation.) If the difference is only quantitative, then, as Cooper (1987) pointed out, we should not use a terminological distinction that connotes qualitative differences. If transference varies only quantitatively, then an intrinsically different type of transference should not be posited and used to differentiate psychoanalysis from psychotherapy. Moreover, clinical experience clearly reveals, in my judgment, that the intensity of transference varies according to patient, analyst, and treatment moment, not just according to the frequency of sessions.

Within a positivistic scientific tradition, interpretation is viewed as an objective observer's delineation of fact. From a relativistic scientific position we know that the explanations contained within interpretations are the analyst's theoretically based organizations of the data. These interpretations, as Stolorow (1990) recently pointed out, are suggestions. They are suggested explanations emanating from the subjective vantage point of the analyst. Interpretations are a particular type of suggestion aimed at illuminating, understanding, and explaining the functions and origins of schemas. Interpretations differ from other types of suggestions (for example, the analyst's self-revelation that he or she was not feeling critical) aimed to affect the transference. Recognizing that interpretation is a form of suggestion vitiates the often made distinction between interpretation and suggestion for distinguishing these supposedly two distinctive procedures, psychoanalysis and psychotherapy.

Supportive statements are also differentiated from interpretation that is used to discriminate psychoanalysis from psychotherapy. The meaning of "supportive" rests heavily on one's theories as to what in the patient is supported and how it is supported. Interpretation, at its best, is, from a self-psychological perspective, supportive of consolidating selfhood. Additionally, the Menninger Project (Wallerstein, 1986) found, in contrast to expectations based on theory, that supportive statements appeared in psychoanalysis as well as in psychoanalytic psychotherapy. This finding both vitiates the distinction between psychoanalysis and psychotherapy and alerts us to a broader range of analytic activity than is currently included in our theory of technique.

I am reminded of an incident that happened over ten years ago between a new patient and myself. During the first session the patient, a recent graduate, informed me that she was going on her first job interview that day. During our second session, two days later, the patient paused after the first ten-to-fifteen minutes and for some reason—deviating from prescribed analytic procedure, but perhaps not from "ordinary human intercourse"—I inquired as to how her job interview had been. Of course what I considered to be an innocuous question emanating out of human concern and interest could be, and most surely would be, criticized for intruding with a nonanalytic remark, the use of suggestion, manipulation of the transference, imposing my agenda, and so on. To my surprise, my patient broke down into tears. In our exploration to understand what had occurred, (the most important analytic task), we discovered that the question about her job interview had been a question that her father would never have asked. My question conveyed to her a sense of acknowledgement and interest on my part that served as a profound beginning of a new relational experience, wherein the self–selfobject connection was in the forefront. I am sure that this is not a rare event, but we need to include events such as these in our discussion as well as in the theory of psychoanalytic treatment.

In addressing the psychoanalytic situation, Miller suggests that ". . . the theory guiding a therapist's work is less important than the core therapeutic process itself; the content of interpretations is less important than the formation of the self–selfobject bond, its maintenance and internalization." Miller is implying that the self–selfobject bond is established through ministrations including, but not limited to, interpretation, again opening the door to the inclusion of a wider range of actions within the theory of psychoanalytic technique. This corresponds with Kohut's (1984) delineating the importance of the "personal presence" of the analyst.

There has been a long-standing debate in psychoanalysis about the relative importance of affective bonding versus cognitive insight as "curative" agents (Friedman, 1978). Self psychology, with its emphasis on a specific type of affect bonding, has substantially altered the balance, which previously was top-heavy with cognitive insight. However, both are crucially important and are intricately interwoven in a curative experience. In his effort to delineate the core therapeutic process, I believe Miller, in this presentation, has inadvertently underemphasized the importance of interpretation, the specificity of its content, and the guiding theory. Theories and interpretive content, I believe he would agree, are vitally important in either facilitating or disrupting the self–selfobject connection and ongoing self-consolidation—what Miller refers to as the core therapeutic process.[1]

Interpretation is often juxtaposed with responding to or "gratifying" the patient's needs, the latter occurring only in psychoanalytic psychotherapy. Originally embedded in the positivistic scientific

---

[1]Miller refers to the finding that different psychoanalytic schools achieve success, (suggesting that more than one theory can be facilitative), to buttress his argument that the core therapeutic process is the ongoing, nontheory dominated self–selfobject connection. However, apart from the contaminating factor that some of these theories overlap, the outcome data and outcome criteria are currently far too gross to conclude that the use of various orientations does not result in substantial differences in outcome.

stance, interpretation has been viewed as an objective observation that not only obscures the contribution of the observer to the perception, but also conceals the fact that its delivery is the analyst's response to the patient. Accordingly, in the continued, heated debate over gratifying or interpreting selfobject needs, some self psychologists suggest that we only interpret and do not respond to selfobject needs. Implicit is the assumption that interpretation is not a response. Clearly, interpretation is an action and, therefore, from the patient's vantage point, a response that can facilitate or disrupt the self–selfobject connection. For example, a cogent, interpretive explanation of a patient's anxiety reaction can provide, via insight, a soothing function.

Suggestion and manipulation are related concepts; suggestion is traditionally viewed in psychoanalysis as a form of manipulation. Recognition that interpretation is a particular type of suggestion imperils once again the "objectivity" of interpretation and potentially taints it, if we insist on using the term, with that perjorative tinge of manipulation.

"Manipulating the transference" essentially refers to the analyst's noninterpretive response to alter the transference or, more specifically, the analyst's attempt to respond directly to the patient's developmental needs and not to repeat the traumatogenic experiences of the past. Once again, contrasting manipulation with interpretation of the transference derives from the positivistic, scientific stance, wherein the analyst is viewed as the objective observer and not the responding participant, whereas interpretation is viewed as a nonresponsive delivery of the objective truth. Interpersonal responses are often suspect and labeled perjoratively as manipulation of the transference. The current relativistic, scientific position enables the recognition that any of the analyst's actions impact the intersubjective field and, potentially, the transference. Interpretive activity is a response of the analyst that often, but not always, is a response different from the repetitive, traumatogenic responses of the past and, as previously noted, can be directly responsive to selfobject needs. Interpretation, despite our subjectively assessed intentions, can be viewed by an outside observer and subjectively experienced by the patient as a form of manipulation. For example, we know all too well how coercive resistance interpretations can be, particularly if a patient wants to leave treatment. No one would claim that manipulation is a justifiable intervention in psychoanalysis or psychotherapy; manipulation is an attribute of an intervention, the origins of which can only be ferreted contrasting manipulation out within the intersubjective field. Manipulation versus interpretation, a specious distinction, cannot be meaningfully used as a criterion for distinguishing psychoanalytic psychotherapy from psychoanalysis.

All of Miller's points and the foregoing negate the distinction between psychoanalysis and psychoanalytic psychotherapy and are summarized as follows:

1. Transference is ubiquitous and does not fundamentally differ from one process to the other.
2. A terminological distinction between transference and transference neurosis should not be made to address a quantitative difference and, therefore, cannot be used as a differentiating criterion.
3. The basic technique is analysis of transference in both processes.
4. Transference is not resolved, but organizational capacity is enriched in both processes.
5. Suggestion is used in both processes, for even interpretation is a form of suggestion.
6. Supportive responses occur in both processes.
7. The core therapeutic process for both processes is the establishment, maintenance, and regulation of the self–selfobject connection, and is facilitated by a broad range of analytic responses, including interpretation.
8. Clinical experience validates that enduring structural change occurs in both processes.

Miller clearly views psychoanalytic psychotherapy and psychoanalysis as more similar than not, and I concur with his view. Where we may differ is that he, I believe, still maintains, in the end, a distinction between the two. He views psychoanalysis and psychoanalytic psychotherapy as two points on a continuum, apparently based on the intrinsic criterion of the ability of the patient and the extrinsic criterion (Gill, 1984) of the frequency of sessions and its impact on regression. As Miller notes, many analysts, including Miller in this volume (see also Gill 1984; Rangell, 1989), have reported the use of analytic procedures and have obtained analytic results with fewer sessions, including once- or twice-a-week, and in an upright posture. What varies is not the process, but the particular intersubjective field that is analyzed regardless of how much time there is for the analysis.

We are in the process of expanding and reconceptualizing analytic technique and recognizing that its application generally does not need to be restricted by extrinsic criteria. What's critical is not the

differentiation between psychoanalytic psychotherapy and psychoanalysis, but the consistent application of expanded psychoanalytic
technique within the work that we do as psychoanalysts, work
designated as psychoanalysis. In this sense, psychoanalytic psychotherapy cannot be substituted for psychoanalysis, it *is* psychoanalysis.

REFERENCES

Cooper, A. (1987), The transference neurosis: A concept ready for retirement. *Psychoanal. Inq.*, 7:569–585.

Fosshage, J. (1990), Toward reconceptualizing transference: Theoretical and clinical considerations. Presented at annual meeting, Division 39, American Psychological Association, New York City.

Friedman, L. (1978), Trends in the psychoanalytic theory of treatment. *Psychoanal. Quart.*, 47:524–567.

Gill, M. (1982), *Analysis of Transference, Vol. I.* New York: International Universities Press.

_____ (1984), Psychoanalysis and psychotherapy: A revision. *Internat. Rev. Psycho-Anal.* 11:161–179.

Goldberg, A. (1990), *The Prisonhouse of Psychoanalysis.* Hillsdale, NJ: The Analytic Press.

Hoffman, I. (1983), The patient as interpreter of the analyst's experience. *Contemp. Psychoanal.*, 19:389–422.

Kohut, H. (1984), *How Does Analysis Cure?* ed. A. Goldberg & P. Stepansky. Chicago: University of Chicago Press.

Lipton, S. (1980), A further contribution to the advantages of Freud's technique. Paper presented to the Philadelphia Psychoanalytic Association.

Rangell, L. (1989), Structural and interstructural change in psychoanalytic treatment. *Psychoanal. Inq.*, 9:45–63.

Stolorow, R. (1990), Converting psychotherapy to psychoanalysis: A critique of the underlying assumptions. *Psychoanaly. Inq.*, 10:119–130.

_____, & Lachmann, F. (1984/85). Transference: The future of an illusion. *The Annual of Psychoanalysis*, 12/13:19–38. New York: International Universities Press.

Wachtel, P. (1980), The relevance of Piaget to the psychoanalytic theory of transfer-ence. *The Annual of Psychoanalysis*, 8:59–76. New York: International Universities Press.

Wallerstein, R. (1986), *Forty-Two Lives in Treatment.* New York: Guilford Press.

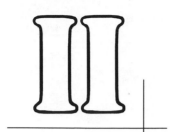

Clinical

Chapter 6

Countertransference in an Intersubjective Perspective: An Experiment

Peter Thomson

O wad some power the giftie gie us
To see oursels as others see us!
It wad frae monie a blunder free us,
An' foolish notion.

Robbie Burns
From poem "To a Louse," 1786

The stimulus for me to undertake this experiment arose from my special interest in the approaches to psychoanalytic therapy of Schwaber (1981a, b, 1983a, b, c, 1986, 1987) and an interest in the proponents of intersubjectivity, Stolorow, Brandchaft, and Atwood (Atwood and Stolorow, 1984; Stolorow, Brandchaft, and Atwood, 1987). It seemed to me that these approaches to psychoanalytic therapy were very promising, especially in the treatment of difficult patients, but that sufficient attention has not been given to the special countertransference problems associated with these approaches. There is a dearth of examples illustrating the countertransference experiences of the therapist. Consequently, I decided I would undertake a research project composed of an examination of the data of my countertransference experiences with my patients over a four-month period.

The four-month period of the study included a two-week vacation, taken after seven weeks of patient treatment. My intention was to try to discover the manner in which my own self-organization interacted with the patient's unfolding transferences. I hoped to find out how the patient's experience during analysis reverberated on my own experience and, thus, affected my responses; and how these responses then affected the patient. For the purpose of this presentation, I selected analytic material from the analyses of two patients. The events are described just as they happened.

HENRY

Henry, a young, single, librarian, was in the fourth year of analysis during the period of the experiment. A prominent feature of this analysis was periods of silence. Exploration of the silences showed them to be expressions of inhibitions arising from shame reactions caused by Henry's parents inability to respond affectively to him in his early life. The material described arose during the first five weeks of the experiment. I will describe the disruption of an archaic mirror transference.

In one session early in the study period, I noted that I reacted to Henry's continuing silence with some inner frustration. He spoke, at this point, of preferring to believe that I was truly nonresponsive and nonreceptive to him. I then commented, "So you feel more comfortable believing I am nonresponsive?" He replied, "Yes, and I am enraged at your nonresponsiveness." I became inwardly angry because, according to my own experience, I had in fact gone to considerable lengths to be both responsive and encouraging.

A day or two later, an event took place that affected the course of the analysis for several weeks. One morning, after a long silence, Henry said, "It is upsetting to have to say this. My friend Rob (who had leukaemia) died over the weekend." I responded, "You must have a lot of feelings about that, and I guess it is difficult to talk about them." I believed myself to have been compassionate, but as this conversation transpired, his view was vastly different. He remained silent for several days, and all efforts to encourage him to speak were of no avail. Finally, four days after the aforementioned exchange, he responded to my saying, "I think you are angry with me." He continued, "Yes, I needed a more intuitive response to my experience. My reaction has been to withdraw and to do things on my own." I noted myself feeling defensive and I wished to protest that I had done my best to empathize with him. Henry continued, "You did not seem to understand how upset I was. I felt you were very distant and harsh. You sounded technical, not genuine or sympathetic. I would have appreciated a more simple and personal comment." For some time, he continued to chide me. My experience of myself, so different from his experience, reminded me of Schwaber's similar experience with her patient, Ms. M (Schwaber, 1983c). I had to work quite hard to decenter from my pressing need to believe that I had only been kind. I made a number of remarks over the next period of time that I considered to be understanding of his feelings, but they were not accepted as such; for example, I said, "I truly appreciate your feeling so mistrustful and that you need the right kind of response." I also said, "Perhaps you could help me to become more usable." The latter statement was a response to his remark that I was of no use to him.

Henry's feeling that it was futile to talk to me, along with his anger and negativism, continued for two or three more weeks. He said, "If the quality, the tone and language, of your response isn't exactly right, it leaves me enraged. My sense is that you are far away from what I am experiencing. You suggested at one point that I fear to let you come closer to me. That infuriates me, it is so far removed from where I am."

Gradually, Henry's rage dissipated. My concretized sense of guilt and responsibility failed to take into account the occurrence of the triggering in the patient Henry, at the time of Rob's death, of a heightened sensitivity to a traumatic response.

INTERSUBJECTIVE INTERPLAY AS AN ORGANIZING THEME

I comment on this vignette in terms of the intersubjective field, with emphasis on my own input. I first noted my frustration with Henry's continued silence. Upon self-reflection, I recognized the influence of my classical training, which induced in me a prereflective need to regard his silence as a resistance. This aversive attitude caused me at times to match his silence with my own, and at other times to make excessive efforts to push Henry to speak. Unquestionably, my attitude had its effect on the intersubjective field, leading him to experience me as nonreceptive. Thus my comment, "So you feel more comfortable believing that I am nonresponsive" contains a denial of my contribution to his experience. His remark in response was "Yes, and I feel enraged at your nonresponsiveness." His remark can be understood, therefore, as quite fitting, although at the time I saw myself only as responsively encouraging.

The event that affected the analysis for some time, Henry's news of his friend's death, along with my response to it, must be understood in the light of my prereflective attitude. Although I thought I had been compassionate, the intersubjective field had already been coloured by my response to his continued silence. I must add, however, that another powerful determining factor was Henry's early life experience. But one can see how my prereflective attitudes interfered with my capacity to empathize. The silence was finally broken when I recognized and interpreted his anger with me. He was then able to tell me how he experienced me as harsh or technical, which can now be understood as my "classical" demand that he analyze; but at the time, I could hardly decenter from my belief that I had only been kind.

My next series of remarks, for example, "I truly appreciate your feeling so mistrustful" were, I think, a counterreaction to my feelings of failure. The latter feelings were a concretization of my sense of responsibility for his disappointment in me; I was thereby prevented from pursuing a genuine empathic inquiry into the source of his experience of me (Brandchaft and Stolorow, 1988).

Henry continued for another two or three weeks to feel that it was futile to talk to me, that I was far away from his experience. Why did his rage finally dissipate? I have no definitive answer but I think that as Henry sensed I was more in touch with his experience, this began to change the intersubjective "weather." I also have the strong impression that Henry's negative feelings gave expression to healthy adversarial strivings. A little later on, he commented on how he was pleased to, as he put it, have attained the freedom to "rant and rave." I believe that the material I described illustrates the complex mutual regulation and dysregulation of intersubjective interplay to be an organizing theme of analysis.

Before turning to the second patient, I will outline the work of Schwaber and that of Stolorow, Brandchaft, and Atwood on inter-subjectivity and then relate the work to countertransference. Schwaber's work is outlined in a series of papers published during the last decade (Schwaber, 1981, 1983a, 1983b, 1983c, 1986, 1987). The approach to intersubjectivity can be found in two recent books. These are *Structures of Subjectivity* by Atwood and Stolorow (1984) and *Psychoanalytic Treatment: An Intersubjective Approach* by Stolorow, Brandchaft, and Atwood (1987).

Schwaber

For approximately the last decade, Schwaber has been promulgating her thesis that the influence of the observer, the therapist, must be taken into account in the psychoanalytic situation (a view first put forward by Kohut, 1977). Her views are very clearly enunciated in her (1983c) paper, "Listening and Psychic Reality." In this paper, as in others, Schwaber uses many examples from the psychoanalytic literature to demonstrate how analysts of all theoretical persuasions have been obstructed in their listening and understanding of their patient's material by failing to take into account the influence of their theories and their own personal approaches upon the patient's material. As a result "the analyst attunes to a reality other than that of the patient's inner world, assuming the position of silent arbiter of what is or is not distorted in the patient's perceptual experience" (Schwaber, 1986 p. 911). She is at pains to demonstrate that analysts are participators, inescapably involved in bringing about what is happening in the psychoanalytic process. Schwaber (1983c) states, "The shift in perspective is one in which the organization of behaviour, of intrapsychic experience, is seen as the property of the more inclusive system of which the individual is a part. Such a move has considerable impact on the gathering of psychoanalytic data". Schwaber (1981b) quotes Sander's (1975) opinion that the change from viewing the organization of behaviour as the property of the individual to conceptualizing it as the property of a more inclusive system, of which the individual is a part, represents a major turning point in developmental research. "Listening from within the patient's experience, weaving the perception of the analyst's contribution, silent or stated, into the elucidation of the subsequently emerging material assigns different meaning to our understanding of transference and resistance" (Schwaber, 1983).

Schwaber wishes us to understand that, as psychoanalysts, we have not been listening from the vantage point of the patient's intrapsychic reality. Our own truths, in particular our theories, have tended to take precedence. As a result, we have been viewing the patient's experience of us and of his reality as distorted and our own as true. We have also failed to take into account all the influences that the analyst's presence and personality, in his silence or in his interventions, are having on the patient's material and behavior.

Intersubjectivity

The intersubjective viewpoint first appeared in Stolorow and Atwood's study of the interplay between transference and countertransference (Stolorow, Atwood, and Ross, 1978). They considered the impact of the correspondences and disparities that exist between the analyst's and the patient's respective worlds of experience on the treatment process (Stolorow, Brandchaft & Atwood, 1987, p. 2). Stolorow and Atwood, thereafter joined by Brandchaft, attempted to describe the conditions under which such phenomena obstruct or facilitate the unfolding of the psychoanalytic dialogue. Countertrans-ference, considered in this context to be inclusive of all that comprises the analyst's organization of self-experience, for good or for ill, clearly makes a major contribution to these conditions.

The essentials of intersubjectivity (Stolorow, Brandchaft, and Atwood, 1987) are outlined in these two passages, which originally appeared in *Structures of Subjectivity* (Atwood and Stolorow, 1984):

> In its most general form, our thesis . . . is that psychoanalysis seeks to illuminate phenomena that emerge within a specific psychological field constituted by the intersection of two subjectivities—that of the patient and that of the analyst. . . . Psychoanalysis is pictured here as a science of the *intersubjective*, focused on the interplay between the differently organized subjective worlds of the observer and the observed. The observational stance is always one within, rather than outside, the intersubjective field . . . being observed, a fact that guarantees the centrality of introspection and empathy as the methods of observation . . . Psychoanalysis is unique among the sciences in that the observer is also the observed.
>
> Clinical phenomena . . . cannot be understood apart from the intersubjective contexts in which they take form. Patient and analyst together form an indissoluble psychological system, and it is this system which constitutes the empirical domain of psychoanalytic inquiry.
>
> The intersubjectivity principal was applied to the developmental system as well:
>
> Both psychological development and pathogenesis are best concep-tualized in terms of the specific intersubjective contexts that shape the development process and that facilitate or obstruct a child's negotiation of critical development tasks and successful passage through develop-mental phases. The observational focus is the evolving psychological field constituted by the interplay between the differently organized subjectivities of child and caretaker [pp. 1–2].

The intersubjective approach is closely related to, and an out-growth of, self-psychology. Intersubjectivity, however, places special emphasis on the examination of the minute and subtle effects of the analyst's real presence and interventions as subjectively experienced by the patient. "The analyst seeks consistently to comprehend the meaning of the patient's expressions, and centrally, the impact of the analyst from a perspective within rather than outside the patient's subjective frame of reference. We have referred to this positioning as 'the stance of empathic enquiry' " (Brandchaft and Stolorow, 1988).

The analyst is unable to claim that his knowledge, theory, or interpretations, have any ultimate validity. As Brandchaft and Stolorow (1988) stated, "Access is then provided to the specific and idiosyncratic, not standardized or theory-dictated, way in which the patient is organizing his experience of the analyst and the meanings which the experiences have come to encode." The patient is free to question the analyst's interventions or silences and to react with total spontaneity without his behaviour being considered distorted or mistaken. But this places the therapist in a much more vulnerable position. Since pathology is now no longer viewed in terms of processes located solely within the patient, it no longer protects the therapist from the various ways in which he himself and his theories are implicated in the phenomena he observes. As Brandchaft and Stolorow (1988, p. 12) indicated, there is no longer the presence of a "cordon sanitaire" as is the case when the concept of distortion is utilized. Brandchaft and Stolorow describe this situation for the therapist as "frequently like feeling the sand giving way under one's psychological footing. Seeing oneself and the world consistently through the eyes of another involves a real danger that the analyst's own organization of self-experience and perspective will come under threat" (p. 12). My second case presentation offers illustrations of this experience and includes details of the threat to the therapist's self-organization as well as the mutual feedback cycle that ensued.

It may well be that the special value of the intersubjective approach is in allowing the greatest scope to the revelation of the patient's subjective reality. As Kohut said, "If there is one lesson I have learned during my life as an analyst, it is the lesson that what my patients tell me is likely to be true . . . that many times when I believed I was right and my patients were wrong, it turned out, though only after a prolonged search, that my rightness was superficial whereas their rightness was profound" (Kohut, 1984, pp. 93–94). Many patients suffer from a primary difficulty in their lack of a sense of reality about their inner experience. As Brandchaft and Stolorow (1988) suggest, the patient's ability to sustain a belief in their own subjective reality was derailed because their perceptions as children communicated to the caretakers information the caretakers did not want to hear, and so the patient's perceptions and affects became the source of continuing conflict. Such structural weaknesses predispose to borderline psychotic states. These conditions have been treated by the intersubjective approach, with special attention being paid to restoration of the patient's "core of subjective truth" (Stolorow, Brandchaft, and Atwood, 1987 p. 106–172). The intersubjective approach to these more than averagely disturbed patients is especially liable to give rise to countertransference problems for the therapist.

According to Stolorow and Lachmann, (1984/1985) the future of transference lies in the concept of organizing activity. Thus, transference would be the assimilation of the psychoanalytic relationship into the patient's world. Conceived in this way, transference was seen by these authors as an expression of the universal striving to organize experience and create meanings. We should therefore assume that the analyst's transference, which we call countertransference, must represent his own attempts to organize his experience of the patient and of the psychoanalytic relationship. That this attempt to organize his experience may be thrown into disarray will be demonstrated in my experience of the second patient.

The nature of the analyst's countertransference is influenced by the analyst's theoretical orientation to psychoanalysis (Wolf, 1983). This being the case, an analyst who uses one of the two approaches already focused on may be expected to encounter some unique difficulties. Let me first refer to the work of Schwaber (1983c). She gives an illuminating account of the particular problems that she encountered with two patients, Ms. M and Mr. K:

> I reflected on my countertransference, trying to ascertain whether it might have interfered with my ability to recognize the meaning of Mr. K's defensive stance or Ms. M's unrelenting sense of injury. Yet, however relevant a factor this may have been it did not touch on the full complexity of the question. There seemed to be another dimension, more critical, at issue. It was that I felt a particular *resistance to being experienced in this way*, as central to another's experience, while so different from how I felt myself to be. Each of these factors—the centrality of my unwitting participation in another's experience, as well as the lack of concurrence with my own experience of myself—seemed to stir a resistance which is not just my own, but may have more ubiquitous significance: a resistance to the acknowledgement that the truth we believe about ourselves is no more (though no less) "real" than the patient's view of us—that all we can "know" of ourselves is our own psychic reality [p. 329; italics added].

Schwaber then speaks of this resistance as a deeply-rooted pull back to the secure position of the external observer, attempting to assess the patient's experience as determined by processes independent of the analyst's presence within them. Here then is a special snare; that is, the need to avoid acknowledging the patient's view of us as having its own truth. I would, however, in disagreement with Schwaber, argue that there is indeed a countertransference here in the form of a defense by the analyst against a blow to the sense of self conveyed by the patient's view of him or her. Yet the experiment to be described leads me to believe that these difficulties can ultimately be turned to good effect. As the analyst becomes accustomed to the patient's scrutiny, he will find himself not simply allowing the patient full scope to observe him, but will find himself sometimes inviting the patient to do so when he or she hesitates. But to reach this stage of acceptance may not be easy and may require periods of under-standing and working through of narcissistic sensitivities. As the authors of these two approaches, as well as McLaughlin (1981), have all indicated, the yield in greater access to the patient's inner experience makes the process well worthwhile. The centrality of narcissism or of the analyst's vulnerability in countertransference has been testified to by both Gunther (1978) and Wolf (1983). Gunther believes that the very nature of the psychoanalytic relationship is such that it inevitably impinges upon the analyst's narcissism. Countertransference, he believes, appears in the reactions, defensive or otherwise, which the analyst experiences due to such impinge-ment. How much more liable to narcissistic injury must be the situation where the analyst cannot erect the "cordon sanitaire" (Brandchaft and Stolorow, 1988) that leads him to view the patient's behaviour as determined by processes independent of his or her presence within them. In order to work fruitfully and relatively comfortably in these new approaches, it must behoove a therapist to both monitor and master his reactions. And it was partly with this in mind that I undertook the experiment. Ultimately, the analyst, by means of inner processing, may be able to convert his anger, hurt, or other aversive reactions into signals so that they no longer block access to the kernels of truth in the patient's observations.

Stolorow, Brandchaft and Atwood (1987) refer only briefly to these countertransference problems (in their new paper, however, Brand-chaft and Stolorow (1988) refer to the threats to the analyst's psycho-logical self). Stolorow, Brandchaft, and Atwood, (1987) in a commen-tary on projective identification, cite a reference from Kernberg (1975), in which the latter describes an episode in Ingmar Bergmann's movie *Persona*. There, Kernberg describes the reaction of a nurse to a coldly destructive patient. The nurse develops an intense hatred for the sick woman and treats her cruelly at one point. Stolorow, Brandchaft and Atwood disagree with Kernberg's view that the nurse's experience was an instance of projective identification. They believe rather that "the nurse demonstrated her own narcissistic vulnerability and propensity for rage reactions" (p. 114). The authors then add the following brief but significant sentence, "We have observed such factors at work in ourselves and regard them, as to some degree universal in therapeutic relationships" (p. 114). They write here also of the patient's fear of the analyst's narcissistic vulnerability, and of being held responsible for the analyst's frustration. It appeared to me that here the authors focus on a central problem in the insubjective approach that requires a good deal more attention.

In psychoanalytic therapy, the empathic bond functions (or fails to function) in both directions. Each partner is continually organizing and being organized by the other. There is thus a mutual process that results in the perpetual formation of new intersubjective fields. The analyst, whether aware of it or not from his vantage point, is expecting the patient to contribute to his own self-regulation via self-object ties.

The second patient was the only one during the experiment with whom I experienced a countertransference reaction in the more classic sense of a neurotic or pathologic state. It was, however, quite intense and prolonged, involving the experience of a good deal of stress from approximately the sixth to the fourteenth week of the study period. I believe this episode illustrates the threat to my sense of self that arose from the loss of a needed selfobject link with an affirming patient. It also demonstrates the necessity for self-tolerance in the working through of a period of narcissistic vulnerability. It is an example of a two-way disruption of self-regulation. Also illustrated are the patient's experiences of the analyst's threatened reaction to her intense affect states during selfobject disruption (Stolorow, Brandchaft, and Atwood, 1987, p. 14).

Diane

Diane, in her early thirties, was a housewife. She was unhappily married and had small children. There was a history of several psychotic episodes that she described as involving "powerful delusions and hallucinations."

For several weeks prior to the events to be described, I had been experiencing rising tension in the presence of this patient. I had assumed that archaic needs and their accompanying strong affects were beginning to emerge from repression as she began to regress in an archaic selfobject transference. I had already noted, in myself, a tendency to be reassuring to Diane in my interventions. I retrospectively understand this to have been an unconscious need to reassure myself, an attempt to ward off the various effects of her emerging intense affects upon me.

During the sixth week of the study, at the start of a session, I noticed I was very apprehensive. After a silence, Diane said that the lack of visual communication, in lying on the couch, made her feel very much alone. I had been beginning to become aware that my silence seemed to produce such intense feelings of aloneness in her. In sessions just prior to this, she had been describing how alone she had felt in midadolescence after her oldest sister (a significant selfobject) had suddenly left home after a series of altercations with the father. The patient then went on to say that her alone feelings must be a problem for me. I said, "You mean, it is as if there is something wrong about it for me?" She answered, "Yes, you are concerned about it." Rather than explore this, I then made a "reassuring" statement, which I now see as a defensive effort to allay my own apprehension. I said, "Well, there could be two kinds of concern . . . concern as interest or caring, and concern as worry that something is wrong. I felt concern only in the first sense." She remained silent for six to eight minutes. I finally asked, "Did my remarks somehow stun you?" She answered, "Well, maybe . . . my mind wandered off." There were a few further exchanges that I felt were getting us nowhere. I sensed I had been out of tune and finally said "I think I must have cut you off." Immediately she began shrieking "Yes, why did you have to do that?" I asked, "At what point did it occur?" She continued with great vehemence, "Why do you have to ask? You should know. It means I am alone and have to do the analysis all by myself." I said, "It shouldn't have to happen that way." Still yelling, she went on, "Well, it is that way. Why do you have to do that?" I answered, "I think I cut you off when I talked about concern, I thought I was trying to reassure you." She shouted, "Well, it wasn't reassurance. You don't want to hear my intense emotions." I answered, "That is not true." Diane went on, "Then why did you have to do it?" I answered, "I didn't realize I had done it, until later. I guess you are right that there was some intensity of feeling I wanted to avoid." Still speaking with great passion, she replied "Then how can we work together if you are afraid of my emotions?" Then I said, "I think we have been able to work together in the past and we will be able to in the future. I just need to catch myself before it happens." (Note my apologetic attitude.) There the session ended. I was much shaken by the intensity of her anger and by my own anxious, guilt-ridden responses to it.

This session ushered in a period of stress for me. I had long known that my major countertransference "Achilles heel" lay in my reactions to blatantly angry female patients. A basic self-image of myself as a loving, caring, nondestructive, well-motivated, and competent therapist would be threatened by the criticism of women. I will elaborate on this shortly.

Nothing much happened during the week that remained until the vacation period; we both had distanced ourselves. A dream she had during this week clearly indicated her sense of me at this time. The dream was of a rabbit with an injured paw. The rabbit was also resentful. She also spent part of this week comparing me unfavourably with the psychotherapist (a woman) whom she had seen, once weekly, for some years, after the last psychotic episode. My own experience during this week was of feelings of mea culpa and a well-justified fear that Diane might leave analysis.

On the first day back after the vacation, I began by asking her, "How has it been going?" The question seemed to aggravate her. She answered, "What am I supposed to say to that?" She continued in very critical terms regarding the analysis and spoke of quitting. I then drew her attention to the disruptive effects of the aforementioned session. Now she began yelling again: "Your attitude to my analysis is cavalier. You have no interest in it but for your own purposes. Why did you cut me off? Why can't you get it right? You are afraid of my strong feelings." This was repeated several times. She also spoke of her fear of becoming psychotic again. In the grip of the continued threat to my self-image, I found it hard to sit through the session. However, this time I made no attempt to defend myself. I was becoming aware of the need to tolerate and understand my countertransference as the probable key to my becoming again usable as a selfobject.

The next day, her vehement censure continued: "I don't think you have ever been with me emotionally." Other criticisms were that I failed to protect her from bad decisions in her life, that I was self-indulgent in using her as a learning experience, and that my responses to her dreams were superficial. The last criticism particularly galled me because I believed I had been able to understand her dreams in some depth. I think it was the vehemence of her criticism as much as the content that made me question myself and doubt my competence to analyze her. (Recently, I read *The Taming of the Shrew* prior to attending a stage performance of the play. Reading Katharina's diatribes was nothing like the impact of hearing the passion of their utterances in person.) Diane left this session sobbing bitterly and saying she did not want to be in analysis any more. I indeed feared that the analysis might be about to be broken off. I could easily have colluded with her wish to quit at this point.

She began the next day with a long silence, which I broke by asking if she had any further thoughts or feelings. She answered, "I just see you as an adversary." I said, "I think I can understand what you feel. I agree with some of what you have said, though, I don't think it is as bad as you believe. I do want to be with you in your emotional experience. When I cut you off I didn't realize it until later. Realizing it makes all the difference." She replied, "I don't know. It is like a bad marriage and I have already got one of those. Analysis promises to help, then it lets me down. It is exhausting and discouraging. You have never been with me emotionally. I don't think you are capable of it and my emotionally violent reactions are due to that knowledge." I then said, "Perhaps you could speak, in more detail, about your experience that I am never with you emotionally." She answered, "I feel a great distrust of you. I can't afford to let go. There is something unchangeable about your unconscious. It manifests itself in your strange reactions to my dreams." I asked, "What strange reactions?" She said, "You seem to respond superficially, you want to get them over with." (My own sense of my response to her dreams was in marked contrast to this.) She continued, "Most of the activity of the analysis takes place outside of here. You make endless mistakes. I can't stay around while you learn. I want to stop the analysis." This was uttered at the end of the session with the patient half shrieking and half sobbing.

It would take too much space to continue to describe the sessions in any detail. After this, I brought her back to the first big disruption, which had occurred during her feelings of aloneness. We were gradually able to understand that these feelings, precipitated by her sister's departure from home, also had value for her in providing her with her first sense of having an authentic self. This, however, was soon lost due to the gross intrusiveness of the mother; and her father's unavailability as a substitute selfobject, because he shortly afterwards developed a psychotic episode precipitated by the break in his attachment to his elder daughter. This shortly ushered in the patient's own first psychotic episode at age 18. When she was just beginning to recover this valued feeling of authenticity in the analysis, she experienced me as cutting it off, just as her mother had intruded on it. All of this took some time to comprehend and is not relevant to my countertransference experience, to which I will now return.

I knew that I had been experiencing Diane as a selfobject who failed to affirm a needed self-image. I also experienced her as failing to regulate and to contain my own strong feelings, though I did not understand their nature as yet. Her experience of disruption and anger due to her aloneness precipitated my own disruption, which, in turn, greatly aggravated hers. In the past, I had recognized that my need to see myself as sensitive, loving, well motivated, and so on had

had an influence on my choice of profession. I had gained some degree of understanding from experiences similar to this one in that my need for such a self-image arose from early experiences. I had come to believe that I had been needed then as a gentle, loving, selfobject. Women patients who even hinted that I might not be kind or that I might be destructive threatened this quite basic self-image, or template, and threatened to undo defenses against an entirely different but repressed self-image, which contained guilt-ridden anger. My anxiety with this patient arose from the threat of the emergence of such unregulated affect along with attendant guilt. This was the reason for the mea culpa attitude, which pulled me towards concretizing the feeling of responsibility for the patient's misery (Brandchaft and Stolorow, 1988).

My experience of Diane as a selfobject who failed to affirm my sense of self is illuminated by the following quote from Alice Miller (1979): "the amazing ability on the child's part to intuitively perceive and respond to the need of the mother and to take on the role assigned to him. This need brought love for the child, he could sense he was needed and this gave his life a guarantee of existence" (p. 49). The pursuit of psychoanalysis as a vocation provides many analysts with a similar guarantee. As Miller (1979) says "the pursuit of this strange profession contains the root of the analyst's narcissistic disturbance" (p. 54). My countertransference reactions and their underpinnings illustrate this quote. As I proceeded with the self-analysis of my experience with Diane during the next few weeks, I became, more than ever before, painfully aware of an ego-alien rage originating in early childhood and causative of my feelings of personal fault.

Intersubjective Interplay

I will now add a few comments in terms of the intersubjective field.

During the few weeks prior to the described fragments of analysis, the rising level of tension in both participants heralded the arrival of a new and stormy intersubjective field; retrospectively, this can be seen as motivated quite separately in each partner. For Diane, the analyst's ordinary analytic silence reactivated her experience of the lack of empathic presence in either parental selfobject. In particular, her experience of the loss of her elder sister during adolescence reactivated the period leading up to her first psychotic bout. The threatened emergence of Diane's strong affects now disturbed my equilibrium, owing to my unconscious need for an affiliatively affirming selfobject (Lichtenberg, 1988). My "reassuring" remarks at the time were efforts to maintain my equilibrium. Such attempts were doomed to fail. My loss of self-regulation now had its impact on Diane, resulting in her outbreak of narcissistic rage. The mutual disruption of regulation processes that was now occurring gives witness to Lachmann and Beebe's (submitted) proposition that experience in both early life and in transference is organized through simultaneous and interdependent processes of self-regulation and interaction (or mutual regulation).

Diane's rage induced in me mea culpa reactions, especially due to the threat to my self-image as a loving, caring therapist. My state was clearly sensed by the patient, who perceived the analyst in her dream as an injured and resentful rabbit. For a short period, we both aversively withdrew from each other.

By the time of the return from vacation, I fully realized that with the patient in such a state of fragmentation, my most urgent task was to take my own disrupted state in hand. I did not find this at all easy. To see oneself through the eyes of another did not exactly feel like a gift at this time. However, I was at least able to refrain from defending myself and to somewhat shakily return to the exploratory stance (Lichtenberg, 1988) by encouraging her to enlarge upon her experience of me. Gradually, the patient settled down and recovered sufficient self-cohesion for us to take a look at her reactions to my ordinary analytic silence. It became evident that this silence had evoked in Diane her experience of the absence of an empathic selfobject presence in both parents. She had placed more hope in her father. At this juncture in the analysis, her experience of her father centered around her experience of great disappointment at his ultimate unavailability following the loss to her of the presence of the elder sister.

Basch (1988) said that a very strong affective reaction in the therapist interferes with his capacity to understand the patient's affective state and the significance of his or her message. Lichtenberg (1983) spoke of analysis as a unique interaction, which proceeds with strain at its junction and a search for insight through empathy and introspection. I would conclude from my experience with this case that the search, necessitated by such interactional strain, must include the analyst's inquiry into those prereflective attitudes that form the underpinnings of his character. Unless he does so, he may not come to understand how he inevitably repeats the failure of the patient's early environment. Such a search of the self requires tolerance and empathy for oneself.

CONCLUSION

What can be learned from this experiment?

1. It is valuable to the analyst to understand his self-structure and prereflective attitudes. It is especially valuable for him to understand his areas of self-vulnerability, along with his reactions to, and defences against, these vulnerabilities.

2. Although intersubjectivity is neither an interactional nor an interpersonal theory, it is a two-person as well as a one-person psychology. That is to say, although the focus of the analysis is still the subjective intrapsychic experience of the patient, a major influence on the experience is the therapist himself. We thus need to understand both sides of the intersubjective unit.

3. As I illustrated, the therapist is often disconcerted to find that the patient's experience of the analysis is entirely different from his own. During the subsequent, essential effort of decentering, the therapist may come to learn a good deal about himself.

4. The more the analyst comes to know about his own reactions, the less likely he will be to concretize, that is, rationalize his motives in, for instance, his theory about what he is doing. Thus, with Henry and Diane, my feelings of failure stemmed from a prereflective attitude that led me to believe that I was personally responsible for the disappointments and that I should therefore be able to relieve them.

5. A significant reason for the analyst to understand and deal with his narcissistic vulnerability is that if he does not do so, the patient, who is aware of this vulnerability, will be forced to restrain and restrict himself or herself for fear of damaging the therapist.

6. The analyst's prereflective attitudes and/or accompanying concretizations may prevent him from sustaining an attitude of empathic inquiry. This is illustrated in my interaction with Diane.

7. Self-regulation and selfobject bonding are two-way processes. When serious disruptions occur, the therapist himself may temporarily lose his self-regulatory capacity. The restoration of the selfobject tie may sometimes depend on the therapist coming to understand the unconscious causes of his or her own disruptions.

8. Right up until the end of his or her career, an analyst will be faced with situations he or she has not encountered before, and these situations will produce reactions that he or she could not have anticipated. The effort to understand these reactions may turn out to be valuable bits of research for his own benefit and occasionally also for the benefit of the field of psychoanalytic therapy.

9. In all human communication, the differences in individual organizing principles create serious barriers to communication. Psychoanalysis, from an intersubjective viewpoint, represents at attempt to understand these communication barriers from both sides.

REFERENCES

Atwood, G., & Stolorow, R. (1984), *Structures of Subjectivity: Explorations in Psychoanalytic Phenomenology*. Hillsdale, NJ: The Analytic Press.

Basch, M. F. (1988), *Understanding Psychotherapy: The Science Behind the Art*. New York: Basic Books.

Brandchaft, B., & Stolorow, R. (1988), The therapeutic alliance (a view from within). Paper presented to Toronto Psychoanalytic Society.

Gunther, M. S. (1978), The endangered self: A contribution to the understanding of narcissistic determinants of counter-transference. *The Annual Psychoanalysis* 4:201–224. New York: International Universities Press.

Kernberg, O. (1975), *Borderline Conditions and Pathological Narcissism*. New York: Aronson.

Kohut, H. (1977), *The Restoration of the Self*. New York: International Universities Press.

_____ (1984), *How Does Analysis Cure?* ed. A. Goldberg & P. Stepansky. Chicago: University of Chicago Press.

Lachmann, F. M. & Beebe, B. (submitted). Dimensions of the transference.

Lichtenberg, J. D. (1983), Psychoanalysis and Infant Research. Hillsdale, NJ: The Analytic Press.

_____ (1988), Rethinking the scope of the patient's transference and the therapist's counter-transference. Presented at 11th Annual Psychology of Self Conference, Washington DC.

McLaughlin, J. T. (1981), Transference, psychic reality and counter-transference. *Psychoanal. Quart.* 50:639–664.

Miller, A. (1979), The dream of the gifted child and the psychoanalyst's narcissistic disturbance. *Internat. J. Psycho-Anal.* 60:47–58.

Sander, L. (1975), Infant and caretaking environment: investigation and conceptualization of adaptive behaviour in a system of increasing complexity. In: *Explorations in Child Psychiatry*, ed. E. J. Anthony. New York: Plenum, pp. 129–166.

Schwaber, E. A. (1981a) Empathy: A mode of analytic listening. *Psychoanal. Inq.*, 1:357–392.

_____ (1981b), Narcissism, self psychology, and the listening perspective. *The Annual of Psychoanalysis*, 9:115–132. New York: International Universities Press.

_____ (1983a), Construction, reconstruction, and the mode of clinical attunement. In: *The Future of Psychoanalysis*, ed. A. Goldberg. New York: International Universities Press, pp. 273–291.

_____ (1983b), A particular perspective on analytic listening. *The Psychoanalytic Study of the Child*, 38:519–546. New Haven, CT: Yale University Press.

_____ (1983c), Psychoanalytic listening and psychic reality. Internat. Rev. Psycho-Anal., 10:379–392.

_____ (1986), Reconstruction and perceptual experience: Further thoughts on analytic listening. *J. Amer. Psychoanal. Assn.*, 34:911–932.

_____ (1987), Models of the mind and data-gathering in clinical work. *Psychoanal. Inq.*, 7:261–275.

Stolorow, R., Atwood, G. & Ross, J. (1978), The representational world in psychoanalytic treatment. *Internat. Rev. Psycho-Anal.*, 5:247–356.

_____ Brandchaft, B., and Atwood, G. (1987), *Psychoanalytic Treatment. An Intersubjective Approach.* Hillsdale, NJ: The Analytic Press.

_____ & Lachmann, F. (1984/1985), The future of an illusion. *The Annual of Psychoanalysis,* 11/12:19–38.

Wolf, E. S. (1983), Empathy and counter-transference. In: *The Future of Psychoanalysis,* ed. A. Goldberg. New York: International Universities Press, pp. 309–326.

Chapter 7

Commentaries

SELFOBJECT TRANSFERENCES, INTERSUBJECTIVITY, AND COUNTERTRANSFERENCE
Anna Ornstein

In discussing Dr. Thomson's "Countertransference in an Intersubjective Perspective," I will focus on the following: (a) I shall reexamine his clinical examples to see whether or not the intersubjective perspective has optimally safeguarded his empathic listening perspective. (b) Whether or not the intersubjective perspective provided him with a better tool for following the analytic process as opposed to taking the emergence of selfobject transferences into consideration. (c) Finally, I will raise some general clinical–theoretical questions related to intersubjectivity and selfobject transferences.

In his introductory remarks, Dr. Thomson familiarized us with the clinical theory that guided him in his work; the work of Evelyn Schwaber, and the intersubjective approach as articulated by Stolorow, Brandchaft and Atwood (1984, 1987).

"The intersubjective approach," he says, "is closely related to, and an outgrowth of, self psychology." As a clinical theory, therefore, the intersubjective approach should be an advance over self psychology; it ought to safeguard the empathic listening perspective more effectively, and it ought to be a better guide in the conduct of psychoanalysis than is the clinical theory of the psychology of the self.

In reviewing Schwaber's work, Dr. Thomson reminds us that

93

Schwaber (1983) promulgated the idea that the influence of the observer, the therapist, must be taken into account in the psychoanalytic situation.

It is difficult to distinguish this statement from Kohut's description of the selfobject transferences. It was the observation that the analyst had an impact on the patient's self-states that had put Kohut "on the trail" of the selfobject concept. This idea was put forward by him in 1966 in "Forms and Transformation of Narcissism," and had its precursor in his 1959 paper, "Introspection, Empathy and Psychoanalysis." Kohut removed the hyphen between the self and the object for the very reason Dr. Thomson quotes Schwaber, namely, after he had repeatedly observed that the analyst's impact on the patient's self-states had a central significance in the process and in the outcome of an analysis.

The nature of the selfobject transferences affects the whole of the treatment process. The manner in which countertransferences (the attitude and feelings of the analyst toward the patient) determine the form that resistances will take and the way in which the working through of habitual defenses may be accomplished. This added dimension of transference and resistance was stressed before by Ornstein and Ornstein, 1975: "[a dimension] which is contributed to by the analyst, one that can be readily overlooked when the clinical manifestations of resistance and transference are viewed exclusively as phenomena of intrapsychic origin. Their interpretation, then, is likely to disregard the analyst's possible contribution to their form, content, intensity and occasional intractability" (p. 221).

Dr. Thomson's contributions are of significance because they not only stress the importance of the analyst's impact on the patient's self-states, but also because they describe in detail how he, as the analyst, was affected by the patient's hostile attacks. He described vividly how his own disorganization affected the analysis and how he himself benefited from this experience through self-analysis. Whether the analyst's emotional state ought to be called countertransference in such instances or could be better described as the analyst's transferences in relation to the patient remains an open question. In this kind of mutually regulated self-system, one cannot readily distinguish as to what ought to be considered countertransference (in the narrow definition of the word), and what the analyst's transference expectations are in relation to the patient. Since the main thesis of Dr. Thomson's paper is to demonstrate that psychoanalysis, in essence, takes place in the area of intersubjectivity, that is, between two mutually regulating self-systems, the source of the analyst's affects may not be a decisive factor. Many analysts designate all feelings belonging to the patient as transference and all those belonging to the analyst as countertransference. But the analyst's own, unrecognized, and/or unacknowledged selfobject needs in relation to their patients would more correctly be referred to as the analyst's transference.

THE EMPATHIC LISTENING PERSPECTIVE: INTERSUBJECTIVITY AND SELFOBJECT TRANSFERENCES

The clinical theory of self psychology is based on our increased appreciation of the intrinsic relationship between the recognition of selfobject transferences and the method of empathy.

In the first case of Henry, it appears to me that, had Dr. Thomson, in addition to his own feeling state, considered that what he was witnessing was an emerging selfobject transference, he may not have become so deeply affected by the "sense of guilt and responsibility" that he lost his empathic listening perspective. Empathic immersion in the patient's inner world is a process that is made possible by the analyst's ongoing effort to decenter from his or her affective state. In this case, the exclusive attention to intersubjectivity without regard to the emerging transference interfered with the analyst's efforts to establish and maintain empathic contact with the patient's inner experiences; the intersubjective approach failed to safeguard the analyst's ability to listen from within the patient's perspective. What makes self psychology such an attractive psychoanalytic theory is exactly this: There exists an inseparably close linkage between the phenomenon of selfobject transference and the empathic mode of observation. There is no other way in which the analyst can recognize and appreciate his or her impact on the patient (which is the essential aspect of a selfobject transference) but by the continued effort to decenter from his or her own reaction; only then can the analyst immerse herself or himself in the patient's subjective experiences. Losing sight of the way in which the patient is making use of the analyst, that is, loosing sight of the selfobject nature of the relationship, results in the analyst also losing the empathic listening perspective.

SELFOBJECT TRANSFERENCES AND THE PROCESS OF WORKING THROUGH.

The effort to remain in empathic contact with the patient's experiences and the recognition of selfobject transferences have far reaching significance for the whole of the analytic process. Although Dr. Thomson restricted himself to the discussion of the way in which his intersubjective approach had alerted him to the importance of his countertransference reactions, I believe that his theoretical frame of reference had consequences for the way in which he conceptualized the analytic process as a whole.

Dr. Thomson quotes Evelyn Schwaber, saying that what constitutes particular danger points in the therapeutic process are times when the patient's perception of the analyst is markedly different from the analyst's perception of himself. This would be in keeping with a strictly intersubjective approach to the analytic process. I would maintain, however, that what is of equal importance in an otherwise well-progressing, analytic process is the patient's reaction to the analyst inadvertently repeating what had originally proven to be traumatic to the patient. I believe that this is what occurred in the case of Diane.

In response to the analyst's ordinary analytic silence, Diane experienced intense loneliness. This reminded Dr. Thomson of an earlier session when the patient described how alone she felt in midadolescence after her older sister, a significant selfobject, had suddenly left home. Fearing that he had injured the patient in some way, Dr. Thomson became apologetic and the patient perceived him as a "rabbit with an injured paw." Feeling emotionally abandoned, Diane reacted with narcissistic rage and angry attacks on the analyst ensued. With honest self-scrutiny, Dr. Thomson tells us how these attacks disorganized him and how this experience eventually promoted his own self-analysis. This is a state of affairs that we are all familiar with, and the honest reporting of these experiences by Dr. Thomson is to be deeply appreciated. The patient's continued rage was in sharp contrast to the analyst's self-image "as a loving, caring, nondestructive, well-motivated and competent therapist."

In this instance, the analyst's ordinary analytic silence elicited the repetitive aspect of the transference: the reexperiencing of the original trauma of the intolerable state of aloneness. What the analyst experienced as disruptive to himself was the discrepancy between his own perception of himself and the patient's perception of him. But this is not what appears to have been disruptive to the patient at first. What created the rage and the disruption in the patient was that the analyst's ordinary analytic silence elicited the repetition of an earlier, genetically significant, traumatic experience. The question has to be raised whether or not, in this instance, close attention to the transference could have guided Dr. Thomson to an interpretive rather then to an apologetic response.

With the patient in a state of fragmentation, Dr. Thomson wisely decided that his most urgent task was to take his "own disrupted state in hand". Only then was he able—though still somewhat shakily—to return to the exploratory stance by encouraging the patient to enlarge upon her experience of him.

Encouraging the patient to enlarge on her experience of the analyst constituted an essential aspect of the repair of the ruptured therapist–patient tie. Stolorow and Lachmann said in relation to the technique of repair: "The singular importance of analyzing the patient's experience of ruptures in the transference bond is found in the impact of such analysis in constantly mending the broken archaic tie and thereby permitting the arrested developmental process to resume once again" (Stolorow & Lachmann, 1984, 1985, p. 33).

However, I question whether this is all that has to be done under these circumstances. Eliciting the patient's experiences of the analyst is only the first step—though a crucial step—in repairing the broken tie. The other equally important second step, in my view, is to include reconstructive interpretations into the analyst's responses.

SOME GENERAL CLINICAL-THEORETICAL ISSUES RELATED TO INTERSUBJECTIVITY AND SELFOBJECT TRANSFERENCES

What is important to remember in this context is that the nature of the selfobject transference is different from the way transference has been conceptualized in classical psychoanalysis. Whereas classical psychoanalysis conceptualized transference as primarily repetition and displacement from the archaic objects of the past, selfobject transferences contain two aspects: although they are being shaped by the experiences with the analyst in the present, they also contain repetitions. Disruptions in the analysis signify the repetitive aspects of the transference, and such inevitable disruptions represent psychopathology. In adults with a variety of personality and behavioral disturbances, "a broken archaic tie" cannot be analytically "mended" without the working through of those defense organizations that have evolved, over a lifetime, into a final common pathway in response to various kinds of anxieties. It is at times of disruptions that the patient's vulnerabilities and their attendant defense organizations become exposed, which make such interpretations not only possible but also emotionally meaningful. By reconstructive interpretations, I mean interpretations that include the genetic source of the patient's vulnerabilities and the specific, idiosyncratic manner in which the patient habitually protects himself or herself from retraumatization.

Reconstructive interpretations have several analytic functions: They promote self-reflection, insight, and an empathic acceptance of one's own childhood self. If they are successful in fairly accurately encompassing the patient's subjective experiences, they result in the recall of those traumatic childhood memories that are experientially most closely related to the current transference disruption. This is how Kohut put it: "If the repeated interpretations of the meaning of separation from the analyst on the level of the idealizing narcissistic libido are not given mechanically, but with correct empathy for the analysand's feelings . . . then there will gradually emerge a host of meaningful memories which concern the dynamic prototypes of the present experience" (Kohut, 1971, p. 99).

Habitual defense organizations that had limited patients in their ability to establish satisfactory selfobject relationships can best be worked through in relation to the repair of the inevitable disruptions of selfobject transferences. The recall of childhood memories, self-acceptance, and the working through of habitual defense organizations assure psychic continuity that, in turn, constitutes a fundamental aspect of psychic recovery.

In the case of Diane, the analysis got back on track once the analyst "brought her back to the first big disruption, which occurred during the feeling of aloneness." Importantly, empathic contact was reestablished when Dr. Thomson shifted to the exploration of the meaning that the analyst's "ordinary silence" had for the patient.

In summary, I raised the question as to whether or not what Dr. Thomson experienced as countertransference in these analyses was related to his failing to take the emerging selfobject transferences into consideration, and, as a result, losing his empathic listening perspective. The recognition of selfobject transferences is closely linked to the empathic mode of observation, which, in turn, requires an ongoing effort on the part of the analyst to recognize and to decenter from his own subjectivity. Further, I raised some general questions regarding the relationship between intersubjectivity (as this was demonstrated by Dr. Thomson's clinical example) and selfobject transferences. This question, I believe, has to be raised because differences in theoretical orientation affect the whole of the analytic process, specifically, the manner in which the repair of disruptions in the analysis is undertaken. The latter is an important aspect of the analytic process as it is intrinsically tied to the process of working through.

REFERENCES

Kohut, H. (1959), Introspection, empathy and psychoanalysis. *J. Psychoanal. Assn.*, 7:459–483. Also in: *The Search for the Self*, ed. P. H. Ornstein, Vol. 1. New York: International Universities Press, pp. 205–232, 1978.

———— (1966), Forms and transformation of Narcissism. *J. Amer. Psychoanal. Assn.*, 14:243–272. Also in: *The Search for the Self*, ed. P. H. Ornstein. Vol. 1, New York: International Universities Press, pp. 427–460, 1978.

_____ (1971), *The Analysis of the Self*. New York: International Universities Press.

Ornstein, A. & Ornstein, P. (1975), On the interpretive process. *Internat. J. Psychoanal. Psychother.*, 4:219–271.

Schwaber, E. A. (1983), A particular perspective on analytic listening. The *Psychoanalytic Study of the Child*, 38:519–546. New Haven, CT: Yale University Press.

Stolorow R. & Lachmann F. (1984/85), Transference: The future of an illusion. *The Annual of Psychoanalysis*, 12/13:33. ed. Chicago Institute for Psychoanalysis. New York: International Universities Press.

Stolorow R., Brandchaft B. & Atwood G. (1987), *Psychoanalytic Treatment: An Intersubjective Approach*. Hillsdale, NJ: The Analytic Press.

COUNTERTRANSFERENCE IN THE ANALYTIC PROCESS
Bernard Brandchaft

It is a special pleasure to discuss this valuable and courageous contribution of my friend and colleague, Peter Thomson. The paper calls attention to a relatively neglected area the analyst encounters when, guided by the principles of intersubjectivity, he or she attempts to analyze the central clinical phenomena and the states of mind of more difficult patients. It is basic to Dr. Thomson's approach that the difficulties encountered in the treatment of such patients can only be comprehended as occurring within a field in which the impact of the analyst on the patient's experience makes a continuing and *codetermining* contribution to the evolving events. I stress *codetermination* because one of the very great contributions of the intersubjective perspective is that it provides a clarifying focus with which to delineate the roles of each of the participants to the unfolding interaction. This in turn helps to understand better the nature of psychoanalytic transformations and what is required to bring these transformations about. The emphasis placed by self psychologists (including myself) upon the contribution of the analyst, when he is experienced as failing in a selfobject transference, to derailments and impasses in the therapeutic process sometimes has been misunderstood so as to minimize or obscure the contribution of the patient to the dialogue (Adler, 1989; Hitchcock, 1989). I believe that, where such misunderstanding occurs, unwarranted clinical compromise and collusion with archaic defenses can result, a point to which I shall return later in my discussion.

Thomson's interest in exploring the impact of his patients, Henry and Diane, upon his own self organization led him to prolonged reflection on the alterations in his states of mind. In order to do this, he had to move away from the more comforting tendency to hold his patient's psychological make-up to account for his state of mind, and toward an understanding of the contribution of his own already existing structures to the ongoing process. That such turning inward is crucial in the analytic course cannot be overemphasized, for what Thomson transcended, the tendency to blame another for his own state of mind, will be seen to have been the counterpart of the process in which he was the target, in which Henry and Diane were resolutely immersed. Without the self-reflection that Thomson describes, the ingredients were present for familiar outcomes, stalemate, or negative therapeutic reaction. Such outcomes become likely when patient and therapist each defends his own distinctive perspective and perceptions from the threat to self-demarcation posed by the other's conflicting perspective and its perceptual base (Brandchaft, 1983; Brandchaft & Stolorow, 1990).

Turning inward, Thomson became able to identify and focus upon various more deeply lying aspects of his own experiencing. He had not been aware of these at first, but only of his annoyance and frustration at Henry's silence and unresponsiveness to him, that is, the effects of frustration of archaic selfobject needs of his own. Without such awareness, Thomson could have no knowledge or control of these factors or the part they had been playing in their impact upon Henry, his silence, and what was beneath it. He was as effectively isolated from Henry as was Henry from him, each of the pair by configurations originally designed to protect but now rendering higher mental functions inaccessible.

In each of the cases, Thomson became aware of an oppressive sense of guilt and failure. An archaic organizing principle of his own had been activated and had begun to shape his experience. He became aware that he was feeling responsible, not only for his own but for Henry's and Diane's disturbed states of mind, their disappointments in him, and the particular pathways these disappointments took. The underpinnings of any distinctive sense of self of his own were being eroded and with them the foundations of what sort of person and analyst he really was. These foundations were being surrendered to Henry's and Diane's forceful expression of *their* reflection of him. His subsequent efforts took the form of attempts to restore his sense of self or the relationship according to patterns laid down in earlier times. He found himself possessed by urgent needs to deny or "fix" or "repair" whatever he had done wrong in his patient's eyes, and to restore the relationship by presuming to become the kind of analyst Henry and Diane wished or felt they needed him to be, and, failing this, by apologies for not being that kind of analyst.

So far, the experience Thomson relates is by no means as unusual as his candor in reporting it. There are, I would venture to say, few among us for whom that particular quicksand, or some similar, is not quite familiar territory. What was more unusual was the process of sustained self-reflection that enabled Thomson to recognize and transcend the nonreflective patterns of his own experience. By this process, he was able to unburden his mind and free it to begin to understand the experience of his patients.

He became aware that it was not Henry's silence nor Diane's relentless disappointment and rage alone that had its particular impact upon him but the special and idiosyncratic meanings activated within him that threatened his own differentiated sense of self.

Were it not for the analyst's own way of organizing his experience of himself and his patients, and for his unrecognized archaic selfobject needs from his patients being activated, his understanding and hence his responses might well be very different. One might well, then, comprehend that Henry's and Diane's expressions of criticism, disappointment, profound despair, or stubborn withdrawal speak eloquently to their *experience* of profound selfobject failure, repeating and echoing damaging, developmental failures. He will recognize that it is not only his patient's feelings but importantly their hopes that are being injured. He will be aware that such crucial experiences are not a reason to abandon analysis but to utilize it to attune himself to the fears that such expressions generate in patients. He will thus recognize the opportunity to provide an environment in which Henry and Diane can come to feel safe in expressing fully what and how they feel. He will appreciate that Henry's silence and Diane's rages are for them their only available means of self expression, for reasons which will, in good time, emerge if the channels of authentic self-expression are kept open. This aspect of the therapeutic interaction, its "holding" function, is quintessential to the process of psychoanalytic repair of disjunction and distinguishes it from a countertransference enactment. In situations of the kind being described by Dr. Thomson, from an important perspective, nothing has gone wrong with him, in the patient, or in the interaction between the two. The role that each of the players was enacting in the common scenario, up to that point, had been predetermined, not by anyone's virtue or competence or lack thereof, but "by that unfathomable selection that decrees that each of us shall be the child of his particular parents" (Kennan 1989, p. 244) and the complex subsequent events that shaped him and no other. Henry's silence and Diane's expressions of criticism and disappointment will be appreciated as vigorous expressions of attempts at revitalizing their own threatened selfdemarcataing processes. Once a milieu of trust had been reestablished in the patient's experience of his affect state being "contained," the analytic effort could focus on the specific selfobject failures as part of the continuing sorting out of misunderstandings and misattunements on the part of the analyst from the invariant and enduring meanings being triggered in the patient.

When such crucial attempts at self-differentiation and self-delineation arise in analysis, particularly because characteristics or interventions of the analyst unwittingly pose threats to the patient's precarious sense of differentiated self, they frequently are not recognized as such by either analyst or patient. They therefore fail to elicit the appropriate responsiveness from the analyst. This constitutes a repetition of central developmental trauma and sets the stage for the activation of unconscious principles that shape the patient's subjectivity and give it its repetitive forms.

Thomson notes that the necessary process of introspection, that not so embraceable component of the empathic-introspective stance, is extremely difficult and especially so with patients like Henry and Diane. The intensified engagement of hopes and fearful expectations in such patients will inevitably lead to selectively exquisite attunement to any element in their experience of their environment, including analysis, that is reminiscent of the threat to self-differentiation. Furthermore, for a very long time they will be unable to sustain a sense that there is any enduring significance of experiences that do not confirm these fears, tending to believe that the confirmation has only been delayed.

A patient's insistence that the analyst concretely and literally fulfill his selfobject longings and archaic hopes; a patient's experience of massive or final disappointment if the analyst does not or cannot commit himself to this goal; despairing expressions of the threatening collapse of hopes and desperate condemnations of the analyst for such outcome — all this tends to activate within the analyst similar affects of despair and protest as archaic meanings of his own become preoccupying. At the center of these are the still active residues of his own primal archaic conflict — to give up increasing portions of his own differentiated selfhood in an attempt to preserve the tie, or to bear the responsibility for the inconsolable disappointment and pain of the one who has become dependent on him.

The particular difficulties encountered in the treatment of difficult patients is rooted in this peculiar intersubjective interweaving of the propensity reciprocally to activate and have activated the primitive conflicts that continue to pose serious threats to self-differentiation, self-demarcation, and self-definition. As Thomson describes so well, only the recognition by the analyst of the engagement of such archaic principles can enable him and his patient to escape from the shackles of their enmeshment.

Because the experience of each of the players (analyst and patient) is shaped not only by the circumstance the patient presents to the analyst but by the triggering effect on the analyst's ways of organizing his experience and the unconscious principles determining these modes, the analytic commitment to seek to understand the experience of patients from a perspective within the patient's subjective framework acquires a new and expanded meaning. Failures of the analyst from within the patient's subjective experience, the particular meanings encoded in that experience, what is revived and precisely how it has come to be organized, will all ultimately have to occupy the focus of the kind of sustained self reflective inquiry Thomson initiated in himself. This characteristic, which we and our patients share in common, has been described elegantly by one of the most astute observers of the affairs of our time:

> Everything that is observed, everything that is known or can be known of reality emerges from the interaction between two moving objects, that which is observed and the pair of eyes that are observing . . . for one of the keys to the understanding of the human predicament is the recognition that there is, for the human individual, no reality—no comprehensible and useful reality, at any rate—other than that of an object as perceived by the human mind—no abstract reality, in other words detached from the eye of the beholder. All that we see around us may be considered to some extent as a part of ourselves, the reflection of our own astigmatisms, our own individual perspectives and— sometimes—our intuitions. Unless it is taken that way, we cannot recognize its reality or even know it to be real [Kennan, 1989, p. xiii].

The unconscious principles that organize experience and give it its distinctive stamp have been characterized as belonging to the realm of the prereflective unconscious (Atwood & Stolorow, 1984). They begin to be established very early in life, some time before the capacity for symbolic thought has been achieved. They are determined by the specific conditions or rules that the child experiences as governing his role in the mutual regulation of affectively harmonious relationships with his important caretakers. Breaking these rules and violating these conditions involves renunciation of the only source of comfort within the child's experience. These unconscious principles thereupon provide an unequalled opportunity and otherwise unavailable window into most basic and affect laden childhood experiences, the residues of these, and the impact upon the child's developmental architecture.

As we have maintained in another context, *"developmental trauma derive their lasting significance from the establishment of invariant and relentless principles of organization that remain beyond the accommodative influence of reflective self awareness or of subsequent experience"* (Brandchaft and Stolorow, 1990, p. 108).

The principles that govern the mind's overall information processing are neither clearly evident in behavior nor introspectively directly available to higher levels of mental functioning. They operate in the form of unconscious paradigms and are implicit in repetitive behavioral rhythms or reactive affect states. The detailed and hierarchical systems of these paradigms determine how accurate and salient are any psychological propositions that purport or may be used to conceptualize or reconceptualize clinical phenomena.

Understanding the makeup of subjectivity in this way also carries with it the recognition that these underarching but unconscious enduring propensities determine the limits beyond which enduring transformations cannot proceed. The analytic compact remains hostage to two childhoods, that of the analyst and that of the patient.

Thomson's self-reflective efforts, which enable him to decenter from the constraints and astigmatisms of the countertransference residues of his own childhood and thereby accept the reality of his patient's experience of him, is the first and indispensable step if he hopes to be able to comprehend his patient's experience from within rather than outside. As Dr. Thomson suggests, such efforts do have the therapeutic effect of affirming and consolidating the patient's confidence in his own perceptions. They have additional far-reaching effects in enabling the analyst to recognize and define the patient's discrepant expressions as immensely important vehicles of a reinstated differentiation. Henry and Diane need these expressions to be reflected back as not diminishing to the analyst and therefore a threat to the tie, but as valuable contributions to the analyst's understanding of himself and this particular individual and an expansion of the bond. An analytic environment in which the threat to self-differentiation has been lifted is experienced as a haven of security, as a "safe house" is to a refugee. It establishes a foundation for a truly unique therapeutic alliance (Brandchaft and Stolorow, 1990). Self-differentiating and self-demarcating processes that are evolving will inevitably be accompanied by anxieties and retreats because of the developmental circumstances through which they have been filtered. The analyst's continuing recognition and identification of these retreats, the analysis of the conflicts that bring them about, and the illumination of the underlying invariant organizing principles increases the mutative potential as the bond of trust is strengthened. This aspect of the therapeutic process, in my experience, specifically promotes the development in the patient of an independent center of initiative and a sustaining enthusiasm for an evolving design that expresses the patient's own distinctness. An eagerness to understand his own contribution to the direction his life has taken follows as an intrinsic part of this program.

Finally, this perspective on the nature of intersecting subjectivities provides a framework within which future light can be shed upon a controversy that has plagued psychoanalysis from its beginnings. I am referring to theories regarding the relative contributions to analytic cure of relationship and understanding, and the more specific roles of each in a fabric that enables both the analyst and the patient to be the best they can be.

We are indebted to Peter Thomson for deepening the focus on the analyst's experience and how it is organized. In keeping us aware of the impact of the analyst in codetermining the field that he observes, Thomson preserves and extends an historic legacy left to us by Heinz Kohut.

REFERENCES

Adler, G. (1989), Uses and limitations of Kohut's self psychology in the treatment of borderline patients. *J. Amer. Psychoanal. Assn.*, 37:761–765.

Atwood, G. & Stolorow, R. (1984), *Structures of Subjectivity: Explorations in Psychoanalytic Phenomenology*. Hillsdale, NJ: The Analytic Press.

Brandchaft, B. (1983), The negativism of the negative therapeutic reaction. In: *The Future of Psychoanalysis*, ed. A. Goldberg. New York: International Universities Press.

Brandchaft, B. & Stolorow, R. (1990), Varieties of therapeutic alliance. *The Annual of Psychoanalysis*, 18:99–114. Hillsdale, NJ: The Analytical Press.

Hitchcock, J. (1989), Review of *Psychoanalytic Treatment: An Intersubjective Approach* by R. D. Stolorow, B. Brandchaft & G. E. Atwood. *Psychoanal. Quart.*, 58:666–671.

Kennan, G. (1989), *Sketches From a Life*, New York: Pantheon.

Chapter 8

The Trauma
of Incest: Threats
to the Consolidation
of the Self

Karen M. Peoples

In the mere 11-year span between 1979 and the present, there has been a virtual explosion into public and professional consciousness of the frequency and devastating impact of sexual abuse within the family. The sheer force of recent words and images on the subject of incest, including extensive clinical studies (Finkelhor, 1984; Briere, 1988), and carefully researched incidence and prevalence surveys (Russell, 1986), as well as popular television, theater, and documentary dramatizations, is testimony both to the enormity of the problem and to the weight of factors—cultural and familial—which had hitherto kept this broken taboo shrouded in silence.

Presently, we see coming together important streams of study that, it is interesting to note, ran their own relatively separate courses for a number of years. Flowing through one corner of the field of psychology and psychiatry has been a current of data on trauma and its characteristic response patterns. From the pioneering work of Horowitz (1976) to the more recent contributions of van der Kolk (1987) and others, study of the somatic, affective, and cognitive disturbances wrought by overwhelming life experiences has led clinicians to a much fuller appreciation of the therapeutic needs of such disparate groups as combat veterans, victims of violent crime, and holocaust and disaster survivors.

*The author gratefully acknowledges the incisive and helpful suggestions on this article offered by Dr. Susan Sands and Dr. Joan Hertzberg.

Yet, until the last few years, this crucial field of investigation did not extend its observations to what is perhaps the most ubiquitous battleground, the family.

In another fertile corner of the psychological field, the psychoanalytic study of trauma has been carried out for more than nine decades, but with a far different course and with significantly different real implications for the trauma survivors sitting in consulting rooms around the country. Despite the tremendous complexity and diversity of views in the domain of psychoanalysis, it is not inaccurate to conclude that the main current of analytic thought have been dominated by the presumption of innate sexual and aggressive drives, and that said drives have been considered the primary motivators of behavior, mental life, and personality. The position of actual trauma, once in the foreground of Freud's thinking, has taken a decidedly backseat position relative to fantasy life in standard analytic formulations of psychic disturbance.

Although it has been widely observed that sexual and aggressive tendencies, with their concomitant fantasy elaborations—including incestuous-type wishes—do play an important part in the child's maturation, their status as central organizing principles of psychic structuralization only recently came into question. In particular, it was through the strong tributary of psychoanalytic self psychology, flowing in a channel similar to the one carved by British object relations theorists such as Balint, Fairbairn and Winnicott, that a crucial shift is occurring toward a more environmentally based—or at least environmentally balanced—understanding of the traumatic origins of many forms of psychopathology.

This is not to say, of course, that the hugely significant object relational contributions of Margaret Mahler (Mahler, Pine, and Bergman, 1975) failed to adequately acknowledge the pathogenic part that interpersonal factors can play in child development. But, as Bacal (1985) pointed out:

> Classical analysis . . . fails to make a meaningful distinction between the pathogenic and the pathogenic that is also traumatic—a distinction, I would suggest, that is of great clinical importance. This failure on the part of classical analysts and current object-relations theorists stems from their attempt to understand the effects of the environment in the context of a theoretical position that is essentially a one-person psychology, where excessive or pathological drives are regarded as the determinants of psychopathology. From the self-psychological perspective, this is not an issue, as the theory presupposes that psychopathology results from a failure of environmental response to the needs of the child's developing self [p. 207]

In short, psychoanalytic theory, long dominated by assumptions about the drive-determined, intrapsychic rather than interpersonal genesis of psychopathology, has in many respects failed to adequately acknowledge the needs of patients suffering from actual trauma, and in particular, due to the sway of oedipal theory—from the trauma of incest. Thus, psychoanalysis, although preoccupied with the question of trauma for decades, has significantly obscured and minimized the direct interpersonal contributions to patient symptomatology that occur in cases of incest and child abuse, as Rush (1980), Herman (1981), Miller (1984), Masson (1984) and others have noted.[1]

The risk of some form of iatrogenic repetition—especially in classical analytic settings—of the abuses of power in the original parent–child dyad is quite high in cases of incest. Masson (1984) comments:

> Whether it is openly stated or merely accepted as a hidden theoretical premise, the analyst who sees . . . a patient (with a history of incest) is trained to believe that her memories are fantasies. As such, the analyst, no matter how benevolent otherwise, does violence to the inner life of his patient and is in covert collusion with what made her ill in the first place [p. 191].

This obscuring of incest trauma's dynamic relationship to patient symptomatology was brought to light in recent research studies, in which a significant portion of individuals diagnosed with borderline personality disorder, most of them women, revealed a history of childhood sexual assault. Herman (1987) noted that "data from three pilot studies offer suggestive evidence that histories of childhood abuse may be found in the majority of borderline patients, and that this finding, although common in the general patient population, is significantly more common in patients with a borderline diagnosis" (p. 118). Briere (1984; Briere and Zaidi, in press) identified a post-sexual abuse syndrome that shares many features in common with a borderline diagnosis. And researchers and clinicians in the fast-developing field of multiple personality and dissociative disorders note that as many as 97% of patients with clinically diagnosed

---

[1]For a further discussion of this issue, see the recent, intriguing article by Westerlund (1986), which suggests that Freud's so-called abandonment of the seduction theory was heavily influenced not only by his idealization of Fliess, but also by discoveries, via his self-analysis subsequent to his father Jacob's death, of his father's incestuous abuse of Freud's siblings, and possibly of Freud himself.

multiple personality disorder have a history of childhood sexual abuse (Institute of Noetic Sciences, 1984).

It is clear from its increasing popularity that psychoanalytic self psychology has offered a crucial corrective—at least on the American scene—to the general analytic picture of childhood trauma. Kohut's emphasis on empathic attunement in the therapeutic relationship has provided a powerful fit with current understandings of the developmental requisites by which the child comes to feel, and say by its actions, "I am a valued person in my own right." However, little has been written from a self psychological perspective—aside from Ulman and Brothers' valuable recent work (1988)—on the specific dynamic consequences of incest trauma, especially as they pertain to the development of a sense of self.

Thus, we appear to be at a point in which the convergence of two powerful streams of thought, trauma theory in general psychiatry and intersubjective approaches in psychoanalysis, can enable mental health professionals to shine a much more focused light on what has heretofore, (as recently as ten years ago), been the murky and often forbidding realm of parental betrayal via the sexual exploitation of children. Although the currents of research and practice in the field of psychological trauma have been continually broadened and refined to the point that special inpatient psychiatric units are now being opened to treat the widespread occurrence of dissociative disorders, as yet there does not exist a cohesive framework for understanding the developmental implications of such early trauma for the structural integrity of the sense of self. In a similar vein, despite the "goodness of fit" between self psychology's conception of traumatic parental failure and recent advances in infant research (Brazelton, 1981; Stern, 1985; Beebe & Lachmann, 1988), both of which speak to the core interactional processes by which children become a self, there is little self psychological material that accounts for the familiar symptomatic portrait of acute and delayed trauma reactions: numbing, intrusion, constriction of intellectual and/or social functioning, explosive rage, and so on (van der Kolk, 1987). In particular, there is an absence of material on the more severe effects of dissociation, a defense along the same continuum as disavowal (Kohut, 1971, 1977) but one that, in its extreme forms, essentially structures the self as a tormented collection of highly conflictual and unstable fragments.

The specific linkages between childhood incest trauma and forms of disturbed functioning in adult life are being laid out with increasing directness in a large number of research studies (Brown, 1988; Smith, 1989; Briere & Zaidi, in press). These disturbances include such phenomena as the aforementioned chronic and extreme employment

of dissociation, crippling shame and guilt, sexual dysfunction, mas-
ochistic or self-injurious behavior, severe anxiety and depression,
eating disorders, and substance addiction and other forms of compulsive behavior. Yet these overt symptoms appear to be the mani-
festation of a more critical underlying interference in self-structure:
they appear to represent severe impairments in the healthy development of a sense of *entitlement* to *agency* and to *subjectivity*.

This chapter seeks to provide an approach to clinical intervention
that integrates an understanding of traumatic stress response patterns into an overarching comprehension of the impairment to
segments of self-experience that is inherent in severe incestuous
abuse. This impairment to the crucial experience of entitlement to
one's being-in-the-world is particular to all incest survivors; however,
because of its reinforcement by powerful cultural processes, this
impairment to entitlement appears especially insidious in female
survivors. Whether it is the core self-experience of free ownership
over one's emotional responses, as when one feels "This is *my* body
shaking with anger," or the sense of authorship of one's behaviors, as
when one enjoys the thrill of saying, "This creation came uniquely
from my ideas"; or further, when one knows the pleasure of being a
subjective agent with freedom of will and desire (Benjamin, 1988)
saying, in effect, "I am the one who wants!," such experiences lie at
the heart of the child's ability to establish herself as the vital,
"independent center of initiative" Kohut championed (Kohut, 1971).

And it is just such crucial self-experience of entitlement to agency
and subjectivity that is most seriously endangered when incestuous
abuse occurs. In its more severe forms in cases of chronic and sadistic
violation of the child, the devastation of these key components of
selfhood—particularly in the female child assaulted by a trusted male
in a position of authority over her—frequently culminate in an
internal holocaust in which the survivor helplessly relives again and
again her early subjugation, this time by the ghostly but tangible
hands of persecutors who are now within her, and who continue to
rob her of what is her own.[2]

I will attempt to address disturbances in entitlement to self-agency
and subjectivity in three central domains of self-structure. Adopting
the useful model for assessment laid out by Stolorow and Lachmann

---

[2]It is important for clinicians to note that an increasing number of male clients are
recovering and reporting memories of sexual abuse by a family member. However, the
majority of the cases involve incestuous abuse of a female child. For this reason, I will
refer primarily to the incest survivor using the feminine pronoun. The terms *client* and
patient will be used interchangeably.

(1980), I examine how development of the affective coloration, the temporal stability or identity stability, and the cohesion of the child's self-structure may be disrupted by incestuous abuse, and how the working through of these developmental disruptions in psychotherapy with the adult survivor may be exacerbated by unresolved, chronically patterned trauma responses, requiring the therapist to temporarily assume a more active stance toward the client aimed at stabilizing her self-regulatory functions. Because the aforementioned entails the interweaving of a number of complex dynamic threads, case material will be used to slowly build the supporting fabric.

NEGATIVE AFFECTIVE COLORATION OF SELF

This first domain of self-structure refers to self-esteem and the relative degree to which the sense of self is positively or negatively toned. Contrary to presumptions by early researchers such as Kinsey and Pomeroy, current detailed data on the effects of various types of incestuous abuse reveal that it is a rare occurrence for sexual contact with a relative to be a purely positive one. In a carefully controlled survey of 930 women conducted in 1978, Russell (1986) found that "not a single case of father–daughter incest was reported to be positive in its entirety" (p. 44).

The negative aftereffects of incest, often severe, are cited repeatedly in the literature and consistently include guilt and shame, low self-esteem, and depression (Herman, 1981; Russell, 1986; Courtois, 1988). In particular, intense shame often functions as a major form of resistance to the exploration of abuse memories, because it arises from a deeply held conviction of the patient's badness and sense of responsibility or blame for the abuse. For one patient, the recall of any memories of her father's seductive, intrusive behavior immediately permeated her with an intolerable feeling of being "a slut," as though she had suddenly been stripped naked and the "true color" of her skin had been revealed. She was unable initially to look independently at her father's behavior because it was inextricably linked to her internalized, shamefully bad, self-representation and its powerfully negative, affective color (Boden, Hunt, and Kassoff, 1987).

Impairments to self-esteem are inherent results of incestuous abuse because of the implied or stated blame placed on the child by the abuser and/or the nonprotecting parent. The lack of recognition of the child's helpless and compliant position relative to the authority of caretakers is rarely identified for the child during or subsequent to the abuse (Herman, 1981; Rieker and Carmen, 1986). Thus she is unable to separate out and feel comfortable with any positive feelings or pleasure she may have derived from the attention or stimulation of the abuser, or to feel entitled to her anger at the abuse, because these are contaminated by the shame and guilt of having presumably participated in a bad and secret act.

For some incest survivors, the abuse may primarily disturb self-esteem without adversely affecting the two other domains of self-functioning identified by Stolorow and Lachmann (1980)—identity formation or self-cohesion. Julia is a case in point. A highly successful, poised, and talented corporate manager in her mid-30s, she maintains successful intimate relationships and has been asymptomatic by clinical standards through most of her life. Nonetheless, her history reveals a pattern of victimization in later life—a rape at 16 and degrading sexual experiences in adolescence and early adulthood—subsequent to a two-year period of seductive manipulation and genital handling by a caretaking uncle in Julia's early latency. A bout of intense depression punctuated by binge eating and serious loss of self-esteem occurred as Julia's marriage broke up in her late twenties. And more recently, symptoms of immune symptom depletion triggered an erosion in self-esteem and left her with threatening feelings of vulnerability.

In general, however, this patient's sense of identity has been quite stable, and she has not been prone to serious experiences of self-fragmentation. Yet she was, for the first two years of treatment, unable to feel touched by her successes in any real way. Despite the appearance of poise, calm and comfort with herself, periodically a sense of underlying badness would surface, which she interpreted as a destructive part trying to "sabotage" her growth, a part firmly convinced that people's love for or appreciation of her was unreal because she was inherently unworthy of it.

Interestingly, these feelings of badness seemed to be restricted to a specific segment, or underlying layer, of Julia's emotional life, and did not permeate her entire self-sense. She would remark how she somehow felt "disconnected" from her accomplishments in a "deep" way even though she intellectually took pleasure in her accomplishments. Similarly, she was disturbed that she was only able to "let in" her lover's caring for her so far; it did not touch the deeper core of her, in which lived the belief of her unworthiness.

It became increasingly evident over time that this negative coloration to a core layer of her self-sense was connected to a dissociated aspect of her experience most directly related to the invalidation of her perceptions of reality by others. Her abuse by her uncle most directly characterized situations in which she was manipulated, confused, and frightened but was not permitted to believe this was so. This was compounded by her Christian Science mother, who believed pain and problems did not truly exist. As a result, Julia's reactive, negative affects (Stolorow, Brandchaft, and Atwood, 1987) were consistently either denied or, worse, were construed to be positive.

Thus, Julia repeatedly sought to rid herself of her negative emotions by disavowing their meaning for her and detaching herself from their experiential impact. In addition, she developed a hypervigilant, defensive stance of intellectually evaluating the weaknesses of others so that, if necessary, she could manipulate and intimidate them with her power, poise, and insight into their psychology. In fact, she prided herself on her powerfulness and self-control and was unable initially to discriminate between their skillful, constructive use and the defensive, destructive aspects of both.

Although we slowly progressed toward an understanding of the need for Julia's rigid defenses against vulnerability, the most significant opportunities for working through occurred when her unresolved trauma reactions surfaced. At unexpected moments, as I would question Julia or remind her of early events that pertained to this material, Julia evidenced a mild form of dissociation in which she reported that she was "spacing out," or "going away right now," or trying to hear what I was saying but she was too disconnected from it. On one occasion, she reported feeling very "weird" and experienced a dissociative alteration of perception (Spiegel, Cardeña, and Spitzer, 1989) in which my chair suddenly seemed very far away; she laughingly asked if I had moved it, knowing I hadn't.

Julia tended to dissociate in these sessions whenever states of helplessness were inadvertently triggered in her, states that reactivated or recalled earlier experiences of being shamefully dominated. Similarly, outside of session, interpersonal events that resembled those moments in the past in which she had felt subtly subjugated or exploited tended to throw Julia into a state of numb detachment. In addition, her dreams would occasionally take on the nightmarish quality that these states of numbness were a reaction to, and from which these states protected her.

Due to her characteristic intellectualizing style, in which she responded to my empathy temporarily, then typically moved to a position quite distant from her immediate experience, these dissociative moments served as important vehicles for accessing the unintegrated layer of Julia's emotional life. We worked first to simply increase Julia's tolerance for closely observing and slowly reliving these dissociative experiences and the emotional events that led up to them. Created by the unbidden return of split-off affects and memorics, these dissociative experiences contained the key emotional conclusions that soured Julia's self-esteem.

For Julia, although her core sense of agency—of being the author and director of her actions—was not impaired, her capacity to experience pleasure and mutuality in the exercise of her power was obstructed by shame and by a deep fear of exploitation, a fear that prompted her to exploit others. Her sense of power and agency had a primarily defensive quality. Although she could intellectually be satisfied when observing her skill at confronting others, her emotional freedom to take pleasure in this exercise of self-assertion while remaining open and sensitive to others was unconsciously contaminated by a shame-ridden mistrust, founded in the belief that she was to blame for naively allowing her uncle not only to sexually exploit her but to disarm her judgment. Thus, the core of Julia's negative coloration of her sense of self lay in the humiliation of her trusting openness to others, especially her trust in the underlying motives of others' bids for intimacy. In this way, Julia's ability to surrender her guardedness in moments of mature emotional and sexual merger (Ghent, in press) was ensnared in developmental conflict in which she experienced a part of herself as actively sabotaging her conscious desire to see herself as strong, in charge of interpersonal encounters, and able to protect herself from manipulation.

The restoration in Julia of a healthy sense of entitlement and self-esteem was directly linked to the working through of the self-blame and shame associated with having failed to actively stop her uncle from his molestation of her. And yet these affects related to her experience of helplessness were typically split off from Julia's day-to-day sense of herself. Thus, the bulk of the integrative work in therapy took place in the aforementioned moments of sudden vulnerability when her dissociative reactions were triggered. These moments were like the sudden appearance of crevasses of light breaking open the snowy crust of Julia's self-control, and provided occasions for important contact and repair, not unlike those moments of empathic rupture of which Kohut (1971, 1977, 1984) spoke. As such, of course, they also held heightened potential for the replication of her earlier trauma. Indeed, it was during a period of increased feelings of vulnerability when I attempted to question Julia about possible ambivalence regarding therapy—questions she experienced as critical and manipulative—which gave me the first clues to her deep sense of self-blame as well as to her degree of feeling overwhelmed psychologically. She didn't dissociate in this session—she walked out—something she did not recall having done when we terminated two years later.

Julia's defensive hypervigilance and need for control diminished gradually as we worked in those vulnerable moments to expand her capacity to tolerate the dissociated and disavowed feelings, and to disconnect their linkage to the self-blame that had required these feelings to remain so covert in the first place. Later, I will examine the different levels and kinds of activity required by the therapist, still operating within the empathic vantage point, when trauma symptoms resurface in the treatment.

Thus, in patients like Julia, delayed trauma responses may arise only episodically and to a relatively mild degree, at times of stress or in the face of specific triggering events. These episodic responses are typically linked to specific, isolated aspects of a patient's overall sense of self, aspects impaired by shame, and deeply hidden self-blame. The recovery, transformation and integration of such painful affect states and negative self-representations may be impeded, however, by the very trauma responses that signal their presence.

TEMPORAL STABILITY

Although Julia suffered from what Stolorow et al. (1987) would consider a relatively mild self disorder, with impairment only in the domain of self-esteem, and from relatively mild post-traumatic symptoms, more serious self disorders occur following incestuous abuse when the developmental task of identity formation is disrupted. Spiegel et al. (1989) recently reviewed the literature pertaining to the effects of traumatic situations, such as disasters, war, or physical assault, upon identity stability. Reactions of survivors included a range of conscious detachment experience,

> from a distinct loss of the sense of self to experiences of feeling detached from one's objective or subjective self (i.e., depersonalization) or sensing that the surrounding environment is somewhat unreal or dreamlike (i.e., derealization) [p. 2].

In addition, Cardeña et al. (1989) identified common immediate reactions of dissociation between observing and participating selves, a sense of distance from bodily sensations—including numbing, anesthesia, or a sense of floating outside of one's body—a sense of distance from thoughts or emotions, as well as the adoption of a different identity than usual.

Developmentally, these serious disruptions in one's sense of continuity or self-history (Stern, 1985) may become structured into the child's overall self-sense when opportunities for repair and integration of the traumatic material are absent subsequent to the dissociative episode. Thus, not atypically, the child experiencing repetitive abuse is left with insufficient psychological means to bridge dissociated states with the more normal experience of the day-to-day self-sense. Although splitting internal experience, such dissociative disruptions to the continuity of identity do not necessarily result in protracted disintegration of the self. Rather, they result in the developmental derailment of diverse segments of experience that, because they cannot be safely integrated into the overall psychic structure, remain developmentally immature—much as Kohut (1971, 1977) described in the specific separating off of archaic grandiosity in the vertical split personality organization.

Margaret, a 38-year-old single parent, came into therapy three and a half years ago stating that she felt "out of control" with herself, "obsessed" by thoughts of her ex-boyfriend, and like her "resources were dwindling." She suffered from dreams in which her father and ex-husband were experienced as a vague "oppressive presence," and was unable to control compulsions to drink, binge eat, and sleep for long periods of time as well as to voyeuristically spy on her ex-boyfriend. She frequently felt plagued by "spooky," "creepy" presences that seemed to lurk in the background—although she was afraid that admitting this meant she was going crazy—and ghosts were actual characters in a number of her early dreams. Blankness would often cross her face in early sessions, and she reported being on "mental overload, like overloading a circuit." I often wondered in the first year of treatment whether Margaret would be capable of connecting affectively and cognitively with her experience and its significance. Despite her awareness of serious depression, anxiety, and feelings of anger, talking with her felt as though "no one was home."

Four months into treatment, Margaret reported a dream that characterized the domination, sexual invasiveness, and trauma to which she was subjected by her father, along with the dissociative quality of her reaction. In the dream, Margaret is in a room where she has somehow ingested helium, and has floated to the ceiling. At first, this seems interesting. (Note the initial detachment.) A cat is looking up at her from the floor. Then she realizes "this stuff is toxic and will cause permanent brain damage"—she has to get it out of her system. She then notices that her father is in the room and that there is a large sewing needle sticking in her leg. She asks her father to take it out so it will let the helium out. He doesn't think there is a problem; he ignores her, refusing to take her seriously. She insists, and begins to get upset, increasingly panic stricken. He finally does so, and she floats down from the ceiling. Her father then wants to give her a shot, but she has already had this needle in her leg and she doesn't want something else that will hurt her. She says no but worries what she will do if he insists. She realizes that even though she is an adult and has every ability to refuse, she is plagued by a vague uneasiness, vulnerability, and creepy sense of dread related to doubts about her ability to withstand him.

For Margaret, the conscious experience of being an adult—the efficient supervisor she was by day in the corporate office—was markedly disconnected from the ghosts and terrors that threatened her unconsciously. In this regard, her sense of identity was kept incomplete due to a dynamic, horizontal repression of relevant memories (Kohut, 1977). In fact, just prior to this dream, Margaret felt a "strange need to nap . . . as though to process some message or get some understanding I couldn't get while awake."

In addition, Margaret's experience of continuity and stability in her sense of identity had been seriously disrupted by a vertical splitting apart of states of severe vulnerability from states of intactness and strength (Kohut, 1977). This discontinuity in her felt sense of identity occurred only in the context of intimate, interpersonal relationships. That is, as long as Margaret was able to avoid intimate relationships, she remained quite functional and experienced herself as stable, bounded, and clear about her goals and direction. However, it is when she entered into relationships with men, driven by her needs for closeness and affection, that she reported "losing herself" and would suffer an intensification of compulsive symptoms.[3]

This temporary loss of identity has been manifest in Margaret's intense and rapid idealizing mergers with men early on in relationships. Although providing considerable soothing and affirmation of her value as a needed object, the merger also quickly begins to threaten Margaret's sense of separate selfhood, that is, her value as a *subject*. As one might suspect, she tends to select men who are

---

[3]Although this type of vertical splitting differs from Kohut's (1971, 1977) discussions, in which it is the selectively and inappropriately mirrored archaic grandiosity of the child that pathologically splits off from the needs of the nuclear self, resulting in a false self-structure, the usefulness of expanding the concept of vertical splitting in self psychology is evident. The many forms in which false self-structure can occur has been indicated by the British object relations school. It remains for self psychologists to address this question further, and to examine specifically whether a vertical splitting of archaic idealizing needs may occur. I believe this was so in Margaret's case. Furthermore, it remains to be examined whether vertical splits in the grandiose pole versus those in the idealizing pole tend to occur along gender lines. I concur with Ghent (in press) and Benjamin (1988) that they do, although these authors did not formulate their hypotheses in the lexicon of self psychology.

grossly incapable of recognizing her independent existence, but who narcissistically crave the mirroring she provides them through her adoration.

Typically, within six weeks these intense mergers would present such a threat to Margaret's identity that she would flee them in a state of panic, feeling that she was losing her sense of direction, will, judgment, and capacity to take care of herself, as well as fearing that she was going to be dominated, used, then callously discarded. When such panicky break-ups would ensue, Margaret would feel a sickening sense of self-loathing, and voices reminiscent of her father would play in her head about how "trashy, sleazy, and worthless" she was. Thus, there ensued a bout of serious compulsive behaviors, primarily designed—we learned over time—to distract her from her merger needs and fears, to ward off the shame associated with them, and to maintain self-esteem by reestablishing a sense of boundedness and self-agency, however limited.

Interestingly, this destabilizing sense of loss of her autonomy is reflected in Margaret's uncanny feeling that her 14-year-old daughter has been living out Margaret's emotional life for her—in particular, Margaret's ability to assert her own needs and desires in the face of a dominating male. In numerous dreams, including one very recently, Margaret is faced by a threatening ghost or by her assaultive ex-husband, and is in danger of capitulating to his intimidating power, unsure if she can withstand him, when the baby in the dream—often identified as her daughter—angrily protests in a way that disrupts the threat and seems to free Margaret to decide against her attacker.

Clearly, what is evident is a shackling of Margaret's sense of agency and intentionality at a level even more disruptive than Julia's. In Margaret's case, her healthy movements toward self-assertion in latency, such as wishing to develop friendships outside her stifling home atmosphere, apparently proved a grave, narcissistic threat to her seductive, paranoid father. In her early years, Margaret felt she was "in heaven," the center of her father's adoring universe. She had trouble recalling and integrating these feelings with the "creepy," frightening experience of intrusion associated with his insistence that her bed remain in the parental bedroom until age 12, within arm's reach of her father's side at night, or with his watching her in the bathtub, or trying to paw at her.

"Heaven" collapsed for Margaret when, around age 10 or 11, her father began to ragefully turn on her, soon abandoning Margaret altogether and turning to her younger sister. His destructive manipulation of her efforts at self-assertion and the sexualized distortion of those efforts led Margaret in adolescence to the "path of submission and depression" so aptly described by the Stolorow group (Stolorow et al., 1987). In this version of developmental conflict, the child finds that the only way to maintain vitally needed selfobject ties is to completely subordinate her needs for self-demarcation and self-assertion.

Margaret's case is, of course, not unique. Shame and intense self-loathing colored her self-concept. Alcohol and food abuse, depression, anxiety, and compulsive sexuality characterized her behavior away from work. A serious paralysis of her sense of entitlement and agency marred her capacity for maintaining intimate relationships. But of central importance for our therapeutic work together—particularly for the establishment of a sense of authority or permission to maintain her own desire in the face of her intimate partner's wishes—were unresolved trauma reactions.

We were unable to proceed steadily toward the exploration and integration of relevant early material because to do so threatened to precipitate a phase of intrusive symptoms characteristic of traumatic stress reactions, including nightmares that left her feeling "taken over," intrusive blaming judgments that at times had a hallucinogenic intensity (Cardeña et al., 1989), marked panic at the resurgence of certain affect states, and a sense of dread that her future had been completely abrogated. When, after a year and a half of treatment, Margaret was able to decide to abstain from alcohol, she entered a phase of intense flooding of affects that threatened to seriously overwhelm her.

The difference for Margaret was that, despite the instability of her sense of identity, she was able to stave off experiences of serious fragmentation, mostly through frantic, compulsive behavior. As we worked to understand the function these behaviors served and to help her slowly replace the more destructive ones with beneficial, self-soothing, and care-taking behaviors, she gradually gained an increased tolerance for the most threatening affect states—those related to her father's insidious sexual intrusion, psychic domination, and subsequent abandonment.

Stolorow et al., (1987) refer to identity stability as a critical second dimension of self-structure having to do with the individual's capacity to maintain an integrated, cognitively elaborated self-schema over time. Experientially, this is felt as a sense of continuity and sameness to one's sense of self, despite changes of context, mood, physical condition, and so on. Severe forms of temporal instability—or identity discontinuity—may be seen in fugue states and multiple personality disorder.

Clients like Margaret experience disruptions of their self-organization in the two domains of self-esteem and identity, reflective of midrange or moderately serious self-disturbance (Stolorow et al., 1987). As I have attempted to show thus far, the resolution of Margaret's self-disturbance was complicated by the persistence of dissociated and disavowed traumatic affects. Unlike other individuals in this moderately severe range, Margaret maintained a relatively stable level of ego functioning, as evidenced by her ability to sustain an effective work life aside from her interpersonal difficulties. Nonetheless, she initially presented many of the apparently borderline features typical of many individuals with serious abuse histories, including a marked constriction in her capacity for cognitive elaboration and articulation of her experience, marked lability in intimate, interpersonal relationships, and intense compulsivity and impulsivity in her behavior.

It may be apparent by now that significant degrees of overlap exist between the dissociative symptoms of traumatic stress and the symptoms that characterize borderline personality disorder. Briere and Zaidi (in press) and Herman and van der Kolk (1987) most clearly demonstrated from research findings the linkage between early sexual abuse trauma, particularly incest, and their borderline-type sequelae in later life. It is often inevitable, following such pernicious betrayal of the child, by father *and* mother, that serious impairments occur in the child's developmental capacity to effectively structure emotional and cognitive experience.

What is important to stress here, however, is that clinical evidence indicates that these same severe symptoms often recede dramatically when their roots in early traumatic experience are identified, understood and actively addressed in the context of an empathically sustained therapeutic relationship. The tendency to rely chronically upon dissociative or splitting defenses to ward off overwhelming emotions and bodily sensations can be effectively diminished when the therapist assists the patient to regain much-needed control over her own experience, resulting in greatly stabilized overall functioning that facilitates the more interpretive, symbolic work of therapy.

This process will be examined in more detail shortly. First, it is necessary to assess the consequences for the adult incest survivor whose sense of self as a child was not only rendered "bad" or inconstant, but whose moment-to-moment existence as a cohesive, subjective agent was under dire threat.

SELF-COHESION

In the two preceding cases, in which disturbances in self-esteem and identity were explored, I drew primarily on the work of Stolorow and his colleagues (1987; Stolorow and Lachmann, 1980). These authors present a particularly lucid extension and refinement of Kohut's compelling work that is firmly grounded in the phenomenology of self-experience and that is congruent with the developmental unfolding of the sense of self illuminated by infant research. In their continuum of self-disturbance that I am utilizing here—from disruptions in self-esteem, identity and, now, self-cohesion—these authors identify the critical importance of two developmental needs.

Somewhat different from Kohut's original two lines of mirroring and idealizing needs, these authors specify two domains in which optimal caregiver responsiveness is required. One concerns the child's developmental strivings, which broadens the need for mirroring affirmation from Kohut's focus on grandiosity and exhibitionism to the full range of excitement, exhilaration, mastery, accomplishment and self-assertion associated with the exercise of one's innate potential. The other concerns the child's vital need for connection to a "regulating other" who can assist the child in managing reactive affect states. Although their discussion of this latter domain does not, in my opinion, adequately address the phenomenon of idealization, especially in its more mature forms, their understanding is extremely useful regarding the ways in which one's affective experience can become conflicted and rendered the *destroyer* of the self that deeply needs connection with others.

Rarely do we see situations in which an individual's own feeling states become so alien and anathema as in cases of early, chronic, parental sexual abuse of the child. In these family situations where physical and emotional violence, betrayal, and active disconfirmation of the child's reality become routine terrors, basic trust has often been profoundly shattered. Existence as a coherent fabric is repeatedly rent and disassembled by the unpredictable intrusion into the child's bodily and psychic boundaries. Protest is often brutally stifled. Her desperate emergency attempts via dissociation may even be closed off to the child, as in cases where the father realizes that his daughter is not feeling the rape because she has learned to crawl psychically into a tiny crevice in the wall; at this point the sadistic father forces her to look him in the eye.

Such assaults aim not solely to achieve satisfaction through use of the child's body but are geared toward domination over and, in some cases, extinction of the child's very sense of self. The young victim's subjectivity itself becomes the abuser's prime target. As such, subjectivity also becomes simultaneously the child's most precious possession and most potentially dangerous vulnerability.

It is surprising to witness how many children physically surviving such deadly environments grow up *not* to be psychotic. Nonetheless, they often live as adults with a level of existential vulnerability that turns day-to-day functioning into a debilitating struggle against terror and despair. Such individuals often experience a continual, underlying threat of fragmentation of their internal capacity for organizing reality. This sense of threat not infrequently erupts into actual, terrifying breakdowns in self-structure. Unlike the fear of falling apart recounted by many individuals at moments of vulnerability, survivors of violent incestuous abuse not uncommonly describe such moments of fragmentation in torturous terms, such as "I'm being blown apart, or ripped apart."

Tracy is one such individual whose sense of self was not only stained with self-hatred and interrupted by feelings of derealization and confusion, but was subject to overwhelming losses of self-cohesion. The first of six children born to a meek, depressed, and impoverished mother, Tracy was the light of her mother's bleak life for the first two-to-three years. A very dependent woman and daughter of alcoholic parents, Tracy's mother dwelled in fantasies that their perfect mother–daughter love was all she, the mother, needed. Her reliance on her daughter for narcissistic supplies persisted throughout Tracy's life in the form of an intense enmeshment.

When Tracy was 4 years old, her mother remarried. At age 5, her stepfather began forcing Tracy to masturbate and orally copulate him. Tracy fearfully sought her mother's protection at this point; her mother appropriately managed to mobilize to leave the situation, but was dissuaded by her own father, who convinced the mother that she needed the marriage and that Tracy was lying. Tracy's fate was sealed here—any protest quashed. Soon after, Tracy's stepfather began a pattern of rape, intimidation, and humiliation that lasted for seven years.

In addition to the overwhelming physical violation she suffered, Tracy could find no safe place to retreat psychologically. Just when she would begin to hope he had lost interest in her and that she might have an inviolate space in which to be alone, he would seek Tracy out and take slow pleasure in first encroaching on, then invading her. When she would show excitement in something outside the home, especially when she would show desire, such as for the pair of white cowboy boots she so badly wanted at age 8, he would entice her by first seeming to join in her excitement, only to use it maliciously against her later. The boots she could have. "Don't you want them terribly?" he would observe (but at what cost to her body and soul?). "How are you going to repay me?" he would ask.

At age 9, Tracy was compulsively overeating to numb her feelings of rage, shame, and despair; by age 10 she was bulimic. At age 12, she began using drugs and alcohol, and by age 15 was resorting to cutting herself with razors to relieve the overwhelming tension of her inner life.

When Tracy entered treatment with me at age 24, she had been hospitalized twice for apparent suicidal gestures related to her use of the razor. Although important for her protection, these hospital treatments failed to address the fact that her cutting was not motivated by a wish to commit suicide (Smith, 1989), but was in fact a desperate attempt to regulate her imploding emotions and thus restore her vitally needed self-cohesion.

At such times of fragmentation, she was plagued by the intrusive reexperiencing of accusatory voices that ridiculed and taunted her. These were not the hallucinations of psychosis, for Tracy clearly knew they were inside her own mind; they were complex hallucinatory phenomena common to the intrusive phase of posttraumatic stress disorder, and they were of terrifying intensity. Tracy also experienced a number of the somatic symptoms that accompany this kind of reexperiencing, including dizziness, palpitations, a sense of spinning, as well as physical numbness (Cardeña et al., 1989).

The first task of therapy was to help Tracy manage these disabling symptoms of fragmentation. Although the process of structuralization in cases of such serious self-disruption is by no means a simple or rapid one, the therapist's active, timely assistance in the diminishing of the patient's primary and secondary responses to trauma is of crucial importance. Helping the patient to de-escalate chronic somatic and affective states of "battle alert" provides a vitally needed sense of safety and helps create an internal "armistice," thus facilitating the building of a stable empathic relationship in which to conduct the more finely-tuned, working-through process.

To elaborate, the following quote from Fink (1988) indicates the severe disruption of the core self sense of affectivity (Stern, 1985) typical in patients with serious dissociative disorders following traumatic abuse:

> Mistrust of affectivity is a cornerstone of dissociative pathology. The severely traumatized individual has not learned to rely on stable affective experience, but instead experiences emotions as disintegrating. Either as a primary response to trauma, i.e., an inability to integrate overwhelming neurophysiologic stimuli, or as a secondary response based on the conditions implicit in the traumatic circumstances, the MPD (multiple personality disorder) patient is unable to rely on a secure, well-modulated pattern of affective arousal. There is then a resultant insecurity as to how affect will be experienced, an

insecurity as to whether the physiologic components of affective states will follow a predictable pattern of increasing and decreasing intensity or whether they will be experienced unpredictably and as chaotically disorganized and overwhelming [p. 45].

The overloading of the autonomic nervous system results in high levels of stress and chronic fatigue. Attention to this bodily experience is a must because it is in the body that the survivor repeatedly registers the threat of trauma. This attention to the bodily experience can be approached by a variety of means, including progressive relaxation, creation of a hierarchy of soothing visual imagery, hypnosis, and instruction in basic self-calming activities (Brown and Fromm, 1986), as well as carefully monitored medication, where indicated. For example, for the first nine months of her twice-weekly treatment, Tracy would curl up in a ball on the sofa and quiver. She looked like a frightened rabbit who could not discern the source of the danger she sensed was all too near. For many weeks, the majority of the sessions were spent helping her "ground" or "anchor" herself in her bodily experience in the present, helping her find her breath and utilize it to slowly release her muscle tension, and creating detailed images of safe and nourishing experiences.

Tracy was tormented by hellish internal imagery associated with the sadistic, accusatory attacks of her stepfather, which triggered a panicked feeling of being trapped. Before we could begin to untangle the emotional significance of these brutal memories, Tracy had to experience some distance from and control over their impinging force. Before she could even begin to approach the demons within her, Tracy needed a clear internal space in which to recover her own psychological equilibrium. This meant helping her unlearn her automatic strategy of dissociation and discover the ground in which to be safely alone in the presence of both internal and external others (Winnicott, 1965; Benjamin, 1988; Ghent, in press).[4]

The path toward this internal space was not a smooth or even

---

[4]A crucial distinction must be made between facilitating detachment—via a strengthening of the patient's observing self—and dissociation. Reexperiencing and reintegration of disavowed affects are a necessary part of the healing process, and it is important to help the patient avoid the tendency to dissociate, especially the patient who chronically dissociates. What is sometimes missed in this effort is the importance of slowly facilitating the patient's self-control over the distancing process, bringing it under conscious volition as a step toward restoring the patient's overall self-regulatory capacities. Conscious detachment from, and observation of, traumatic memories provides a necessary balance to the process of reexperiencing, and both must occur in a graduated fashion concomitant with the patient's increasing sense of control over her internal experience.

visible one, but rather something Tracy and I both groped intuitively for in the moment-to-moment interchange in the session. Finding the path required attunement to the physiologic, postural, and gestural features of Tracy's nonverbal behavior that signaled shifts in her internal tension states. These shifts often occurred in rapid sequences and reflected the dynamic fluctuation of dissociated ego states that Watkins and Watkins (1979) describe. For example, Tracy consistently required my regulatory assistance in relaxing her muscle tension—being guided step by step by my voice and sometimes requiring a calming hand on her shoulder—before she had enough distance from the pressure of her anxious images and sensations to continue describing them—in halting words and through drawings.

Intervention at the level of secondary response to trauma is more complicated because it has to do with "the conditions implicit in the traumatic circumstances"—namely, the meanings and intentions associated with the abuse. These meanings are kept alive by the conscious and unconscious expectational sets and shattered archaic, narcissistic fantasies (Ulman and Brothers, 1988) of the patient which often fit hand in glove with configurational elements of present situations. Incest survivors are typically so hypervigilant for danger that a single cue reminiscent of the early trauma can trigger an explosive chaining of associations that re-create the entire original scenario in the experience of the survivor. For example, a critical remark by a boss or co-worker can precipitate a dominolike collapsing of self-esteem, as deep-seated feelings and cognitions spring up of self-loathing, doom, and hopelessness. To prevent this collapse, the individual may internally scramble to escape the crippling self-blame she experiences. The individual may, in her rage and fear, need to project this blame outward because experiencing any shred of it toward herself so thoroughly threatens her or his tenuous self-esteem, identity, and cohesion.

Here is where self psychology and trauma theory come together so fruitfully. As these case examples have attempted to illustrate, unresolved trauma responses can have a strong, disruptive effect on the progress of the therapy, because the incest survivor's ability to reflect upon her experience and tolerate the affective storms it brings, especially self-blame and self-hatred, may be short circuited by spontaneous and chronically employed dissociative reactions. An understanding of these reactions and timely intervention with them may not only significantly stabilize the therapeutic relationship, but can also provide the patient with an important cognitive tool by which to explain to herself the unpredictable upsurgence of sensations and feelings to which she is subject.

None of these interventions, however, will prove very useful without the sustaining presence of the therapist's empathic immersion in the patient's experience. In particular, self psychology teaches us that it is the therapist's capacity to repair the ruptures that occur in the therapeutic bond that is so crucial to the transformation of those deeply embedded expectations of injury the patient carries. The mirroring and, most importantly, the affect regulating and affect integrating functions that the therapist serves are vital to the restoration of the incest survivor's sense that there is a space in the world of human beings to which she is entitled and in which she can visibly and audibly embody her own aspirations. Without such restoration and repair, the incest survivor may be able to do only that—survive, falling into what Krugman (1987) referred to as the secondary elaboration of trauma—that is, a characterological adaptation of depression, avoidance of intimacy, and overall impoverishment of her life sphere.

The important work that Kohut began toward recognition of the central needs of the self for responsive attunement has been elaborated by recent writers in a manner that is directly applicable to the needs of the incest survivor.

Julia, Margaret, and Tracy all experienced varying degrees of unresolved traumatic symptoms that both disrupted and provided a vehicle for important affect integration work. The capacity to desomatize affective experience—that is, to prevent somatic signals of emotional arousal from spreading like wildfire into diffuse bodily alarm—is a developmental capacity that is chronically disrupted in cases of severe physical and sexual abuse, because it is typically in such cases that both parents fail repeatedly to provide the requisite selfobject responsiveness.

As Stolorow and Socarides (1987) outlined,

Through countless experiences . . . the caregiver, by comprehending, interpreting, accepting and responding empathically to the child's unique and constantly shifting feeling states, is at the same time enabling him to monitor, articulate, and understandingly respond to them on his own [p. 72].

This responsiveness allows for the differentiation of one's own feeling states from another's, the discrimination of different kinds of feeling states within one's own continuous being, and the crucial ability to not only tolerate affects but to utilize them as helpful signals in the service of self-preservation. Stolorow and Socarides continue: "When affects are perceived as signals of a changing self-state rather than as indicators of impending psychological disorganization and fragmentation, the child is able to tolerate his emotional reactions without experiencing them as traumatic" (p. 72). Without such signaling capacity, "the emergency of affect often evokes painful experiences of shame and self-hatred, arising originally from the absence of positive, affirming responsiveness to the child's feelings. Emotionality thereby comes to be experienced as a solitary and unacceptable state, a sign of a loathsome defect within the self that must somehow be eliminated" (p. 72).

The sudden arising of affect, the return of unbidden memories, the unpredictable emergence of bodily sensations, all may represent not only the degree to which the incest survivor is still being internally traumatized and abused, but also reinforce her experience that she has lost ownership over and authorship of her own actions, body, and emotions.

CORE SELF AGENCY AND SUBJECTIVE AGENCY

This consideration leads to the theme of entitlement to agency and subjectivity, which has been woven throughout the discussion. Fink, mentioned earlier in reference to impairments in self-affectivity, offered an important integration of dissociative data with Stern's (1985) work on the core self—the second of Stern's four developmentally arising and continuous domains of self-experience. Fink suggested that it is the organization of the core self, via bodily based experience, that is most adversely affected by severe physical and sexual abuse and its dissociative sequelae. The organization of critical muscular and sensory capacities involving motor plan execution (self-agency), physiological arousal (self-affectivity), body boundaries (self-coherence) and continuity of perceptual experience (self-history), he argued, is more likely to be disrupted than is the subjective sense of self, Stern's third domain of self-experience. It is, of course, this third domain, developing through the empathic attunement of caregivers, which is of such relevance to self psychologists due to its implications for narcissistic disturbance.

Fink (1988) comments:

> Physical trauma may cause particularly *physical* psychic wounds with resultant deficits in the realm of bodily somatic self perceptions. The consequences of physical and sexual trauma for the young child obtain most directly to uncertainty for the individual's perceptions of and relation to his or her body . . . The magnitude of incestuous trauma disturbs the child's gradually emerging security in the sphere of his

existence as a physical being. Disturbances in the realm of core self mirror the quality of dissociative experience [p. 46].

I agree with Fink that the profound disturbances of identity and bodily coherence that manifest in severe dissociative disorders, such as multiple personality or atypical dissociative disorder, as well as in some of the severe clinical manifestations of borderline personality disorder, are indicative of derailment in the domain of the core self, as Stern (1985) described it. However, there is also a crucial aspect of agency, typically associated with core self experience, that lies at the heart of the domain of subjectivity, the domain of the subjective self. This is the experience of intentionality. As Stern demonstrated, it is through the sharing of attention and intention by which the toddler enters into communion with others and begins to learn about empathy and mutuality. And it is in those all-important moments when the caregiver recognizes, understands, and responds to the toddler's shifts of attention and intention that the child comes to feel a sense of being recognized as a person in her own right—as a center of independent initiative and volition.

To truly be seated in her own subjectivity, however, the child must discover and recognize the independent initiative and intentionality of her caregivers. The child requires caregivers who can not only accept her affects and assertions of control without retaliating, withdrawing, or collapsing, but who can assert their own selfhood without having to obliterate the child's selfhood. As Benjamin (1988) pointed out so eloquently, it is the breakdown of mutuality—the mutual recognition of each other's subjectivity—that results in the patterns of domination and submission so characteristic of human relationships, and that are so distortedly enacted in the incestuously abusive family.

In case after case of chronic incestuous abuse, one parent typically invades and crushes the child's will or coerces it into submission through guilt, while the other parent denies, withdraws from, or collapses in the face of the child's emotional assertions against being violated. Benjamin emphasized the moments of connection and contact under conditions of mutuality as central to the child's sense of pleasure in discovering reality. She cited Winnicott's notion that reality is not just something that must be adapted to, but is rather

a positive source of pleasure, the pleasure of connecting with the outside, and not just a brake on narcissism or aggression. Beyond the sensible ego's bowing to reality is the joy in the other's survival and the recognition of shared reality. Reality is thus *discovered*, rather than *imposed;* and authentic selfhood is not absorbed from without but discovered within [p. 41].

It is not difficult to see how the incest survivor's experiences obstruct and threaten to obliterate her sense of subjective agency, a feeling of pleasure in, and entitlement to, being alive, visible, and vocal—that is, as Benjamin stresses, to be recognized as a *subjective* other. Central to the therapeutic process with many incest survivors is the need to be free of the fear that the other's self-assertion will destroy her own self-assertion, and the paradoxical, sometimes deeply unconscious fear that assertive efforts of her own—including and, in particular, the expression of her anger—will destroy or debilitate the other.

This brings us finally to the important question of transference and countertransference in the therapeutic relationship.

TRANSFERENCE AND COUNTERTRANSFERENCE

In survivors with severe abuse histories, the need to have the therapist serve vital selfobject functions frequently exists in agonizing conflict with the visceral expectation of further traumatization by, and failure of, the therapist to meet those needs. The patient often maintains a hypervigilant stance in relation to the therapist, and may experience the therapist's lapses in attunement as major injuries, necessitating rapid retreat, in consciousness and sometimes in action, to a position of safety to preserve the self from further threat.

Yet this withdrawal, although serving a crucial protective function, also threatens the patient's needed ties to the therapist. The essential treatment task in such instances, as self psychology so clearly demonstrates, is the consistent identification of the points of injury or disruption in the empathic bond, and exploration of the impact they have upon the patient, including the conscious and unconscious fantasies they generate or shatter. For example, in the midst of communicating her experience, Tracy repeatedly and furtively scanned my face for signs of irritation, disgust, or tiredness. If she believed I was feeling such a response, her face would shut down, her muscles would tense, and the transference relationship would suddenly spring from background to foreground (Stolorow et al., 1987), necessitating my speculations and queries about what my responses meant to her.

The therapist's exploration and communication to the patient of the meaning of such disruptions of her self-organization, in the context of the patient's immediate experience of the therapist, and later, in the context of her early trauma history and derailed developmental movement, are, as we know, central to the integration of the patient's disavowed or dissociated affect states and to the restoration of the forward momentum of the treatment.

Incest survivors from families in which caregivers routinely required the child to attend to their own narcissistic equilibrium will often be exquisitely attuned to fluctuations in the therapist's self-esteem and self-cohesion. Deeply-rooted fears of having, ultimately, to again surrender her own needs in the service of the therapist's subtle requirements for mirroring are common. Thus, for example, even the therapist's mild displays of confidence in the patient's movements forward may be received as evidence of the therapist's need for the patient to improve in order to enhance the therapist's self-esteem.

The problem of defining appropriate therapeutic boundaries and parameters of therapist responsiveness looms large in the treatment of incest survivors, where disconfirmation and active distortion of the reality of the abuse is often the normative reaction from the social surround (Rieker and Carmen, 1986). As I attempted to establish an in-depth analytic stance that simultaneously acknowledged the enormity and the dynamics of the cultural problem of sexual abuse, my conception of the therapeutic "container" necessarily changed over time. I was initially concerned that I might reinforce my clients' sense of victimization by empathizing too emphatically with the horror of their abuse or that I might infantilize my clients by occasionally offering active assistance toward the restoration of a modicum of comfort in response to their states of dissociated terror, for example, by extending my hand to hold. What emerged from this cautious exploration of flexibility in boundaries, without impeding the depth of analysis, however, was a deepened appreciation that it is the therapist's empathy itself that is, indeed, the container. Rather than predetermined or rigidly fixed rules for setting limits and boundaries, it is the consistency of the therapist's understanding, moment-to-moment in the analytic encounter, that forges the type of stable yet malleable self-selfobject matrix that enables the patient to sustain forward momentum along the developmental path.

With the caveat that therapists, of course, must in all cases refrain from emotional and sexual exploitation of their patients, and must certainly avoid acting on grandiose fantasies that one can or should become active in the patient's life outside treatment, I do believe that, in the more severe cases of trauma I have described, the therapist must assume an active stance—at least initially—within the treatment process of validating the incest survivor's reality and safeguarding her fragile sense of self.

Still, as Goldberg (1990) noted, there is a great deal of ambiguity about what is the appropriate stance of the analyst or therapist. I agree with Goldberg that therapists working from a self-psychological perspective are particularly susceptible to being shackled by the expectation of perfect attunement to their patients. And the comments made here regarding the incest survivor's exquisite fear of misattunement may reinforce such oppressive expectations. Conversely, therapists who adhere to a rigid stance of apparent neutrality and who fail to validate the reality of the patient's trauma, repeat the noxious interpersonal experiences the incest survivor suffered originally.

In the process of resurrecting her own tenuous belief that she is truly entitled to be seen and heard in the world of others—that is, in the process of reclaiming her own right to be recognized subjectively—the incest survivor in treatment may be markedly unable, for a long period of time, to grant recognition or mutuality of any kind to the therapist. This is usually due precisely to the fragility of her sense of entitlement to agency in her core and subjective domains of self.

If this process eventually becomes very difficult for the therapist to sustain, is this because of specific vulnerabilities in the therapist's self-esteem that require attention? Often, this is the case. But is it not also perhaps difficult because of a basic and normal need by the therapist to be minimally recognized in his or her own right as a human being in a meaningful human encounter? Kohut (1971) eloquently addressed the struggles of the analyst, working with a client in an archaic merger transference, who must learn to tolerate this fundamental lack of recognition as a subjective agent. Sustaining affective immersion in the experience of a client in desperate need, yet terrified and rejecting of contact, may require a profound capacity in the therapist to demonstrate consistently an even and positively toned neutrality. Yet, in some instances, the apparent breaching of that neutrality through active provision, as when Kohut (1984) responded to the plaintive need of his severely depressed client by extending his fingers for her to hold, lifts the coffin-lid of the patient's despairing self-isolation sufficiently to allow the first tendrils of true mutuality to form.

The desire for a clear and tangible definition of the analytic therapist's role begins to take on an urgent quality at times in the face of the intensity and horrific nature of our abused clients' early sufferings—the enormity of which is just beginning to be exposed to many therapists. Questions can become quite agonizing, such as whether, and how often, to speak with a client by phone between sessions, and how to define those parameters therapeutically.

It is perhaps partly due to the changing understandings about early childhood abuse that the theoretical debate over "gratification" versus "abstinence" has become so heated. Insinuated through the debate and arising in our own private moments of grandiosity or desperation seems to be the notion that a precise, unchanging, and secure boundary within which to operate is an attainable ideal. The desire to avoid role ambiguity and the therapist's difficulty in tolerating ambiguity over time are especially intensified by the often rapidly shifting functional capabilities of our clients who have been severely abused.

Self psychology has been pivotal in bringing this debate into the center of analytic discourse, and in thus opening up for discussion ground that is unavoidably murky—and invariably rich and fertile. In the unfortunate (yet paradoxically propitious) absence of a perfectly stable definition of our role, it seems we can only grope our way through these murky areas with our patients, respecting and trusting that the eventual discovery of true mutuality, and the healing power such genuine contact provides, will in time be found, if only because we are groping together.

CONCLUSION

The challenge to establish a psychoanalytic model of developmental assessment that adequately encompasses the critical contributions in the literature on trauma reactions, on the one hand, and that can effectively describe and explain the development of the self and its intrapsychic functions, on the other, is just beginning to be met. It is increasingly clear that psychoanalysis must broaden its knowledge base to encompass the significant and exciting advances in the fields of cognition, affect development, infant research, and psychosomatic medicine, for example. As psychoanalytic theorists and practitioners, we must be courageous enough to allow our most preciously held organizing perspectives to be deconstructed—and perhaps even shattered—in the service of explanatory models that enhance our ability to facilitate the healing of psychic trauma. Only when we constantly face and move through the disruptions to our own narcissistic equilibrium brought on by shifts in our beliefs about self and world do we have the opportunity to rectify and minimize the iatrogenic forces at work within ourselves and within our theories. Then we have an opportunity to truly end the silence that has surrounded the trauma of incest for so many years.

REFERENCES

Bacal, H. (1985), Optimal responsiveness and the therapeutic process. In: *Progress in Self Psychology, Vol I* ed. A. Goldberg. New York: Guilford Press, pp. 202–227.

Beebe, B. & Lachmann, F. (1988), Mother-infant mutual influence and precursors of psychic structure. In: *Frontiers in Self Psychology: Progress in Self Psychology, Vol 3.* ed. A. Goldberg. Hillsdale, NJ: The Analytic Press, pp. 3–25.

Benjamin, J. (1988), *The Bonds of Love.* New York: Pantheon Books.

Boden, R., Hunt, P. and Kassoff, E. (1987), Shame and the psychology of woman. Presented to the annual meeting of the Association for Women in Psychology, Denver, CO.

Brazelton, T. B. (1981), Precursors for the development of emotions in early infancy. In: *Emotion: Theory, Research and Experience, Vol II,* ed. R. Pluchik & H. Kellerman. New York: Academic Press.

Briere, J. (1984), The effects of childhood sexual abuse on later psychological functioning: Devining a post-sexual-abuse syndrome. Presented to the Third National Conference on Sexual Victimization of Children, Children's Hospital National Medical Center, Washington, DC.

_____ (1988), The long-term clinical correlates of childhood sexual victimization. *Annals NY Acad. Sci.,* 528:327–334.

_____ Zaidi, L. (in press), Sexual abuse histories and sequelae in female psychiatric emergency room patients. *Amer. J. Psychiat.*

Brown, D. & Fromm, E. (1986), *Hypnotherapy and Hypnoanalysis.* Hillsdale, NJ: Lawrence Erlbaum Associates.

Cardeña, E., Spitzer, R. & Spiegel, D. (1989), Checklist for brief reactive dissociative disorder, acute stress reaction research project. Dept Psychiat. & Beh. Sci., Stanford University School of Medicine, Stanford, CA.

Courtois, C. (1988). *Healing the Incest Wound: Adult Survivors in Therapy.* New York: Norton.

Fink, D. (1988), The core self: A developmental perspective on dissociative disorders. *Dissociation,* 1:43–47.

Finkelhor, D. (1984), *Child Sexual Abuse: New Theory and Research.* New York: Free Press.

Ghent, E. (in press), Masochism, submission, surrender. *Contemp. Psychoanal.*

Goldberg, A. (1990), *The Prisonhouse of Psychoanalysis.* Hillsdale, NJ: The Analytic Press.

Herman, J. (1981), *Father-Daughter Incest.* Cambridge, MA: Harvard University Press.

Herman, J. & van der Kolk, B. (1987), Traumatic antecedents of borderline personality disorder. In: van der Kolk. *Psychological Trauma,* B. Washington, DC: American Psychiatric Press.

Horowitz, M. J. (1976), *Stress Response Syndromes.* New York: Aronson.

Institute of Noetic Sciences (1984), Multiple personality: Mirrors of a new model of mind? *Investigations,* 1:1–23.

Kohut, H. (1971), *The Analysis of the Self.* New York: International Universities Press.

_____ (1977), *Restoration of the Self.* New York: International Universities Press.

_____ (1984), *How Does Analysis Cure?* ed. A. Goldberg & P. Stepansky. Chicago: University of Chicago Press.

Krugman, S. (1987), Trauma in the family: Perspectives on the intergenerational transmission of violence. In: *Psychological Trauma,* ed. B. van der Kolk. Washington, DC: American Psychiatric Press.

Mahler, M., Pine, F. & Bergman, A. (1975), *The Psychological Birth of the Human Infant.* New York: Basic Books.

Masson, J. M. (1984), *The Assault on Truth: Freud's Suppression of the Seduction Theory.* New York: Penguin Books.

Miller, A. (1984), *Thou Shalt Not Be Aware.* New York: Farrar, Straus & Giroux.

Rieker, P. & Carmen, E. (1986), The victim-to-patient process: The disconfirmation and transformation of abuse. *Amer. J. Orthopsychiat.*, 56:360–370.

Rush, F. (1980), *The Best Kept Secret: Sexual Abuse of children.* Englewood Cliffs, NJ: Prentice-Hall.

Russell, D. (1986), *The Secret Trauma: Incest in the Lives of Girls and Women.* New York: Basic Books.

Smith, J. (1989), Self mutilation among incest survivors. Unpublished doctoral dissertation. California Institute of Integral Studies, San Francisco.

Spiegel, D., Cardeña, E. & Spitzer, R. (1988), Brief reactive dissociative disorder. Unpublished manuscript.

Stern, D. (1985), *The Interpersonal World of the Infant.* New York: Basic Books.

Stolorow, R., Brandchaft, B., & Atwood, G. (1980), *Psychoanalytic treatment: An intersubjective approach.* Hillsdale, NJ: The Analytic Press.

Stolorow, R. & Lachmann, F. (1980), *Psychoanalysis of Developmental Arrests: Theory and Treatment.* New York: International Universities Press.

Stolorow, R. & Socarides, D. (1987), Affects and selfobjects. In: *Psychoanalytic Treatment: An Intersubjective Approach*, R. Stolorow, B. Brandchaft & G. Atwood. Hillsdale, NJ: The Analytic Press, pp. 66–87.

Ulman, R. and Brothers, D. (1987). A self-psychological reevaluation of post-traumatic stress disorder (PTSD) and its treatment: Shattered fantasies. *J. Amer. Acad. Psychoanal.*, 15:175–203.

van der Kolk, B. (1987), *Psychological Trauma.* Washington, DC: American Psychiatric Press.

Watkins, J. G. & Watkins, H. H. (1979), Theory and practice of ego state therapy. In: *Short-Term Approaches to Psychotherapy*, ed. H. Grayson. New York: National Instit. Psychotherapies & Human Sciences Press.

Winnicott, D. W. (1965), *The Maturational Process and the Facilitating Environment.* New York: International Universities Press.

Westerlund, E. (1986), Freud on sexual trauma: An historical review of seduction and betrayal. *Psychol. Women Quart.*, 10:297–309.

Chapter 9

Envy in the Transference: A Specific Selfobject Disruption

Rachel Wahba

This paper was written in an attempt to look at and subsequently understand envy as a response to a particular disruption in the transference. The impetus to write this article originated a few years ago when I was struck by the intensity with which some of my clients were responding to differences or changes (e.g., when I appeared dressed differently from them in some way, or when I acquired new office furniture). These differences or changes triggered unbearable experiences in the clients and lowered self esteem.

Acutely aware of how important it was for these particular clients to experience us as alike, I found myself feeling responsible for not protecting the sameness, and disrupting their need (and demand) to experience us as alike. Feeling conflicted, I was both challenged and intrigued by the intensity that accompanied these disruptions. Was I doing something wrong here besides not adequately understanding the nature of the disruption? Without having a handle on what specific selfobject need was disrupted, it was difficult at times to remain nondefensive and empathically attuned in the face of acute attacks of envy and narcissistic rage in the client that the experience of difference evoked in these transferences.

As a clinician practicing from a self-psychological perspective, I found Melanie Klein's (1957) seminal work on envy wonderfully descriptive of the intensity and depth of the affect these disrupted transferences evoked, but I experienced her method of understanding and interpreting envy primarily as drive derivative defensive projections essentially unempathic. I was interested in understanding and explaining my clients' envy in a way that would speak more directly to how I was failing to met a specific selfobject need.

Once the transferences were understood as twinship based, the envy and rage could be understood as fragmentation experiences resulting from the disrupted need to feel sustained by the experience of sameness or alikeness. The concept that their envy was a product of the disruption of a specific selfobject need clarified and shed new light on understanding and interpreting envy in these situations.[1]

I will attempt to illustrate with clinical material how this theory explains the emergency of envy as a valid and understandable response to a particular (twinship transference) disruption that is restored when the envy is understood and explained in the working through process. The clients I will be discussing entered treatment seeking a female therapist with whom they felt they shared certain similarities. Although I don't imagine envy in the transference to be a female issue or exclusive to female therapists working with women, my experience with this particular dynamic has been with female clients who had strong twinship and alterego needs.

ENVY

Envy, a powerful emotion, is an affect most of us prefer to deny rather than acknowledge. Joseph Berke (1987), wrote: "We live in a world where envy is continually unleashed and collusively denied. In this respect envy is to this century what sex was to the Victorians, an obsession best avoided and forgotten" (p. 325). A hateful emotion, pathological envy is filled with resentment and desire to possess or ruin what one sees in another. Whether the envy is of a personal nature, for example, the aging, fairytale stepmother unable to properly mirror her blossoming daughter, Snow White, or the dramatized, professional envy of the court musician Salieri in Amadeus, poisoned by his envy of Mozart's incredible genius, envy is an emotion motivated by a need to have and be in control of something. The envier feels desperately diminished and powerless without this prized something.

As much as we may want to deny the fact, envy has been with us forever. We are all familiar with varying degrees and faces of envy: our own envy of others and the fear of being envied. Envious

---

[1]Douglas Detrick, with whom I was consulting at the time, encouraged me to look at these situations as disrupted twinship transferences. This conceptualization was critical to opening up a new way of understanding and interpreting the clients' envy and rage reactions.

responses span a continuum, from failures in empathy (those times when we feel more envy than joy perhaps, in a friend's good fortune, or when, with some guilt, we feel less genuinely sympathetic about another's misfortune than we might if not for the presence of envy), to the most extreme cases where envy culminates in murderous rage.

It is understandable that, in the treatment setting, most of us would rather try to defensively control this undesirable, sometimes shameful feeling and look the other way to avoid seeing envy in ourselves and the people we see in treatment (Allphin, 1982; Cohen, 1982, 1986; Berke, 1985, 1987).

Consciously or unconsciously, envy is commonly confused or disguised as jealousy (Friday, 1985), and generally experienced as a less malignant emotion. In the psychoanalytic literature, jealousy is described as triadic, and envy as dyadic. Jealousy involves feeling left out and less lovable, with the desire to be included or to eliminate the competing rival in a three-person system (originating with the oedipal triangle). Envy is experienced between two people where the envied one is perceived as having something very essential that the envier lacks. In "The Eye of Jealousy and Envy," Evans (1975) describes jealousy as more passive and less active than envy:

> The eye of jealousy is passive in that it seeks not to possess, but rather to torture itself with the danger of being dispossessed; or it looks longingly at what others have, but makes no effort to have. Envy, on the other hand, sees no virtue in being a have-not and is aggressive to a degree in its relentless pursuit of that which belongs to others. (p. 490)

In its extreme, the actively charged, mean-spirited essence of envy might be experienced as: "You have it. I want it. You have that element vital to my sense of well being, and I, not you, should have it. And I will take it away from you. Or I will destroy it or you."

Elaborating on Freud's death instinct, Melanie Klein (1957,) was the first psychoanalytic theorist to delve deeply into the subject of envy. She viewed envy as an antilife, instinctual, motivating force that is negative and spoiling. The Kleinian infant is born with a certain amount of, and propensity for, envy that she or he is driven to unleash. The inevitably frustrated infant experiences all that is good as residing in the mother or breast, and this infant, unable to control the breast-mother, is driven to spoil and destroy. In accordance with this theoretical model (Segal, 1981), if the mother is "good enough," she can take in and contain the destructive projections of the infant, and in this manner detoxify the noxious affect. This maternal response makes the infant feel that his or her envy is not so overwhelming and omnipotent. In treatment, the therapist/"good enough mother" takes in and neutralizes these noxious, innate feelings. The instinctually driven infant's envy of mother's breast (and container of all that is good) is thus gradually tamed.

Moving away from treatment informed by instinct theory to Kohut's self–selfobject theories of development, envy can be understood and approached from a different perspective. However, the focus of this article is not to determine whether envy is primarily a constitutional "given" or whether it is reactive to narcissistic injury. The intention here is to look at when and how envy may be evoked as a response to a specific selfobject disruption in the transference, to understand the nature of the resulting transference disruption, and to restore the empathic bond.

SELF PSYCHOLOGY

Central to self psychology is the concept of selfobject experiences (Kohut, 1971, 1977, 1984). Selfobjects provide specific psychological functions that serve to maintain an energetic, balanced, cohesive sense of self. Deprived of the needed selfobject response, the individual will experience a loss in self-esteem, feel depleted and empty, and manifest varying degrees of fragmentation—from mild discomfort to anxiety and rage. Although the form of necessary selfobject responses changes with maturity from archaic merger to more age-appropriate forms, attuned selfobject experiences are needed throughout life to sustain the psychological structure and cohesion of the self.

Kohut conceptualized the self as having three major developmental lines. The mirroring line of development, corresponding with healthy ambitions and self-assertion; the idealizing pole, in which self-affirming values and ideals are internalized; and the alterego/twinship line of development, with its reassuring experience of sameness or alikeness that fosters the acquisition and development of innate skills and talents. Although originally they were subsumed in the mirroring line of development, Kohut (1984) eventually conceptualized alterego and twinship phenomena as a separate and third major selfobject developmental line. Alterego experiences, the most fundamental sense of being human, begins early in life, with the infant's experience of essential alikeness in an emotionally responsive human environment. In his last book, Kohut (1984), wrote of the alterego and twinship experience as creating "a sense of security in the child, a sense of belonging and participating, that cannot be explained in terms of a mirroring response or a merger with ideals. Instead, these feelings derive from confirmation of the feeling that one is a human being among other human beings. (p. 200)

Simultaneously, when alterego and twinship needs are met and alikeness is experienced, potential for learning is stimulated and innate skills and talents are enhanced and developed (Kohut, 1984). An example of the effectiveness of the alterego experience that we are all familiar with in the mental health field is apparent in the various self-help groups. Alcoholics Anonymous, Adult Children of Alcoholics, Alanon, and a variety of other self-help groups meeting specific needs are formed and focused around similar experiences, similar interests, and the development of problem-solving and life-enhancing skills and tools. Groups for adults sexually abused as children, wellness communities, cancer support groups, and groups mobilized around AIDS, bring together people who are alike in some way and meet both alterego and twinship needs. As Detrick (1985), conceptualizes them, "cognitive tools" are acquired and consolidated: "By tools I am thinking not only of the acquisition and consolidation of skill with tools such as a violin, a car, or a tennis racket, but also believe that in the domain of thinking, ideas, concepts, and problem-solving strategies and operations should be considered cognitive tools" (p. 242).

In treatment, attunement to twinship and alterego needs serves an important purpose in promoting increased functioning, self-cohesion, and the development of skills and competences. Kohut saw twinship and alterego needs as synonymous. Both alterego and twinship selfobject experiences provide the modeling and experience of alikeness. However, the alterego experience is a group dynamic, whereas twinship speaks to the sharing of alikeness and sameness between two people (Detrick, 1986).

Because feeling understood, validated, and accepted are critical elements in a successful treatment process, looking for a therapist that one can identify with somehow is not unusual. On this matter, Kohut (1987) said:

> We will not want to see people who are very different from us when we are upset, when we are narcissistically disturbed, when we have suffered a narcissistic blow. We will naturally drift to people like ourselves, of our own cultural emotional makeup. Then one feels enclosed again; one feels reinforced and supported. [p. 70]

While seeking a therapist who is like you is not unusual, when clients have strong needs for sameness and consciously or unconsciously seek a particular therapist because they are both of the same gender, sexual orientation, race, class, or ethnicity, or, who like them, belong to a specific group, differences can be particularly disruptive and may evoke envy in the transference. Given this dynamic, coupled with the therapist's sensitivity and attunement to this need for alikeness, he or she may feel pressured to try and minimize differences. However, when difference is experienced as threatening (to either client or therapist), and envy goes unnamed and underground, growth can only go so far.[2]

As selfobjects are used to provide what is lacking in the self's structure, the more archaic the need, the stronger the desire to merge and have total control of the vitally needed selfobject experience. The more archaic forms of twinship and alterego transferences are characterized by merger, or oneness, and with maturity, move from oneness, to the-same-as, to alikeness (Detrick, 1985). The inevitable disruptions will bring with it a fall in self-esteem and fragmentation.

When sameness, so vitally needed for a sense of cohesion, self-worth, and the acquisition of skills and tools is disrupted, the sustaining experience of alikeness can fragment into envy. This envious experience may also involve fantasies of the depriving/ different other, who, when not perceived as supportively restoring the balance by providing the necessary selfobject function, is perceived as deliberately hoarding and witholding the necessary supplies.

CASE ILLUSTRATION

Jan

When I left the community mental health clinic where I had worked with Jan for three years, neither one of us was prepared for the feelings that erupted when she began to see me in private practice. She hated the Pacific Heights location of my office. She railed at me for moving to "a bourgeois yuppie neighborhood" that she complained was antithetical to her values. Suddenly experiencing me as

---

[2]Obviously, in psychoanalytic work we strive to understand and interpret rather than directly gratify the need, (in the cases I describe, by my remaining the same as the patient). Although, in hindsight, this approach seems so obvious, finding myself without way to understand these disruptions specifically as twinship disruptions, I felt conflicted and in an impossible dilemma. I could collude and try to avoid evoking or naming the envy, or with my inadequate understanding, inadvertently blame the patient by making experience-distant comments that do not reflect the intersubjective nature of the disrupted self–selfobject system.)

different from her, she raged angrily, "I thought you were like me, with high ideals . . . like an Albert Schweitzer! But you are just like any capitalist pig, out to make money so you can have material possessions . . ." She "accidentally" spilled water on the couch, tracked in mud from outside, and had a hard time each week writing my name on the check. Comparing her salary to my fee she said: "At least at the clinic I didn't have to pay the money to you and I know you didn't make a dollar a minute there! For what? I can't imagine where you get such nerve; who do you think you are to make that kind of money?"

Although extremely bright and gifted, Jan had been unable to successfully channel her talents. Downwardly mobile, she experienced my move from the clinic to private practice as a betrayal. When I attempted to explore how this might be affecting her self-esteem, if it made her feel bad about herself that I was making more money, (wondering if she felt devalued somehow by my move to private practice), she responded that she could be a "money hungry capitalist" too, if she wished. She told me that despite the fact that she felt "grateful" for how I had been with her in the three years we worked together, that she felt treated with a respect she had never known, and that she valued the work we had done, she felt it was impossible to continue to work with someone who "obviously had such different values" (from hers). She terminated treatment three months after the eruption of envy in the transference, vowing to stay away from therapy and therapists she said "for at least 10 years."

I don't know if Jan would have continued working with me in private practice even if I had correctly understood her feelings. My interpretations narrowly focused on her feelings of envy and disappointment but not on how I was failing her as a selfobject. I tried to understand her upset but I did not have a theory that framed it or understood it as a twinship disruption. Although I had known that it was important for Jan to see someone she could feel a kinship with, I felt attacked, guilty, defensive, and "stuck."

In retrospect, I understand the rupture as both alterego and twinship disruptions: loss of a sense of community that the clinic provided, and extreme alienation from the loss of alikeness with me. Although initially it looked like idealization gone awry, that was not the primary issue. With idealization, difference in terms of looking up to and merging with the idealized figure is soothing; in twinship, it is the experience of being the same as or alike that provides a sense of cohesiveness and well being. Looking back, I would now attempt to understand and explain how I injured her by thwarting her need to experience us as the same, and look at her envy and narcissistic rage from this vantage point rather than primarily from the perspective that I had disappointed her by exhibiting materialistic values and triggering her envy by my move uptown.[3]

I wasn't able to restore Jan's sustaining experience of sameness and she left treatment within three months of the disruption. As Wolf, (1988), states, "When selfobjects no longer fulfill their function of sustaining the self and instead threaten self-cohesion and make the self feel helpless, they must be eliminated" (p. 78).

Nelly

Nelly, a 50-year-old woman who immigrated to the United States when she was 35, periodically expressed feeling a deep sense of connection and alikeness to me. I was the first female therapist she had ever worked with although she had been in treatment at various points in her life. That I was from another country like her was also very important to her and she remarked often how "at home" and understood she felt with me.

One winter, after I had returned from my vacation, she came in despondent, complaining about how she was surrounded by people who had more than her. She felt very deprived and resentful of most of her friends, and she thought perhaps the solution was to meet new people who were less established and "more like [her]"; then she wouldn't feel so full of "jealousy and resentment." For the next month, she expressed feeling very hopeless and frustrated with me and the therapy. She felt anxious and depressed that I seemed unable to give her the "tools," she said, that would help her out of her miserable feelings.

I wondered if these feelings were triggered by my having taken two vacations closer together than I had in previous years, and I asked her how she felt about my having gone away twice in 6 months. "I thought of that," she replied, ". . . that definitely crossed my mind, but I was afraid to have 'negative' thoughts about you . . . I began to wonder; maybe I don't know you at all, maybe you voted for Reagan!" It made her feel very anxious to think about me in that way, as so different from her. I asked if my having gone away twice (having vacations that presently felt out of reach for her financially), made her feel different from me and was therefore very upsetting to her. Was she afraid of losing me if she experienced us as separate and

---

[3]The point here is that although Jan was disillusioned with me, it was the break in alikeness that was shattering. She felt sustained when she experienced that I was, like her, an idealizable Albert Schweitzer type. When I "changed," moving from a non-profit, low-fee clinic to private practice, we were no longer similarly idealizable figures. It was the twinship disruption rather than a breakdown of idealizing defenses that made the situation intolerable for her.

different, I asked? She said that it wasn't that she would lose me, but that she would lose what she described as a "connection or a bond"; and experiencing me as different (by having something she didn't have) would make her feel more resentful than she could tolerate. She explained that, if she allowed herself to think too much about my vacations, she would feel alienated, angry, and bad about me, and she felt she couldn't afford to do that because then she might have to leave me.

As we continued to explore these feelings, she expressed how angry she was about my being able to afford vacations that she couldn't afford, and in these sessions, envious feelings that she had been trying to suppress for some time about my "status" as a therapist emerged.

For the next several months, she spoke about how utterly and completely powerless she felt in her life. She hated doing paralegal work and wanted to find another more gratifying field but she felt stuck and unable to make the necessary changes that would allow her to pursue this.

In terms of disrupted twinship, my ability to have and do for myself what Nelly felt incapable of doing for herself triggered her experience of us as different and evoked envy in the transference. The difference she experienced in our "status" as she put it, made her feel even more powerless, as she feared that she would never be able to catch up with the people in her life. With the transference disrupted, she felt diminished and painfully distanced from me. Once her envious feelings were expressed and understood as a result of her disrupted need to experience us as alike, and the empathic bond restored, we were then able to open up for exploration her lifelong feelings of deprivation, powerlessness, and the sense that she did not possess the necessary means or "tools" she said, to plan and manage her own life effectively.

This aspect of envy is captured well by Eichenbaum and Orbach (1988):

> Behind the feeling of envy lies not the spoiling, ungenerous destroying person that is so much the woman's experience of herself when she is gripped by envy. What we find rather is a person so deeply conflicted about her own wants and desires that she is frightened by others' capacity to respond to theirs. She admires the others but can't understand how they can pursue what she feels so unable to pursue. She envies their capacity to give to themselves in a way that feels deeply forbidden to her [pp. 98–99].

Both Jan and Nelly experienced my difference from them as frightening and disruptive. In twinship transferences such as these, where archaic needs for sameness have been mobilized, the disruption can manifest itself as envy accompanied by rage or anxiety. Consequently, as the next case will demonstrate, the more archaic and stronger the need for sameness coupled with a deep experience of alikeness, the more intense the disruption and the envy and rage.

Wolf (1988) wrote, on the nature of narcissistic rage:

> . . . it arises when no self–assertion at all is possible, when the self feels absolutely helpless, vexed, and mortified, that is, paralyzed while agitated to the extreme and in deathly danger of losing its integrity. Such a self state is unbearable and must be altered. The offending selfobject or the totally ashamed self must be made to disappear, violently if necessary, even if the whole world will go up in flames. [p. 79]

Loren

This vignette reflects a piece of a long-term therapy during a period of time when the twinship transference was primarily in place, and the subsequent disruptions acute and volatile.

Loren, a 31-year-old single woman who had many years of previous treatment presented herself passively as she described a life that was isolated, chaotic, and bereft of any sustaining emotional connection. As she spoke, eyes downcast, she made a point of telling me that she did not expect any of this to change.

She specifically wanted to see a female Jewish therapist and told me that she was afraid of finding a therapist who would be "too different" from her. At one point in this initial hour, she glanced up and suddenly brightened as she noticed my Star of David, and, with a warm smile, she pointed to hers. She said that it made her feel good to be seeing someone she could identify with, and her mood markedly shifted from distancing and resigned to a slightly but definitely more energetic attitude. Loren left this initial session remarking happily that she liked the fact that my office was in the same neighborhood as hers. I found myself very aware of her need to experience us as similar, and I said something about how important it was for her to feel understood by me. She agreed, but I remember feeling not quite "on the mark" and thinking there was another factor (in addition to her wish to feel understood) that I was responding to but was not yet quite able to conceptualize. I saw that it was very important for her to experience us as alike, and in subsequent sessions this need became quite clear.

There were many different ways in which she expected me to match her in alikeness. I intuitively respected and saw this need as healthy rather than idosyncratic or defensive. However, there were times when I found myself feeling anxious and pressed (as if I was betraying her if I didn't wear my Star of David), or appeared different, and not like her.

In Loren I saw an isolated and emotionally withdrawn woman who felt alienated and disconnected from people but who hoped for a different experience. She expressed over and over again in the course of therapy, how separate she felt, and, in her words, "never with" another.

Her relationship with her mother was deeply flawed. She described a childhood in which she felt hopelessly pushed aside by an overwhelmed and overburdened mother whom Loren desperately longed to be close to. Her alcoholic father disappeared in her early childhood for many years and she had no siblings or close friends. Although Loren grew up derailed and deprived of this very basic need to experience a sense of human connection with others and consequently withdrew and isolated herself for most of her life, she hadn't stopped hoping that something would change. I began to understand that the "something" she was unconsciously seeking in therapy was the experience of kinship, of belonging and feeling alike or the same as another.

This early transference need for twinship (evidenced in her need to experience us as alike), deepened as we began our work together. The inevitable failures in maintaining sameness evoked envy and rage in Loren. Any difference that threatened our sameness was experienced by her as traumatically injurious to her. At these times, she felt as though she couldn't get anything from me and she would think about leaving. I felt pressured to keep up my (unconscious) end of the bargain—to be like her and to allow her to be like me. When she perceived me as different and her deep sense of deprivation and feelings of inferiority were triggered, she lost all good feelings about herself, me, and the therapy. Her envy flared. She would feel rejected and inferior and respond to me as if her loss of self-esteem was my gain. In her mind, I became a "prima donna," or "queen," she would say, and I "had it all," pushing her away as if she was nothing, and making her feel ashamed and less than me.

In the course of treatment with Loren there were several inevitable twinship disruptions that elicited envy. One December, I picked up a sprig of holly with red berries that I found on the ground in front of my office. I brought it in and put it on my desk. Later that afternoon realizing that Loren was my next client and anticipating her reaction, (anger that by having holly in my office I was celebrating Christmas), I felt anxious and thought about hiding the holly from view. I saw myself think this way, and thought it better to leave the holly where it was, reminding myself that the point of treatment was to work through uncomfortable feelings (hers and mine), not to avoid them. It would have been easy to push the holly out of sight. I knew how she expected me to be like her, and if I outwardly showed a difference, as the holly would symbolize, I anticipated angry withdrawal. And I knew I had to leave the holly where it was, just as I didn't alter my style of dress to suit hers even though it upset her to see me dress differently than her. She walked in and immediately saw the holly, turning away from me and becoming scornful and distant as she commented on "Christmas decorations" in my office, and then spoke angrily about how much she hated everything that had to do with Christmas and how it left her feeling alienated and deprived. Initially, without a way of understanding what was happening other than keenly sensing that my deviating from her expectations of staying the same deeply upset and angered her, I was often left struggling with my fear of eliciting her envy and anger. During the holly incident I, battled with my emerging understanding of being optimally responsive by staying with her feelings and attempting to understand and interpret her disrupted need to feel alike, without having to collude and hide the holly, or difference. When I understood that seeing the holly in my office made her feel different from me, as if I were part of something she could never join and be a part of, she felt less disrupted, but still commented that I should not have Christmas symbols in my office.

Rather than experiencing her as a demanding client who needed to be taught that her needs were regressive and had to be modified, I saw that her need for alikeness was an attempt to get back on a derailed developmental track. My inevitable failures could provide the possibility of working through earlier selfobject failures. By my accepting that she felt failed by me and interpreting her traumatic childhood experiences (now revived in the transference), into words that attempted to make sense of her tremendous emotional reaction to any twinship disruptions, the possibility of working through specific deficits became possible. This process of repeated, verbalized, empathic understanding and explaining of her once again frustrated needs helped to restore and strengthen her sense of self and gradually enabled Loren to become less vulnerable to envious attacks.

Toward the end of our first year of working together, I moved my office to a different neighborhood and shortly afterward I bought a desk and some other furniture for my office. Loren said she liked the new furnishings, and she particularly admired my desk. The following week before our next session, I awoke from a disturbing dream that my office had been trashed and that there was a big empty space where the desk stood.

Loren arrived at her hour very upset. She fluctuated between hopeless despair and thoughts of violently destroying my office. She came in angry and frightened saying, "I don't know what to do; I don't know whether to continue to come here and use this as a safe space or to just sling mud on your white walls. I feel terrible, just terrible. I can't look at that desk. I don't know how I can continue to come here and have to look at that desk. It hurts me to look at it." She continued: "It's beautiful. If anybody should, I should have a desk like that. And I have nothing. I've never had a desk," she said, expressing how angry, deprived, and powerless she felt. I tried to understand how she was feeling. I had it all and she had nothing. What a painfully alienating and discouraging feeling that must be. When I used the word "envy" to describe her feelings, she immediately calmed down, suddenly grounded, and responded to my naming her upset: "Envy," she repeated aloud several times, relieved that there was a name for her terrible feelings, and as if hearing this word for the first time. "That's it," she said; "Envy, that's what this is." I explained that I thought that the desk symbolically represented everything she did not have and that my having it separated us, making her the "have not," and I the "have." I was directly confronted by her envious feelings that I had something of which she felt terribly deprived. More importantly, I came to understand that she was also responding to the break in sameness that she needed in order to maintain a sense of cohesiveness and well-being. She experienced my having something she wanted and admired as somehow taking away from her a vitally needed sense of belonging, of being like me, that the twinship transference provided.

It was a very difficult time. For several weeks she sat with her back to me so that she would not have to look at the desk. She felt overwhelmed and distraught. She did not know if she could bear to continue treatment with me, and she did not know what she would do if she could not continue. She described a pain inside her chest, as "something toxic" burning inside. Sessions when she felt better and more connected to me were spoiled later by dreams that I had ignored her or refused to help her or tried to hurt her. These disruptions were slowly worked through as we accepted the vicissitudes of her disturbing, envious feelings and how they related to her experience of me as similar to her mother, with whom she could not recall ever having a positive shared experience. She spoke about her mother only as burdening her with miseries, one who "kept all the nice and special things for herself," leaving Loren to feel pushed away, left out, "like garbage." And referring to my office, she would say it was the same: "Its all your niceness, nothing mine."

In the weeks that followed, she alternated between admiring and appreciating the desk and wondering if I were silently judging her as a "born loser." I acknowledged how wounded and angry she felt, that the desk symbolized our difference; I understood her that this symbol of our difference made her feel bad about herself, alienated, and rejected. I explained how my moving to a different neighborhood and then getting this desk made her feel as if I were rejecting her and evoked all her old and painful feelings of being deprived, pushed aside, and feeling unsupported and alone. I could understand how she felt disconnected from me and experienced us as not working together anymore, not "with" me in the therapy anymore, our unit of sameness changed by the desk, and how it brought back painful childhood feelings. I thought that as a child she had felt (and in fact was) chronically deprived of the experience of sameness or alikeness. She alternated between positive feelings that we could work through something very difficult (when she felt I was there, with her, to support and help her have good things too) and just giving up (when she felt helpless and alienated from me, when she experienced me as "the queen" who needed to push her away and leave her feeling bad about herself). Moments of creativity and hope (she began refinishing a desk for herself) were coupled with missed sessions, feelings of desperation, thoughts of leaving therapy, fantasies of destroying my office, and suicidal threats.[4] But rather than feeling that "the whole world going up in flames," Loren was increasingly able to tolerate her feelings, and because she felt understood, we were able to continue the work as deeper feelings emerged.

During these months, she made herself a desk. She enjoyed the process of refinishing it and liked her new desk. At the same time, these months were also punctuated by terrifying feelings of being trapped in a vacuum, devoid of any human contact. To soothe herself, Loren composed lengthy dialogues between herself and her mother in her journal. For several months, she attempted to recon-

---

[4]Berke (1985) described despair well: "Rage, fueled by an envious narcissism, does not stop at destroying the object. It aims to eradicate any vestige of attachment in the subject, any remnant of love, need or longing . . . Any loss of pride or self-esteem may herald the onset of a major internal battle (aside from an external one) whereby the forces of disorder, fragmentation and chaos overwhelm those of order, integration, and structure . . . but the conflict often leads to a near total cessation of feeling, thought and perception, and can culminate in suicide . . . so that all tension and excitation vanish" (p. 184).

struct experiences of herself as a child and adolescent who felt chronically deprived of any sustaining relationships, pushed aside and confined to her own inner world, feeling different and alienated from others. Reading these passages aloud to me, Loren recalled childhood memories and remobilized needs in the present, at different points asking for the mirroring and sense of connection she had not gotten elsewhere; "Look at me mother. Smile at me. Am I pretty? I want you to admire me. Talk to me. Am I disgusting to you?" And she would sob. Her archaic needs mobilized, she asked the same of me. Was I happy to see her? Did I have patience for her? Would I wait and not turn my back on her even when she felt so helpless?

An especially poignant moment occurred when she described several young mothers with their children at the park one afternoon. She came in saying, "The mothers were 'with' these children. My mother was never with me. She was more like the wind or an empty space, and there was no way to feel connected to her." With the rupturing of the primary twinship connection, I understood and explained that it made sense how she felt with me as she had with her mother—disconnected, in a vacuum, almost nonhuman.

In this period of time, there were other painful disruptions. Loren saw me outside of the consulting room at a movie theater. She phoned me, very agitated, the next day to say that she was feeling extremely upset, "outside of everything," and unable to get dressed for work. When I asked her if something had happened since our last session, she mentioned seeing me at the theater the night before. I spontaneously responded with: "Oh that awful movie!" And immediately her mood shifted: Suddenly she was energetic and present, saying, "Oh, you thought so too! it *was* a terrible movie wasn't it!" She spoke a bit about her reaction to the movie, and ended the phone call with "Thank you, I'm really glad I called, I think I'll be o.k." I realized later that my empathically attuned commentary on the movie was meant to restore the tie that was obviously severed when she saw me outside the hour. My response helped to reassure her. It was right before the weekend, and I knew that I would not be seeing her until the following week. I intuitively attempted to restore the (disrupted) bond by expressing what I imagined would be a shared experience of the movie.

In our next session, we looked at her reaction to having seen me at the theater and continued working through painful and shameful feelings that seeing me had evoked. "I didn't want to say hello," she said. "I felt angry and embarassed, and I thought to myself you have the right to go to the movies, and I thought you probably enjoy yourself when you are not here. You have a right to do things, but I felt upset. I didn't want to bother you. I could see you and I don't think you saw me, and I could observe you the way you do here with me." As I understood that seeing me there, having a good time, made her feel separate and different from me, she cried, recognizing the familiar experience, "It's my mother again, never 'with' her. Is there something shameful about me?"

Loren's increasing sense of self-acceptance, self-assertion, and of belonging evidenced itself several months later when she saw me again at a movie theater. She later described experiencing the familiar feelings of "embarassment" well up in her, and she began to panic. Sliding into her seat, she wanted to hide, feeling ashamed and rejected. "I saw you sitting there with someone, you had popcorn, and I thought, Oh, you probably really know how to enjoy yourself at the movies, you probably really like the movies," She added; "I like the movies." But this time she described how she had gotten up, walked to the other end of the theater, where earlier she had spotted two of her co-workers, and joined them. She said, "I thought, 'I can go there and be with them if I want to. Maybe I'm bothering them and they want to be alone,' but I did it anyway. And they were so nice, and happy to see me, and I stayed with them. It was nice," she said. As she left the hour she commented, "I've been noticing that I enjoy myself in here sometimes. Does that mean I'm getting stronger?"

As she began to experience having more quality in her life, including people she felt a kinship to with whom she enjoyed similarities, she worried about my envying her. At different moments, when she experienced me being genuinely happy for the good things she was experiencing in her life, she was incredulous; "You're not jealous?" And she would break down crying. She would usually cry when she experienced me as being genuinely on her side and "with her."

Loren's narrow life became richer, and she began experiencing me as someone who could support her in having good things. She became increasing able to tolerate differences, and envy became less of a theme in the therapy. Her envious feelings lost their toxicity as she developed a stronger sense of herself and her capabilities. She began to consider pursuing a career that matched her skills, and for the first time, she had "a best friend" in her life who was accessible and with whom she shared important alikenesses. She was filled with wonder at such possibilities, and she was vibrant as she told me how she and her friend shared similar feelings about things, and how they spoke on the phone several times a week—an experience she had never had before.

DISCUSSION

In the clinical material discussed, the primary transference bond of twinship provided a stabilizing feeling of sameness or alikeness. When this experience of twinship, so vitally needed for a sense of cohesion and self-worth was disrupted, the sustaining experience of alikeness fragmented into envy. With this break in alikeness, a frightening and terrible sense of difference, deprivation, and powerlessness was evoked, erupting in envy and narcissistic rage.

However, in treatment, envy can be seen as a sign that hope still exists. Envy signals the mobilization of thwarted developmental needs and implies a desire to get back on track, to enhance and acquire those innate skills and talents, or tools and competences, that will enable the self to feel cohesive, secure, and sustained.

By understanding and explaining the envy and rage as responses to the disruption of a vitally needed twinship experience, the sustaining transference bond could be restored and derailed development proceed. Understood and interpreted accordingly, envy can be worked through from a highly charged fragmentation product to freedom from an internal prison of inferiority and powerlessness.

REFERENCES

Allphin, C. (1982), Envy in the transference and countertransference. *Clin. Soc. Work J.,* 10:151–163.

Berke, J. H. (1985), Envy loveth not: A study of the origin, influence and confluence of envy and narcissism. *Brit. J. Psychother.,* 1:171–186.

_____ (1987), Shame and envy, In: *The Many Faces of Shame,* ed. D. L. Nathanson. New York: Guilford Press, pp. 318–334.

Cohen, B. (1982), Fear of envy in the psychotherapy relationship. *J. Psychother. Inst.,*

_____ (1986), *The Snow White Syndrome: All About Envy.* New York: Macmillan.

Detrick, D. W. (1985), Alterego phenomena and the alterego transferences. In: *Progress in Self Psychology,* Vol 1, ed. A. Goldberg. New York: Guilford Press, pp. 240–256.

_____ (1986), Alterego phenomena and the alterego transferences: Some further considerations. In: *Progress In Self Psychology,* Vol 2, ed. A. Goldberg. New York: Guilford Press, pp. 299–304.

Eichenbaum, L. & Orbach, S. (1988), *Between Women—Love, Envy and Competition in Women's Friendships.* New York: Viking.

Evans, W. (1975), The eye of jealousy and envy, *Psychoanal. Rev.* 62:481–492.

Friday, N. (1985), *Jealousy.* New York: William Morrow.

Klein, M. (1957), *Envy and Gratitude.* Boston: Delacorte Press, 1975.

Kohut, H. (1971), *The Analysis of the Self.* New York: International Universities Press.

_____ (1977), *The Restoration of the Self.* New York: International Universities Press.

_____ (1984), *How Does Analysis Cure?* ed. A. Goldberg & P. Stepansky. Chicago: University of Chicago Press.

_____ (1987), *The Kohut Seminars,* ed. M. Elson. New York: Norton.

Segal, H. (1981), *The Work of Hanna Segal: A Kleinian Approach to Clinical Practice.* New York: Aronson.

Wolf, E. S. (1988), *Treating the Self.* New York: Guilford Press.

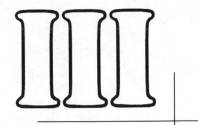

Critique

Self Psychology Expanding: A Consideration of Recent Books by Michael Basch, Arnold Goldberg, and Robert Stolorow, Bernard Brandchaft, and George Atwood*

Estelle Shane

It was just thirty years ago that Heinz Kohut announced to the psychoanalytic world his view that empathy and introspection defined and limited the domain of inquiry in our field. For the next twenty-five years, the leading edge of self psychological thinking was dominated by its founder. To be sure, others, including the authors whose books I am considering here, published significant papers and books, but Kohut clearly shaped the advances in self psychology until the publications of his last posthumous paper and book. Like Freud, then, in his premiere position as the inventor of classical analysis, so it had been with Kohut; self psychology began and remained largely in his hands throughout his lifetime. However, at the same time, and with admirable foresight, he attracted to himself, nurtured, and was nurtured by, a group of extremely talented and creative analysts, dedicated to his vision but certainly not limited by it. Indeed, their views of self psychology do diverge, not just from Kohut's views, but

---

*M. Basch *Understanding Psychotherapy* (1988, Basic Books); A. Goldberg, *A Fresh Look at Psychoanalysis* (1988, The Analytic Press), R. Stolorow, B. Brandchaft, & G. E. Atwood, *Psychoanalytic Treatment* (1987, The Analytic Press).

from one another's, as well, keeping the field alive by infusing it with new ideas. As Arnold Goldberg so cogently reminds us in *A Fresh Look*, all theories are underdetermined, in that they do not allow us to see all that theory needs to encompass; and all theories are wrong; they are just waiting for a better one to come along. The authors whose works are being discussed are prime representatives of this open, scientific stance. Each begins with Kohut's self psychology, but each attempts a refinement, extension, and elaboration; and each volume, in its own way, presents a new vision. The result is three original conceptualizations of Kohut's central goal: to make of self psychology a superordinate framework for encompassing and understanding the psychoanalytic process. Basch builds his theory and approach on the hard scientific data available from infant research, neurophysiology, and communication theory; Goldberg supports his theory and approach with sophisticated philosophy and philosophy of science; whereas Stolorow, Brandchaft, and Atwood devise their theory and approach almost exclusively from within the clinical situation. What can be seen from these three major contributions to the field is strong agreement on many, indeed most crucial matters, with some important differences stemming from their independent approaches that are well worth pondering.

Stolorow, Brandchaft, and Atwood extract three basic contributions of Kohut's self psychology to the science of psychoanalysis. They name: (1) the unwavering application of the empathic–introspective mode as defining and limiting the domain of inquiry; (2) the primacy of self experience; and (3) the concepts of selfobject function and the selfobject transference. I will use their list of Kohut's contributions to psychoanalysis to enter into a discussion and comparison of these three books, and will begin with the first, the empathic introspective mode, limiting the domain of inquiry. What do each set of authors conclude regarding this constraint on the field?

Stolorow, Brandchaft, and Atwood declare, in specific and unwavering agreement with Kohut, that anything that is not in principle accessible to empathy and introspection is not within the bounds of psychoanalytic inquiry. Their overall innovative stance of the intersubjective approach is a natural and consistent application of this position, leading them to their theoretical conclusion. Psychoanalysis, according to them, is the science of the intersubjective, focused on the interplay between the two differently organized subjective worlds of patient and analyst. Because the observational stance remains consistently and persistently within, rather than outside, this intersubjective field, the centrality of introspection and empathy is guaranteed. Although a theory of affect development, written in collaboration with the late Daphne Socarides Stolorow, and a theory of the self are specifically proposed by these authors, these theories seem to be held lightly, in that they are discernable mainly as operationalized in the transference, and the implication is that they are not so much applied to, but are more derived from, and clearly grounded in, the intersubjective field. Mechanistic, heuristic devices are avoided and diagnostic/prognostic presuppositions are strongly discouraged. As in any good analysis, the task of the analyst informed by intersubjectivity becomes that of listening to the patient, observing the unfolding of the patient's subjective experience in interaction with the analyst, and illuminating and interpreting this reciprocal relationship. However, the use of the intersubjective perspective is intended to focus on high power and concentrate exclusively both analyst and patient on the effects of their mutual interaction. Because of this approach, the authors are convinced that the analyst is able to influence the patient's self-organization in a decisive manner.

This is perhaps best exemplified in the way in which pathology becomes understood as a kind of two-person event, a function of both analyst and patient. That is, individuals do come into treatment with specific selfobject needs and specific self-pathology. But how these needs are met and responded to in the intersubjective psychoanalytic field can significantly influence the severity of this pathology, as well as the course and outcome of treatment. For these authors, every diagnosis and every course of treatment can only be comprehended in a real way in the field comprised of the two individual subjectivities, in interaction with one another, joined together by an exclusive introspective–empathic stance. Considerable clinical material effectively illustrates this thesis.

Michael Basch takes a very different view in regard to the relevance of data gleaned from outside this empathic–introspective dyad. Asserting strongly that he would use no reconstructive supposition or theoretical assumption not validated scientifically and extra analytically in infant research, he sets out to elucidate a unifying, explanatory theory for psychotherapy based, not just on empathy and introspection, but also on infant observation, on research in perceptual, cognitive, and affective psychology, on neurobiology and scientific philosophy, as well as on cybernetics, systems theory, and information theory, which, as he says, "have combined . . . to make possible . . . the construction of a theory that encompasses what is important for *human* development" (p. 14). He also takes a very bold leap by dispensing with mind entirely, replacing it simply and directly with brain. He adroitly bridges the conceptual gap between mind and brain by equating the brain's ordering activity with the subjective sense of competence. That is, Basch holds that the brain's main function, creating order, is experienced by the person as competence; competence, then, and the attendant achievement of self esteem, become chief motivational forces throughout the individual's lifetime. Basch presents several major conceptualizations, including a complex developmental spiral; a negative feedback cycle on which a model for thought process is based; and a developmental line leading from affect to emotion, in addition to a comprehensive self-system, which will be addressed later. These scientifically based formulations become the foundation for an integrated, wide-ranging, self psychological, therapeutic approach that is illustrated with extensive and apt case material. As for empathy per se, Basch certainly demonstrates a high regard for its invaluable contribution in the clinical situation. But he also believes that empathy does not necessarily come naturally to the inexperienced therapist. True to his well-established, pedagogic reputation, he dissects and organizes the empathic process in a stepwise fashion to facilitate teaching this elusive but irreplaceable adjunct to the therapeutic endeavor.

Goldberg also takes a strong position regarding the place of empathy and introspection in defining the field of psychoanalysis and self psychology; namely, empathy and introspection alone cannot define the field. Specifically, in several essays, but also running as a rich current throughout his entire book, he makes the point that one cannot have anything other than a naive empathic or introspective capacity without theory, and that that theory cannot be deduced de novo from the psychoanalytic situation but, as in any science, is brought to it in the form of intuition and inference. His thesis, buttressed by an extensive review of the relevant philosophy of science literature, is that theory always precedes observation. Without theory, one would have little or no way of knowing or selecting what among the myriad of data before us is worth attending to. Moreover, without theory, each patient would appear to the analyst as unique, and the profession would not only be more art than science, but also it would lack the essential generalities that can and must be taught and learned by future generations of psychoanalysts. New ideas should be sought, and the unpacking of our more familiar, more global formulations should be undertaken, he tells us, but, this exercise should not be confused with the ordinary practice of psychoanalysis. New formulations are generated out of postanalytic and extra-analytic, as well as analytic reflections regarding the course of treatment. The new formulations are then brought back into the consulting room. It is in this way that we inform and improve our capacity to be empathic with our patients. In a nutshell, empathic understanding cannot be generated exclusively from within the here-and-now analytic situation. For example, Goldberg illustrates in his clinical section of the book how our broad theoretical constructs may be unpacked and then returned to the clinical situation to guide our empathy. It is not sufficient, he tells us, to explain our patients by saying merely that they experienced failure in the requisite idealizing selfobject functions in their surround. We need to understand more about the relationship between such deprivation and its specific effects upon the developing individual. Setting forth a correlation between inadequate experience with an idealizable person and a failure to develop a capacity for self control, Goldberg then delineates the precise characteristics perceived as idealizable by the child; namely reliability, dependability, and predictability, and speculates that it is their absence in the parent that leaves the child unable to regulate and contain himself. Such unpacking of a broad self psychological concept might improve not only our capacity to empathize effectively, but might also increase our knowledge about normal development and good parenting.

Goldberg concludes that one can never limit psychoanalysis to empathy, despite what Kohut says about empathy as defining the field. Although he accepts empathy as our method of observation and data gathering, he warns that if psychoanalysis is to remain a scientific venture, we must be objective rather than merely inferential, we must be able to use a variety of theories to guide our empathic responses, and we must always remain alert to the effects of our own observations on the field that we observe.

The second of Kohut's contributions identified by Stolorow, Brandchaft, and Atwood is that of the primacy of self-experience. Conceptualizing the self as at the center in this way, replacing Freud's instinctual-drive driven, tripartite structural model of the psyche leads inevitably, according to these authors, to perceiving affect rather than drive as the primary motivational system. Basch, too, replaces Freud's biologically linked drive with subcortically triggered affect programs; and Goldberg as well dismisses the dual instinctual drives. Nevertheless, the overall conceptions of the self put forward by each of these sets of authors do differ. Stolorow, Brandchaft, and Atwood criticize Kohut's model of the bipolar self as carrying the potential for reification of self-experience, for mechanistic thinking, and for limiting the number of possible selfobject transferences available for discovery in the analytic situation. They establish instead, not a model of the self, but a description of the self as an organization of experience, conceptualized in terms of invariant principles of organization. It is the invariant principles of organization, structuralized from childhood, that determine and delimit the individual's subjective perspective. For example, in the transference, the patient's experience of the analytic relationship is shaped by his or her own principles of organization, by the "distinctive, archaically rooted configuration of self and object that unconsciously organize his subjective universe" (p. 36).

Basch, too, replaces both the tripartite model and the bipolar self with his own functional self-system, a part of the brain that integrates the affective and cognitive information-processing activities governing the individual's adaptation to the environment. He portrays this self-system as being fully functional only after the individual has attained the capacity for symbolic thought, free will, and the ability to control his or her affects. The fully functional self-system demarcates the beginning of childhood and the end of infancy, and, in its healthy form, is characterized as an open system capable of creativity, free will, adaptation, and learning from experience. This is in contrast to the closed system, which may characterize pathology, wherein unconscious patterns of expectation render the individual unable to adapt to new circumstances, unable to generate new information from them, and unable, therefore, to change the unconscious patterns that are no longer appropriate. Competence and self-esteem, the cardinal signs of a well-functioning, adequately developing self-system, are reduced in the closed self-system, resulting in anxiety, depression, and self-pathology. Despite the distinct differences between their visions of self, (Stolorow, Brandchaft and Atwood's being rooted in pure psychology and Basch's being rooted in the hardwiring of the brain), Basch's concept of the self-system, as influenced by unconscious patterns of expectation, seems comparable to the invariant principles of organization that influence self-experience in Stolorow, Brandchaft, and Atwood's construct. Basch, too, understands transference as bringing old patterns of expectation into new situations, similar to Stolorow, Brandchaft, and Atwood's view of transference as being shaped by unconscious organizing principles; though, as I will illustrate, the organization of transference put forward by these two sets of authors differs markedly, just as their organizations of the self differ markedly.

Goldberg's model of the self is purely psychological and appears more consistent than either of the others, with the basic outline of Kohut's bipolar self, without that model's inelegant metaphor of the tension arc, and without the overly concretized poles and segments that Kohut depicts. Rather, Goldberg's model is informed by the scientific philosophy of structuralism, recalling the hierarchical model put forward in an earlier work coauthored with John Gedo. In his present book, Goldberg describes the self as a structure that is composed of both forms or patterns on the one hand, and of particular contents or meanings on the other. Pathology, which is primary, relates to the forms or patterns of the self, whereas pathology, which is secondary, relates to its contents and meanings. In effect, Goldberg asserts that psychoanalysis, before self psychology, was too preoccupied with secondary pathology; that is, too concerned with the contents or meanings generated by the self-structure; for example, with the myriad ways in which the oedipal conflict was lived out. This emphasis on content was misplaced, Goldberg tells us, as it is the form or pattern that merits our attention. Our concern belongs with the primary pathology related to the integrity of the self. Goldberg provides an example of a borderline patient who, while in treatment, ostensibly progressed from borderline pathology to a narcissistic personality disorder to an oedipal conflict; but once the treatment was ended, the patient reverted to the original borderline functioning. Goldberg pointedly remarks that perhaps too much attention in the treatment had been paid to content, the secondary pathology, and not enough to the primary pathology, namely the form or pattern of organization of the self system. It is, he contends, the overall form of the self that is the essence of self structure, constituted by a variety of self-selfobject relationships.

The third and final of Kohut's contributions to be considered here are the concepts of the selfobject and the selfobject transference. All three sets of authors utilize the selfobject concept, and the definition of selfobject function remains largely consistent among these authors, and between them and Kohut. However, Stolorow, Brandchaft and Atwood, in conjunction with Daphne Stolorow, expand and refine the selfobject concept, contending that selfobject functions pertain to the integration of affect into the organization of self-experience, and the requirement for selfobject ties relates to the need for attuned responsiveness to affect states in all stages of life. In this way, mirroring and idealizable selfobjects are viewed as special instances of this expanded concept of selfobject function in terms of integration of affect. Basch, also recognizing the centrality of affect, presents a developmental line of such affect integration, using the line diagnostically and prognostically, as will be seen.

Turning to their views on how selfobject transferences are organized, each has established a model that encompasses the full range of extant analytic transferences. Stolorow, Brandchaft, and Atwood present two conceptions of transference, appearing in different chapters, with minor discrepancies between them. One model, written in collaboration with Frank Lachmann, defines transference as all the ways in which the patient's experience of the analytic relationship is shaped by his own psychological structures, the patient assimilating the analytic relationship into the thematic structures of his personal subjective world. The selfobject transference is not a type of transference; but a dimension of all transference, fluctuating as figure/ground. That is, even when self-restoration and maintenance are not central, giving way to other facets, such as conflicts over loving, hating, desiring, or competing, the selfobject dimension is never absent but operates silently, its presence enabling the patient to make contact with the frightening and conflictual feelings that have come to the fore. The second model of transference introduced by these authors extends the figure/ground dichotomy with the use of an additional metaphor, the bipolar transference. Here, one pole, the selfobject pole of the transference, represents the patient's longings to experience the analyst as a source of selfobject functions missing or insufficiently provided during earlier years. At the other pole, the pole of conflict and resistance, the patient expresses fears and expectations of a transference repetition of the original selfobject failure. A good analysis is said to be one that shifts from one pole to the other. If one uses both models put forth by Stolorow, Brandchaft and Atwood, it can be seen that all potential transference experiences can be encompassed.

Basch's model of the transference is a three-dimensional, hierarchical grid. One axis represents four possible categories of patient; the categories are not dependent upon symptom, but upon level of affect development and integration. They include: First, those who experienced failure of affective bonding during the first few months of infancy, and who therefore lack the capacity for self-regulation or basic tension control. These individuals are most often diagnosed as borderline. Second, those who learned to be ashamed of their affective responses and who therefore never progress from the level of affect to the level of emotion, that is, being able to put affects into words. These individuals most often are depressed or hypochondriacal. Third, those who have experienced difficulties with affect attunement and who therefore learned that their true emotional states could never be affirmed. These are most often the narcissistic personality disorders. Finally, Basch refers to the category of patient whose self development was adequate, but whose difficulties stem from affective trauma experienced during the oedipal phase of psychosexual development. Basch demonstrates specific modifications in therapeutic approach for each of these categories of patient, which categories represent, as I said, the first axis in Basch's model. The second axis in Basch's model of transference is concerned with the form of transference, the three possible forms being the familiar mirror, idealizing, and alterego. The third and final axis is involved with the content of the transference, and can include, for example, psychosexual issues, such as oral, anal and phallic tensions; or the concern can be with autonomy, creativity, or being a center of initiative; or finally, the content can be consumed by issues surrounding attachment needs. Again, all well-known varieties of transference can be encompassed within Basch's model.

Goldberg's conception of the transference is also, like Basch's, hierarchical. Building upon his structural model of the self referred to earlier, he identifies three levels of transference experience. Although patients may be more likely to relate to the analyst on one or another level, all levels are usually experienced within a given analysis. The levels are therefore to be thought of as aspects of the transference, rather than as discrete transference categories. The first level can be seen in patients whose current concerns are related to the basic building blocks, or underlying elements of their self-structure. The stability of these patients depends upon the apparent contentless aspects of treatment, the rules and regulations of the analytic setting, and the regularities of contact between patient and analyst. The stable transferences with these patients seem to dissolve under the impact of small changes in the treatment, such as a change of an hour, or an extended weekend. Such patients demand settling down, or pacification. Goldberg points out that the major factor in this tension regulation level of transference is that it is free of content or meaning. Patients who may experience this level include, on the one end of the spectrum, individuals who are narcissistically very vulnerable, and on the other, individuals who normally function well. No one, according to Goldberg, is totally immune from this transference proclivity.

Level two is shaped by, and composed of, the familiar selfobject transferences; this second level of transference proclivity serving to regulate and maintain self-esteem. The medium of the self-selfobject relationship on this level is affective exchanges that carry with them the experience of being understood.

Finally, level three is concerned with the many kinds of representations that the self-structure may manifest. It is on this level of transference proclivity where what appears to be conflict may arise; often, this conflict is resolvable by reordering and strengthening the intactness of the self. This third level, concerned with contents and meanings, is where the patient's life narrative is created; however, Goldberg views these narrative creations as merely epiphenomena, rather than as directly related to the formation or dissolution of psychopathology. Yet, it is just these narratives that occupy much of psychoanalysis, and the understanding of them is essential. Furthermore, understanding the meanings of these transferences on this third level does supplement the cure through the achievement of self reflection, a type of self-maintenance.

Each of these three outstanding contributions stands among the very few indispensable guides to self psychology today.

Chapter 11

Three Self
Psychologies
or One?

Frank M. Lachmann

We are at a critical juncture in the evolution of self psychology. Heinz Kohut left a legacy of creative ideas and their implications continued to inspire further explorations. The danger lies in the possibility that, as Kohut's insights are developed, his basic tenents will be elaborated to a point where self psychology splinters into self psychologies. At the moment, we have not yet reached this point. The domain of self psychology continues to be broadened and stretched with divergent contributions, providing points and counterpoints for each other. Before diversity produces fragmentation, it must mean dialog, challenge, and the potential for new views.

Three recent books epitomize three different paths that have evolved from Kohut's contributions. Each steers a different course through unchartered psychoanalytic territory. These are Basch's (1988) *Understanding Psychotherapy: The Science Behind the Art*, Goldberg's (1988) *A Fresh Look at Psychoanalysis: The View from Self Psychology*, and Stolorow, Brandchaft, and Atwood's (1987) *Psychoanalytic Treatment: An Intersubjective Approach*.

Each of the authors pursued Kohut's ideas in his own way. At first glance, their books suggest that pure chance places them within the realm of self psychology. They seem to have about as much in common as the guests in a hotel who share a roof for a night or two and then go off in their separate ways. Each of the authors claim that self psychology provided the springboard and inspiration for his ideas. But, is it really the same version of self psychology that each uses? Is it one self psychology that emerges from their combined efforts or three?

Basch addresses the broad field of psychotherapy and explicates a general theory of mental life as a basis for the art of therapy. Self psychology occupies a central but delimited place in this enterprise. The pathology of "self-experience," the construct he prefers to "self," is treated by investigating cognition, behavior, and dynamics. To do so, he deliberately positions himself outside the frame of reference that defines the domain of psychology as only comprising data that is accessible by empathy and introspection.

Stolorow, Brandchaft and Atwood encompass self psychology within a perspective they have termed "intersubjectivity." Goldberg has delineated a range of subtle issues in the domain of self psychology, emphasizing its uniqueness and applicability as is; he argues for further exploration of this domain rather than its expansion.

The impression of incompatibility of perspective, theory, and treatment predominates between these three books. Can Stolorow, Brandchaft, and Atwood's definition of psychoanalysis as the unwavering application of the empathic–introspective mode be reconciled with Goldberg's advocacy of experience-distant constructs, and with Basch's model of psychoanalysis that draws on neuroanatomy, physiology, and information processing?

Even the place accorded to empathy varies among these authors. Stolorow, Brandchaft and Atwood state that psychoanalysis is defined by the application of empathy and introspection. Goldberg (1988), following Kohut, also defines "empathy . . . as vicarious introspection" (p. 77); but he believes that it is not sufficient for the conduct of an analysis. Basch (1989) holds that vicarious introspection is just a synonym for empathy, so that we are still without a definition for a basic concept in self psychology. Such differences among the authors could pave the way for fruitful dialogs at best and a shattering diversification within self psychology at worst.

Yet, there is some consensus among the authors. *One* self psychology is their fervant ambition, and emerges as their overarching goal. These three volumes bear testamony to the vitality of self psychology, and in their diversity lies its future. The volumes express a debt to self psychology without slavishly reiterating its contributions. Rather than repeating unexamined assumptions from the past, as has been so characteristic in some psychoanalytic discourse, these works point toward new views, new approaches, and new understandings.

To focus on the differences and the similarities of these three perspectives, an approach to psychoanalytic writing used by Bergmann (1988) in his examination of psychoanalytic theories will be applied. From a historical perspective, he formulated five questions that differentiate among theories and "divide" psychoanalysts. They can be stated as follows:

1. How does psychopathology originate?
2. What kind of pathologies, what kinds of patients are not covered by the theory?
3. What is the ideal therapeutic process?
4. What is the overall view, the model of the mind?
5. How do we get from the pathology of the patient to the model of mental health held by the analyst? Or, how does analysis cure?

Yet, even before these questions can be addressed, we are confronted with the dramatically different place that "history" occupies for each of these authors. Goldberg (1989) takes his version of history from Santayana and reminds us that those who forget their history are condemned to repeat it. Basch (1988) emphasizes that history is *not* a hermaneutic exercise, and *not* a product of an agreed upon, shared reality between therapist and patient. Basch reads history in the immutabulity of affects. They are the therapist's Rosetta stone. Basch holds that irrespective of present circumstances and the therapist's personality affects, signals from inner space play themselves out. Affects thus provide a faithful record of past problematic or otherwise disappointing affective communications. This record is shaped by the inborn capacity to respond to stimulation as well as by the caregiver-infant relationship (Basch, personal communication, 1990).

Stolorow, Brandchaft and Atwood see history as George Bernard Shaw sees it. At the end of *The Devil's Diciple*, when asked what will history say to certain occurrences, General Burgogne, speaking for Shaw, answers, "History? history will lie—like always." To Stolorow, Brandchaft, and Atwood, "history," within a psychoanalytic perspective, does not occupy a privileged place. It is a product of interacting subjectivities of people. It is a chronicle of the person's psychic reality, not a revelation of any absolute truths about historical reality. The authors emphasize the extent to which all aspects of the past were organized in a context that has contributed to its shape. When reproduced in a new context, the marks of the old as well as the influences of the new appear.

In spite of these differences, each of the authors of the three books recognizes the importance of "repetitiveness," a historical concept, in mental life. Thus, Goldberg emphasizes the repetitiveness of pathological patterns. Basch emphasizes the immutable retention of affective patterns. And Stolorow, Brandchaft, and Atwood emphasize both the present, as organized according to the past, and the recalled past, as organized according to the present. These three visions of human nature in general, and self psychology in particular, evolve from differing philosophical, scientific–empirical, and artistic perspectives; they may be irreconcilable at the moment but can be potentially complementary.

To return to the five questions that were said to differentiate among a broad spectrum of analysts. For three of these questions there is virtual agreement among all the authors discussed.

First, as to the origin of mental pathology: Although Goldberg (1988) entitled a chapter of his book, "The Unempathic Child," thereby emphasizing constitutional character dispositions and all the unknowns and unpredictables that are encountered in psychoanalytic practice, essentially there is agreement about the origins of pathology. It occurs not through impediments to drive discharge, not through the consequences of inborn, unconscious fantasies, but through the transactions between child and caretakers and how these transactions are experienced, registered, and subsequently transformed in development.

For Kohut as well as for all these authors, self psychology as a theory and as a therapy is linked to a model of development, a model in which affect occupies a central position. Affect regulation and the maintenance of an optimal level of stimulation is achieved through the relationship between parent and child. Affect and the interactions derived therefrom, such as affective attunement, mutual influences between mother and infant, communication, and negotiation are afforded significant, prominent positions by each author. For each, psychopathology is forged in the caretaker–child interaction, given the prewiring, the propensities, and endownment of the child. For each, irrespective of the terms used, affect provides the heartbeat for psychoanalytic treatment.

The second question asks who or what is not treatable? Psychoanalysis initially was confined to transference neuroses and the analysis of oedipal conflicts. Patients suffering from narcissistic transferences were not deemed treatable by classical analysis. Similarly, severe psychotic states were initially considered to be untreatable by psychoanalytic self psychology. But, contributions by Galatzer-Levy (1988), Lachmann and Beebe (1983), Stolorow, Brandchaft, and Atwood (1987), and others have challenged this limitation. Preoedipal and borderline conditions, and even psychoses are understandable and treatable with a therapy informed by self psychology. Thus, there are now virtually no patient groups that would be excluded from self psychologically informed treatment by virtue of their diagnosis.

Now to question three, the ideal therapeutic process. There is a consensus among the authors discussed that, ideally, a selfobject transference is engaged and its vicissitudes are followed, reflected upon, developmentally understood, and contexturally explained so that self-reflection, self-control, and self-empathy can be prompted. However, the extent to which other transferences or other dimensions of the transference are recognized varies among these authors. In one case vignette, Basch (1988) emphasizes that oedipal transferences are a form of selfobject problem (p. 306). For him, transferences, the repetition of patterns of expectations that represent closed systems, are always selfobject transferences. Goldberg discusses a "father transference" (p. 66) and describes the three different types of relationships of a patient with his father and their impact on the transference (pp. 148–149). Stolorow, Brandchaft, Atwood and I (Stolorow et. al, 1987; Stolorow & Lachmann, 1984/85) discussed the figure/ground relationship between the selfobject and other, conflictual, repetitive dimensions of the transference. These differences reflect the struggle within self psychology to capture the complexities of the analyst–patient interaction. They reflect attempts to understand and conceptualize self-experience and thus point to a greater communality of perspective than might be apparent on the surface.

Differences emerge however, as to where to place the curative emphasis in the process of rupture and repair that characterizes the life of the selfobject dimension of the transference. This difference points directly to questions four and five, the analyst's theoretical and metapsychological assumptions and their relationship to the processes of change, cure, or how to get from the pathology of the patient to to the model of health adhered to explicitly or implicitly by the analyst. Here lie the clinical challenges to self psychology from within a self psychological perspective.

The authors have addressed this issue in several contexts. Goldberg (1989) reminded us that self psychology had its origins in the treatment of narcissistic character pathology, and devoted a sizable section of his book to his understanding of character pathology. Might we infer from this that he considers character pathology the primary locus of self pathology, in that character pathology constitutes pathology in the very fabric of the self. Seeing it as primary and intrinsic locates it totally within the patient, makes it the sole property of the patient, and holds the patient responsible for its display in the transference. The analyst, having privileged access to the transference, then proceeds to negotiate with the patient as to the meaning of his experience in the treatment. These negotiations, defined as "a sharing of meanings," are only the means by which the patient is enabled to achieve increased self-control and self-reflection.

Stolorow, Brandchaft and Atwood might question Goldberg's notion that the analyst has "privileged access" to the nature of the transference. But, their requirement that the analyst "decenter" from the structures of his subjectivity would lead to a similar position vis-à-vis the patient's transference. The nub of the difference lies in the place accorded to negotiations. For Stolorow, Brandchaft and Atwood, the exploration of meanings would be tantamount to an empathic immersion in the patient's subjectivity and an exploration of the interface between the analyst's and the patient's subjectivity. It is at that juncture that the patient's pathology has crystallized. For them, analysis of the patient or the patient's pathology is inseparable from the context in which the patient and analyst form a system. For Goldberg, the negotiations are the transactions by which the patient's primary pathology—his intrapsychic organization—is affected. Although Goldberg (1988) states that these "narrative exchanges," add to the cure (p. 139) they seem to be understood as affecting the patient's mediating structures and not the primary pathology. Through negotiation, the patient benefits in that he comes to reflect on the experience-limiting distortions that are a consequence of his character pathology.

To Basch, the negotiations are a form of communication in which affect is engaged. Thereby the patient's limitations in pattern matching are expanded, negative feedback is interfered with, and the sense of efficacy is promoted. And, whereas Goldberg emphasizes the insufficiency of empathy in the curative process, Basch emphasizes its role in dissolving the resistances to the transference.

The power of repetitive patterns is recognized in each of the three books. For Basch, they are subsumed under feedback loops. For Goldberg, they are intrinsic to the concept of character pathology; and to Stolorow, Brandchaft and Atwood, they appear as either figure or ground with the selfobject dimension in the transference. Not only are repetitive patterns organized in a context, but they are continuously reorganized and revived in a context in which the failures and disappointments of the past are repeated and reexperienced. Essentially, they too address psychopathology on the level of character formation. The structures of subjectivity are the warp and woof of character. They (Stolorow, Branchaft, & Atwood, 1989) emphasized the analytic tasks of making conscious these unconscious structures, the repressed, affect-laden experiences that constitute the dynamic unconscious, and the aspects of self-experience that, dimly felt and dimly known, were never permitted to see the light of day. Though this may sound like Freud's early theory, whereby cure was to be achieved by making the unconscious conscious, this is not their main concern. Rather, the concern is that the context in which the conscious-making takes place differs for each of the three kinds of "unconscious." This delineation is presumably Stolorow, Brandchaft, and Atwood's response to the criticism that subjectivity refers only to consciousness, and that psychoanalysis must address mental life below the level of conscious, subjective experience.

All of the authors discussed share a vision of self psychology with significant common elements. Whatever terms they prefer, they have defined the concern of psychoanalysis from a self psychological perspective as addressing and encompassing affectivity, a developmental model, communication, and how one's private world is shaped early in life. In psychoanalytic treatment, we then encounter the character, templates, or repetitive themes that organize experience and distort experience from its potential, had it been permitted to proceed toward the fulfillment of its intrinsic design. Following Kohut, Atwood, Basch, Brandchaft, Goldberg, and Stolorow have rescued and retrieved psychoanalysis, as it was floundering on shallow, rocky shoals. Each steers an innovative course through unchartered, psychoanalytic territory. They may not be charting the same course for self psychology, but they are heading roughly in not too dissimilar directions toward a common goal.

REFERENCES

Basch, M. F. (1988), *Understanding Psychotherapy: The Science Behind the Art*. New York: Basic Books.

_____ (1989), Comments on *Understanding Psychotherapy: The Science Behind the Art*. Presented at the 12th Annual Conference on Psychology of the Self, San Francisco, CA.

Bergmann, M. (1988), What divides psychoanalysts today? Presented at the annual meeting of the National Association for the Advancement of Psychoanalysis, New York City.

Galatzer-Levy, R. (1988), Manic-depressive illness: Analytic experience and a hypothesis. In: *Frontiers in Self Psychology, Progress in Self Psychology, Vol. 3*. ed. A. Goldberg. Hillsdale, NJ: The Analytic Press, pp. 87–102.

Goldberg, A. (1988), *A Fresh Look at Psychoanalysis: The View from Self Psychology*. Hillsdale, NJ: The Analytic Press.

_____ (1989), Reply to Dr. E. Shane's paper. Presented at the 12th Annual Conference on Psychology of the Self, San Francisco, CA.

Lachmann, F. & Beebe, B. (1983), Consolidation of the self: A case study. *Dynamic Psychother*, 1,55–75.

Stolorow, R., Brandchaft, B. & Atwood, G. (1987), *Psychoanalytic Treatment: An Intersubjective Approach*. Hillsdale, NJ: The Analytic Press.

———, ———, ——— (1989) Three realms of the unconscious and their therapeutic implications. Presented at the 12th Annual Conference on Psychology of the Self, San Francisco, CA.

———, & Lachmann, F. (1984/1985), Transference: The future of an illusion. *The Annual of Psychoanalysis*, 12/13:19–37. New York: International Universities Press.

Chapter 12

Reflections on the Future of Self Psychology and Its Role in the Evolution of Psychoanalysis

Raanan Kulka

The departure of key historical figures from center stage of the psychoanalytic movement and the formation of a new stratum of psychoanalysts, whose contribution accumulates in a diffusion of scientific and clinical creativity rather than revolves around single gigantic discoveries, have made the recent years a transitional period in the development of psychoanalysis. During this period, The main effort has been to deepen and further consolidate established insights and to test the possibility of integrating the different trends and viewpoints that have evolved during psychoanalysis's hundred years of existence.

At the same time, it seems to me that within this quiet crystallization, processes are immanent that will lead to a breakthrough in the future development of psychoanalysis as a science and as a unique therapeutic method. The source for such a potential impetus is to be found, I believe, in the theory of self psychology as developed by Kohut. Self psychology, which focuses on the unique human sphere of narcissism, touches on the innermost core of psychoanalysis. It challenges its current boundaries and outlines possibilities of expanding those boundaries toward totally new frontiers. And this is true, both on the philosophical level of psychoanalytic theory as a science, and on the clinical level of psychoanalysis as a method of treating human suffering.

Psychoanalysis attempted to establish its standing as a science by attaching itself to the positivistic sciences while using biological and

175

physical models as metaphors for formulating its own paradigms. In recent years, there has been a noticeable departure from the need to establish psychoanalysis as a science by conventional criteria. The two major expressions of this process are (a) the relinquishing of the necessity for a monolithic theory and the readiness for a plurality of explanations that give meaning to the human condition; and (b) the acceptance of a metaphorical quality for the models that explain the various psychic phenomena.

Although I agree that these processes mark a singificant achievement in the development of psychoanlysis, my position as far as self psychology is concerned is far more radical. Self psychology is not just another model, another metaphor to explain human phenomena. In my view, self psychology expresses psychoanalysis's essential transition from a science that deals with psychic materials through nonpsychic theoretical paradigms, to one that dares build a theoretical paradigm on principles that correspond, in quality, to the materials it investigates.

The demand for a theory that would explain the human being according to the criteria of the natural sciences forced psychoanalysis to apprehend the psyche as a functional system that operates according to a deterministic causality. For many years, psychoanalysis took an apologetic stance in an attempt to maintain its scientific legitimacy, and avoided taking explicit pride in the fact that the unique quality of psychic materials required a scientific approach with a completely different set of rules. To regard the psychic as a teleological system of meaning that can, perhaps, be better understood than explained, really does require a different theoretical paradigm and investigative methods. Not only does this approach not diminish the scientific legitimacy of psychoanalysis, but it provides an opportunity for a fundamental reexamination of various issues in the philosophy of science.[1]

In the attempt to touch on the unique quality of the psychic and to conceptualize the psyche as a theoretical explanation, self psychology made a number of courageous shifts, each involving a partial departure from the haven of psychoanalysis's fundamental concepts. In place of the economic principles that explain the quantitative-energetic facet of the personality, self psychology presented a motivational system of a nonbiological origin, whose development and

---

[1]Thus, for example, the distinction between understanding and explaining is not one of mere semantic subtlety, but reflects my belief that these are two essentially different qualities of the explanatory power of a given theoretical paradigm. But this is, of course, an issue that requires a separate discussion.

operation are channeled by processes having a psychic quality only. Instead of the structural principle, which explains the texture of mechanisms and processes that generate the functions of the personality, self psychology posited its "program of the psychological destiny of the nuclear self," which constitutes a superstructural, organizing framework for human experience. And for the principle of attachment and relationship, which locates the personality in time and space through its ties with an object, self psychology articulated the self–selfobject unit as an entity that presents a hitherto unknown and unformulated modality of relating, and to which the term *relation* in the accepted sense hardly applies.

Even without embarking on a detailed discussion of Kohutian theory, this schematic outline of the main points of self psychology will suffice to demonstrate how the partial departure from the shelter of the main models of classical psychoanalysis exposed the very vulnerability of "psychic" explanations of psychic phenomena. It is no wonder that much of the criticism of self psychology has centered around the obscurity that characterizes much of the theoretical statements of the Kohutian school, an obscurity which has always been judged as reflecting the inherent weakness of these theoretical statements as elucidatory concepts. The external, linguistic weakness of the theoretical fundamentals of self psychology does not prove them to be essentially wrong, and although there is undoubtedly much to be done to crystallize and validate many of the school's principles, it is precisely the criticized weakness that points to a new direction in the quality of the theoretical explanation it offers.

Self psychology has also taken a crucial methodological step forward. Rather than improve external observation methods in order to investigate the subjective phenomenon from an objective distance, self psychology attempts to foster maximal closeness to the "observed"–to the experiencing of the psychic by the subject himself. Self psychology's realization of the almost absurd but unique achievement of touching the subjective from "zero distance" while retaining a scientific stance toward it was made possible by a subtle combination of two major elements: (a) the sophisticated, theoretical conceptualization of empathy and its mode of existence in the dyadic space of the individual and his significant other, and (b) the transformation of empathy into the main investigative tool for the collection of psychic evidence. Such an achievement has a far-reaching implication, in that it represents the creation of a unique scientific position in which the observed becomes his own "explanation." As unintelligible and objectionable as this may sound, I think that it is this unique scientific position, the highest achievement of self psychology, which will allow psychoanalysis to be transformed from a positivist into an ontological science—a science that has as its object being itself. And, indeed, by penetrating into narcissism as a psychic entity unique to mankind, self psychology is dealing with the issue of the meaning and purpose of human existence, with the issue of the purpose of life itself, not from a religious or philosophical perspective but from a scientific viewpoint, which directly stems and touches upon man's immediate psychological experience with himself, the other, and the world.

It is no coincidence that the topic of the last international psychoanalytical congress[2] was dedicated to Freud's essay, "Analysis Terminable and Interminable", on the 50th anniversary of its composition in 1937, two years before Freud's death. In this essay, Freud reflects on the clinical limits of psychoanalysis and the limits of its therapeutic ability to change the human being and ease his psychic suffering. Although this profound essay presents a world view that, to be outlined, would require a life's work, the essay reflects precisely what was continuous and consistent in Freud's essential attitude to psychoanalysis as a method of treatment, an attitude that changed very little throughout his working life. In two of the more moving of Freud's clinical expressions, drawn from very different times in the history of psychoanalysis—one from the cradle of the great discoveries and the other from the verge of his death—Freud outlines his therapeutic credo, and I wish to quote them verbatim.

In the chapter, "The Psychotherapy of Hysteria," in *Studies on Hysteria* (1895), which he wrote together with Breuer, Freud writes:

> When I have promised my patients help or improvement by means of a cathartic treatment I have often been faced by this objection: "Why, you tell me yourself that my illness is probably connected with my circumstances and the events of my life. You cannot alter these in any way. How do you propose to help me, then?" And I have been able to make this reply: "No doubt fate would find it easier than I do to relieve you of your illness. But you will be able to convince yourself that much will be gained if we succeed in transforming your hysterical misery into common unhappiness. With a mental life that has been restored to health you will be better armed against that unhappiness." (p. 305)

In a touching letter to the mother of a homosexual asking Freud to cure her son of his love tendencies, we find an identical fundamental quality:

---

[2]The 35th International Psychoanalytical Congress, Montreal, Quebec, 1987.

By asking me if I can help, you mean, I suppose, if I can abolish homosexuality and make normal heterosexuality take its place. The answer is in a general way, we cannot promise to achieve it. In a certain number of cases we succeed in developing the blighted germs of heterosexual tendencies which are present in every homosexual, in the majority of cases it is no more possible. It is a question of the quality and the age of the individual. The result of treatment cannot be predicted.

What analysis can do for your son runs in a different line. If he is unhappy, neurotic, torn by conflicts, inhibited in his social life, analysis may bring him harmony, peace of mind, full efficiency, whether he remains a homosexual or gets changed. (Freud, 1935, p. 787).

From these two quotes, as from the great essay of 1937, it appears that, for Freud, psychoanalysis touched on the human being's conflictual essence, but left him with his existential suffering.

Self psychology posits a challenge to psychoanalysis's sense of boundary on the clinical level as well, and claims that psychoanalysis must and can treat "common" human misery and unhappiness. In his second book, *The Restoration of the Self*, published in 1977, Kohut quoted the protagonist of Eugene O'Neill's *The Great God Brown*, who, at the end of his long journey into the night says: "Man is born broken. He lives by mending. The grace of God is glue" (p. 287).

This is the faith that lies at the basis of Kohut's dramatic distinction between classical psychoanalysis, which treats "guilty man," and self psychology, which treats "tragic man." It is this faith that, more than anything else, perhaps, embodies the pretensions of self psychology to extend the boundaries of psychoanalysis, even further than the limits that Freud, in "Analysis Terminable and Interminable," called "bedrocks," those limits beyond which there is nowhere to go.

Will the 1990s see the realization of the aspirations of self psychology and the power that it contains for psychoanalysis? This is not an easy question to answer as it relates to the sociological and psychological processes underlying the development of the psychoanalytic movement and the way they will influence psychoanalysis's theoretical and clinical investigation of narcissism.

One of the instructive things that has been occurring in the last two decades, since Kohut put narcissism on the agenda of psychoanalysis, is the immense effort being invested in dealing with the concept of narcissism within the framework of existing paradigms. For example, the valuable contributions of Mahler and Kernberg, with all their differences, represent distinctive examples of what is essentially a similar attempt—using drive and structure as points of departure— to treat narcissism within the context of object relations and their development. This effort derives, in my view, from resistance to the recognition that the experiential aspect of the personality is a separate sphere, and that narcissism is a psychic entity in itself; therefore, the perspectives of drive, structure and object relations cannot contain it. A retrospective analysis testifies to the fact that Freud himself was aware of this fact. It is no coincidence that his own fascinating contribution to the subject, the seminal article of 1914, "On Narcissism," was made at a crucial moment in the crystallization of his theory, when the concept of narcissism was imperative, both for the final formulation of the theory of instinct, with the libido at the center, and for the creation of the theoretical–clinical basis for the structural theory of the psychic apparatus. Interestingly, there is no further development whatsoever of the concept of narcissism in Freud's subsequent writings, as if to suggest that, although the drive and structural models required the concept of narcissism in order to come into being, they did not in themselves provide a suitable context for the development of our understanding of this exclusively human sphere and its place in the human psyche.

Just as the structural model in Freud's theory did not cancel the previous drive model but constituted a kind of higher frame of reference that allowed it a fuller expression, so most of the object-relations theories that came after Freud did not develop at the expense of the drive and structural aspects of the personality. Rather, we tend to regard the object-relations view of the human being, within which both drives and structures are built, organized, and developed, as broader and more exhaustive. Self psychology should be located in the development of psychoanalysis as a scientific discipline and as a method of treatment in the same way. We can trace the development of psychoanalytic theory as an evolutionary process, in which the center of gravity has shifted from energy to structure and experience, with self psychology as the landmark of the final historical transition with which we are all engaged at the moment (Kulka, 1988).

The recognition of self psychology as an essential change, around which the previous achievements of psychoanalysis are organized, is not easy. The notion that self psychology does not refute these previous achievements but equips them with new ways for their complete expression, is difficult to assimilate. At the bottom of these difficulties lie sociohistorical and psychological resistances that many analysts and philosophers of science explored in other contexts. But in the specific case of self psychology, two additional resistances should be noted and their general features emphasized.

One resistance is related to my opening statement: In an era in which there are no longer any giant figures, and in which the explosion of knowledge and its universal dissemination reduces the chances of such figures coming into being, the acceptance of a contribution that is associated with a particular individual as an inevitable change is almost impossible. It would seem, therefore, that very positive processes in the development of culture and science, such as the democratization of scientific authority and the universal-ization of knowledge, also involve the creation of contradictory processes, which can prevent and delay the acceptance of essential changes and developments.

The source of the second resistance is, in my view, no less profound, and belongs essentially to the analytical–clinical encounter. In the past, it was generally agreed in the psychoanalytic community that although the Kohutian theory was underdeveloped, lacking in support, and could not pass muster as a theory, the clinical sphere that this theory touched upon was accepted wholeheartedly. This position has undergone great changes in recent years, and in my view has, in some ways, been reversed. We find Kohutian theoretical elements in wide use in the area of diagnostics, in the partial adoption of conceptual terminology, and also, it should be emphasized, in a more internalized recognition of narcissisim as a human phenomenon no longer necessarily identified with pathology or as a mere transi-tional period in human development. At the same time, it seems that in the clinical area, we find greater and more rigid resistance towards the therapeutic stance derived from Kohutian concepts. This issue is connected with empathy and the unique position of being a selfobject to someone else; the demand self psychology makes on the analyst is almost inhuman, or at any rate very complex and at times intolerably difficult.

What, in fact, is the psychic situation of being a selfobject? To become a selfobject, you agree to give your self "up" for the sake of the "selfhood" of an other that is embodied in you—to be for him[3] *his self* outside of himself, so that he may observe *his selfhood* in you, recognize *himself* in you, internalize *his self* through you. He thus becomes a unique self, not by a process of identification in the accepted sense of the term as occurs between two selves who constitute objects for one another, but through processes of becoming that are very far from being clearly and fully formulated, even in self psychology. The experiential significance of this situation for the analyst is one of great loneliness, at times a complete abrogation of

---

[3]I have chosen the conventional "him" rather than "him/her" in the following description purely to avoid cumbersomeness.

sources of narcissistic satisfaction, a virtual giving up of one's own psychic place—a kind of acceptance of "being erased", which is not identical to being nothing, or nothingness. On the contrary, this is a situation that demands a most intensive psychic presence, having complex characteristics of passive activity and the dissolution of boundaries between self and other without breaking a single boundary. I know that this dialectical presence, which moves between totally contradictory poles, sounds at times as verging on mystical romanticization; but this is not the case, and it requires a very persistent theoretical and clinical effort to decipher the complex elements of the special therapeutic presence required from the analyst by self psychology.

In such a situation the human effort of the analyst to fight for his existence as an object for the other, the patient, to become an existing selfhood, and thus by definition to depart from the position of selfobject, is only natural. The stressing of object relations in the accepted sense, of defense mechanisms, primarily splitting, projection, and projective identification, and the emphasis of reality and reality testing as the ultimate goal for the patient to achieve—these are only some of the grooves to which the analyst might revert as a refuge from the unique hardships of the analytic stance required by self psychology.

The combination of significant sources of resistance to the psychic position demanded of the analyst, and the quality of cultural and scientific development that, in the second half of the century, no longer focuses on key figures whose appearance provokes immediate resistance, will, I think, determine the shape of the next decade in psychoanalysis. This decade will be a period in which integrative eclecticism continues to constitute the natural solution and this integration will be expressed in a legitimization of a horizontal perspective of the four models of psychoanalysis: the drive model, the structural model, the object-relations model, and the self model. The clinical imperative will be to work, not through a rigid adherence to one of the models, but with an ability to use all four models and to move among them flexibly and freely. Even though this position will also have to overcome a number of resistances, such as the wish for a single explicatory principle or the difficulty of cognitive and emotional oscillations among different positions, this stance will, I believe, dominate the next decade.

Although I see this horizontal development only as a transitional stage, my vision does not touch on what the factor will be that will bring about the deeper assimilation of self psychology as a supraordinate framework for psychoanalysis. But I am fairly sure that this assimilation will not be caused by any dramatic event, and will not grow out of new conceptual insights. The modest, and industrious, yet determined and persistent accumulation of clinical work, based on the tenets of self psychology, will eventually bring about self psychology's recognition as the future development of psychoanalysis.

REFERENCES

Freud, S. (1895), Studies on hysteria. *Standard Edition*, 2:253–305. London: Hogarth Press, 1955.
_____ (1914), On narcissism: An introduction. *Standard Edition*, 14:78–102. London: Hogarth Press, 1957.
_____ (1935), A letter to the mother of a homosexual. *Amer. J. Psychiat.*, 107:786–787, 1951.
_____ (1937), Analysis terminable and interminable. *Standard Edition*, 23:216–253. London: Hogarth Press, 1964.
Kohut, H. (1977), *The Restoration of the Self*. New York: International Universities Press.
Kulka, R. (1988), Narcissism and neurosis—An opportunity for integration in psychoanalytic theory and technique. *Internat. J. Psycho-Anal.*, 69:521–533.

Chapter 13

Heinz Kohut
Memorial Lecture:
Toward a Level
Playing Field

E. S. Wolf

Heinz Kohut (1959) inaugurated a major conceptual revolution in psychoanalysis with his publication of *Introspection, Empathy and Psychoanalysis*. By moving empathy from having been merely an ancillary theoretical and technical maneuver into a position of pivotal centrality, Kohut set in motion a series of theoretical and clinical developments that culminated in psychoanalytic self psychology. Many aspects of psychoanalytic theory and psychoanalytic clinical practice were deeply affected by these developments. I shall attempt to demonstrate that the psychoanalyst's analytic spirit, the psychological posture with which a therapist approaches the task of analysis, has undergone a number of subtle but decisive permutations. Specifically, I am pointing to an attitudinal change that has transformed a quasiauthoritarian psychoanalytic milieu into a more egalitarian and empathically sensitive ambience. The roots of these shifts antedate Kohut's emphasis on empathy. It is as if a sea-change of Western sensibility was reflected in psychoanalysis in the theoretical concepts introduced by self psychology and found expression in the alterations of the clinical analytic ambience.

However, it is not easy to trace the reciprocal influences of psychoanalytic theory and psychoanalytic practice, and even more difficult to relate more general cultural changes to the subtle modifications of analyst–analysand interactions. Galatzer-Levy and Cohler (1989) commented that "a shift in what psychoanalysts hope to achieve through their investigations" (p. 3) has been observed. The emergence and development of psychoanalysis did not come about in a vacuum but have occurred in a cultural context that has itself been changing at an unprecedented pace. In addition, the transplantation, mainly in the 1930s, of many leading psychoanalysts from a rich and fertile, but repressively constricted, middle European hothouse into the generously welcoming, wide-open spaces of America has had a shock-like and liberating effect to which, perhaps, we are still too close for an objective evaluation.

I shall focus on the relatively small area of the changing relations between analyst and analysand. I have chosen the clinical, psychoanalytic situation as my field of observation because after 34 years of immersion into psychoanalysis as analysand, student, and psychoanalyst, this clinical, psychoanalytic situation is the most intimately familiar aspect of my psychoanalytic experience. Prolonged intimate contact with the facts and fancies of clinical psychoanalysis has shaped my judgments and licenses me to express the convictions that I have acquired. As such this is a statement of personal opinions reasonably grounded in subjective experience, rather than a well-evidenced and documented, objective, scientific treatise; but in that respect it is no different from most of the psychoanalytic literature. Indeed, as the science of subjective experience, psychoanalysis has yet to develop the methods and criteria that would allow an objectification of its findings on a level comparable to the natural sciences. Perhaps, future sophisticated psychoanalytic research may succeed to ground our impressionistic findings on more carefully controlled data.

THE ANALYST-ANALYSAND RELATIONSHIP

The first of these changes we want to consider is the relationship between analyst and analysand. In spite of Freud's aim to create a basic science—analogous, perhaps, to the basic laboratory sciences underpinning clinical medicine—psychoanalysis has not escaped the burden of its origin in asylums and sick beds. Most psychoanalysts thought, perhaps still think, of neurotics as sick patients. Except for Freud himself, most psychoanalysts carried into their professional work the attitudes and habits of physicians. Physicians do things to patients, whose main responsibility is to be open to the physician's investigations of the most private and intimate parts of their bodies, as well as to be cooperative with the physician's ministrations. It looks like a one-way street.

Freud himself seems to have been relatively free of this medical-authoritarian tradition. Perhaps this absence of a "father knows best" posture was an expression of Freud's deep commitment to truth finding. It is well known that Freud was first and foremost a questioning researcher. Relatively late in his career, under the pressure of growing family obligations, he reluctantly began the clinical practice of neurological medicine. Learning and sharing his insights was Freud's highest ambition. The reports of their analyses with Freud by Wortis (1954), Doolittle (1956), Blanton (1971), Riviere (Ruitenbeek, 1973, pp. 128–131, & pp. 353–356), Grinker (Ruitenbeek, 1973, pp. 180–185), De Saussure (Ruitenbeek, 1973, pp. 357–359), and Alix Strachey (Khan, 1973) all testify, not only to his curiosity, but also to the human and friendly relationships that Freud had with his analysands. The cordial ambience that reigned in Freud's consulting room stands in sharp contrast, however, to what I shall call the "standard classical" psychoanalytic posture. Long before Lipton (1977) elaborated the differences between Freud's technique and the standard classical technique (called "modern technique" by Lipton), the latter had been commented on by others both favorably and unfavorably. According to Lipton (1977, p. 262), "modern technique," based on ego psychology, emerged after Freud's death and was fully established by 1948 when Kris (1951) repudiated Freud's technique with the Rat Man. Lipton mentions Sherwood (1969, pp. 72–73), Mannoni (1971, pp. 115–118) and Eissler (1950, p. 100) as primarily favorable commentators on Freud's technique with the Rat Man, whereas he mentions Kris (1951), Kanzer (1952, P. 18), Grunberger (1966), Weiner (1973) and Beigler (1975) as primarily critical. Lipton speculates that the emergence of this modern technique might be related to the increasing domination of psychoanalysis by ego psychology, and that it may have developed as a reaction against Franz Alexander's concept of the corrective emotional experience.

The post-Freudian, modern technique of psychoanalysis became the dominant mode of psychoanalytic practice in this country after World War II. The decades of the 40s and 50s were the acme of the reign of ego psychology; the psychoanalytic literature was filled with the explorations of the structure of the ego and its functions. Scientific research and knowledge was accepted as the supreme goal of the analytic enterprise. Not only psychoanalysis but Western society generally had made "a holy cow" of science. The pursuit of scientific careers was the primary goals of increasing numbers of students even before the dazzling discoveries of nuclear physics and the space age. The conviction that the technology of chemistry and physics could solve all of our problems became almost universal. The rush to the application of scientific research to the production of consumer goods led to a profusion of products, with hardly anybody noticing that it also entailed a poisoning of the environment. It was not just commercial greed but adoration of the new god called science that became the guiding value all over the world.

In psychoanalysis, this same spirit was enhanced by the publication of the *Standard Edition of the Complete Psychological Works of Sigmund Freud* during the 50s and 60s. In his influential book, *Freud and Man's Soul*, Bruno Bettelheim (1983) elaborated on the inadequacies of James Strachey's translation of Freud into English. He deplored Strachey's substitution of medical terms for ordinary language and the removal of the personal element from Freud's style. Above all Bettelheim objected that *seelicher Apparat* and *Seelenleben* have become "mental apparatus" and "mental life." Prawer (1983) commented that Bettelheim "rightly objects to such high handed, ideologically suspect procedures, and adduces sufficient quotations to prove beyond doubt that Freud wanted and needed the emotional and historical resonances of "Seele" [soul], the secularized term he habitually used to denote the inmost essence of the human personality" (p. 812). Bettelheim also blamed the deprivation of these needed resonances on the same people who sought to make psychoanalysis the private reserve of physicians rather than that of the secular *Seelsorger* envisaged by Freud (1926) in *The Question of Lay Analysis* and in the letter to Pfister (Freud, 1928) on *The Future of an Illusion*. (Freud, 1927)

One may reasonably conclude that the concept of the human soul, which in its secular dimensions was central to Freud's vision of the human personality, was purged from the English translation of his writings. It seems to me that the conceptual and spiritual void thus created by the mechanistic skew of the *Standard Edition* is now being filled with the concept of the self, as introduced by Kohut, to represent that secular essence of being human. Thus psyche, a Greek word for soul, and an essential part of Freudian psychoanalysis, has become again a respected "citizen" of contemporary psychoanalytic thinking. It remains to be pointed out, however, that Strachey's scientismic translation of Freud was not the aberrant misdeed implied by Bettelheim's overheated polemic. I think that any good translator working in the context of the explosion of scientific knowledge during the first half of the 20th century was bound to produce a translation in harmony with the spirit of the times.

The effect of the ego psychological scientification of the analytic situation was to turn the analytic ambience into one of relative coldness and sterility. Justification was found in Freud's (1912) metaphor comparing the analyst's activity to that of a surgeon. (1912, p. 115): "I cannot advise my colleagues too urgently to model themselves during psychoanalytic treatment on the surgeon, who puts aside all his feelings, even his human sympathy, and concentrates his mental forces on the single aim of performing the operations as skilfully as possible. Under present-day conditions the feeling that is most dangerous to a psychoanalyst is the therapeutic ambition . . ." (p. 115). And further, Freud (1915): "The treatment must be carried out in abstinence. By this I do not mean physical abstinence alone . . ." (p. 165). One can only conjecture why Freud so unequivocally exiled compassion from the therapeutic armamentarium of his students. Perhaps he had good reasons to distrust their judicious management of their countertransferences, and therefore recommended suppression instead of self-analysis. In retrospect it seems that Freud gave a "Do as I say, not as I do" kind of recommendation.

Stone (1961, p. 15) appears to suggest that Freud's attitude was a self-conscious protest that he was a medical man, not a man of letters, and that the medical situation per se carried with it certain traditions derived from the doctor–patient relationship. He refers to Lewin (1946) who called attention to the fact that the medical man's first "office" is the dissecting room and his first "patient" a corpse. The medical student is supposed to learn emotional detachment. Lewin suggested that much of the psychological relationship to the cadaver is carried over to living patients. He recalled that in many of the best hospitals therapy, in theory, was considered irrational. Therapeutic nihilism meant that, after a thorough examination and diagnosis, there was nothing to do but wait for the clinical pathological conference. For the budding physician-analyst, the psychoanalytic situation may easily be unconsciously misunderstood as if it were like the morgue. These interpretations by Lewin are somewhat fanciful and certainly polemically exaggerated, but they do underline that there has long been a growing awareness of disturbing distortions in psychoanalytic technique.

It is particularly the idea that the analysand must be first and foremost a patient that seems to me to have no justification in clinical reality and appears to be a residue of our medical ancestry. Even so enlightened an analyst as Stone (1961) stated his belief that "[P]sychoanalysis, as a genuine process, finds its only adequate motivation in the suffering and the need for help of the patient . . ." (p. 16), and he supports this belief by asserting the essential importance of the phenomenon of transference together with his conviction regarding the unique transference value of the physician. No one will argue the need for help as an important motivation for a person's turning to another for aid and comfort. But has our analytic experience really demonstrated the superiority of physicians as magnets for transferences? I think not. Greenson (1967) believed that the patient's ". . .

suffering should be sufficient to induce him to enter the psychoanalytic situation as a *patient*" (p. 360). It is Greenson's contention that only one who feels himself a patient can be analyzed beyond a superficial depth, and he asks whether the prospective patient has ". . . enough motivation to bear the inequality, the unevenness of the relationship between patient and analyst that the analytic situation calls for?" (p. 360). Greenson struggles with the proper attitude of the analyst to his patient. But he is not yet ready to replace patient with analysand. There are no hints of an understanding that dissatisfaction with the state of the self or of the world may well be signs of health and yet can be sufficient motivations for the hard work of analysis. Nor does he mention the motivating pleasure of exploring the new and novel that is part of the inborn gift of life from birth on. For Greenson (1967), the heart of the matter is how to balance the attitudes of deprivation and incognito with compassion and concern. "A certain amount of compassion, friendliness, warmth, and respect for the patient's rights is indispensable. The analyst's office is a treatment room and not a research laboratory. We can feel a reliable kind of love for our patients because they are all in a sense sick, helpless children, no matter what else they may use as a facade" (p. 391). Clearly, Greenson already came a long way from the model of the cold surgeon without human sympathy. Still, he continues to be caught in a conflictful dilemma. For him, the analytic situation remains tilted in inequality. On one hand, the analyst up there trying to remain courteous without assuming an attitude of superiority, authoritarianism or mystery; while, on the other hand, looking down on the patient as a sick, needy child who is to be understood in a kind of ". . . mothering activity, a form of feeding, nurturing, protecting, teaching the patient-child . . ." (p. 378). He wonders whether the process of obtaining insight may be a remnant of strivings for omnipotence (1967, p. 397) and he is critical of some of his colleagues for being more concerned with the purity of psychoanalysis than with improving their therapeutic results (1967, p. 404).

I think I have produced enough evidence for my suggestion that the traditional, classic, analytic technique resulted in an ambience of authoritarian distance, not to say coldness, of analyst versus a patient who was looked upon as sick, perhaps childlike, and who was treated in a mode reminiscent of the medical-surgical model of the ancestry of psychoanalysis. It is not often pointed out that the traditional environment, with the detached, objective analyst who pretends not to feel or care, and who acts as if he knows the patient's thoughts and feelings better than the patient himself, is bound to arouse anger by depriving the patient of needed recognition, concern, and even respect. Traditional technique is likely to create an adversarial ambience, in which the patient's evoked anger is easily but mistakenly interpreted as the patient's aggressive drive. I recall how I experienced my first analysis as a humiliating procedure carried out by an uncaring and even spiteful man whose Olympian pronouncements I recognized only much later to have been his habitual defense against his uncertainty and low self-esteem, albeit that my narcissistic grandiosity was a chronic provocation to him. My experience, unfortunately, was not unusual at that time and many potentially creative young psychiatrists were decisively discouraged from pursuing promising analytic careers by experiencing or hearing about similarly painful psychoanalytic encounters.

How is the situation today? Vastly different, I think. For those who were influenced by Kohut, either directly or through his writings, this change will not come as any surprise. In an analysis or in a psychoanalytic psychotherapy conducted within the framework of self psychology, the obsolete authoritarianism has given way to a reciprocal relationship of equal participants in a mutual, interactive process. Long stretches of silence and nonresponsiveness have become a rarity. The self psychological analyst is an interested participant whose attunement to the analysand becomes evident when his comments reveal a deep understanding of the analysand's experience, especially affective experience, during the analytic session as well as of the analysand's extra-analytic interactions and experiences. The therapist is not restricted to making interpretations, but questions, clarifications, comments, and suggestions and self-revelations can usefully be made within the on-going process without interfering with the gradual unfolding of an analyzable transference relationship. It is difficult to do justice to the subtlety of change because everything I have mentioned may at times also be part of the more traditional, classic technique. The most important and compelling aspect of the self psychological technique is the consistent and systematic posture of empathy, of seeing the psychological world from the point of view of the analysand and not from some supposedly neutral perspective. To understand from an empathic point of view should not be misunderstood as necessarily implying that the understanding analyst is in agreement with the analysand's view. There are many ways to express one's understanding, for example, by one's tone of voice, by the phrasing of one's comments, by one's acceptance, (whether in agreement or disagreement), of the reality of the other person's perspectives. One might say that the authoritative certainty of the analyst has been replaced by a democratic recognition of multiple, competing uncertainties. Above all, empathic attunement is affective attunement, an understanding and resonance with the other's emotional experience; the one-way street has been opened to two-way traffic. To distort and dismiss empathic attunement as "collusion" is doing a disservice to analysts and analysands.

I cannot quantify these changes. I cannot measure how much traditionally oriented psychoanalytic treatment has changed from a few decades ago. I doubt that our traditionally minded colleagues conduct their analyses in the kind of cold and authoritarian atmosphere that was the model thirty years ago. Our whole culture has moved into a more egalitarian mode, from which even the most isolated analyst in his consulting room is not totally immune. Today's patients and clients, especially the younger ones, would hardly tolerate the deprivations and incognito that Greenson mentioned as necessary in 1967.

DEVELOPMENTAL CONSIDERATIONS

Tolpin (1986) first elaborated on how traditional ego psychology sees babies as undifferentiated, narcissistic, greedy, driven, and sometimes sadistically and enviously torn between good and bad part objects; this in contrast to the view held by contemporary self psychological psychoanalysts, who observe integrated babies in mutually reciprocal and responsive interactions with their mothers (the metamorphosis of "Freud's baby" into "Kohut's baby"). Murphy (1980) pointed out that although the ego psychological "concept of adaptation included active dealing with the environment, the terms 'adaptation' and 'adjustment' tend to be used with the connotation of fitting in, as if the environment were something static out there and the infant is a pliable thing to be somehow squeezed into it" (p. 324). The earliest psychoanalytic writers were concerned primarily with the baby's drives' seeking satisfaction and their reflection in experiences of frustration, deprivation and overindulgence. The psychoanalytic situation was fruitful in providing data that could be used to reconstruct developmental sequences. Classically, the view of infancy implied a baby without an ego; the mother, therefore, had to be the infant's ego. The intense communicative activity between infants and mothers had not yet been studied. Instead, the accent was placed on the apparent narcissistic state of the infant. Even Kohut did not think that infants had developed a cohesive self before eighteen months of age. Without ego or self, the general impression of infants was of weak parasites living in symbiotic relation to their environment. The mother was conceptualized as making her observations and judgments and then autonomously acting upon the infant. It is not difficult to recognize here the aforementioned model of the physician with his patients.

In contemporary developmental psychology, the view of the infant is different (Stern, 1985). Part of this change came about by adding to the data obtained from adults in psychoanalysis the data obtained from close and systematic observations of infants with mothers. Moreover, the same factors that brought about a change in the analytic situation and its ambience probably also have influenced the way contemporary observers look at infant–mother interactions. It is, of course, not the infants and the mothers that have changed, but the theories of the observers, which now allow data to be collected that before could not be noticed. Mothers and infants are now seen to be in reciprocal interactions, influencing each other. The metaphor of a one-way street having become a two-way road is applicable here as well. No longer is it only the mother acting on infants; instead, one can study now the emergence quite early, perhaps at birth, of an infant as an independent center of initiative, who actively seeks selfobject experiences via interactive transactions. Reciprocity of influence is seen where once only unidirectional effects could be registered. To use the language of politics, one might say that the relationship between parents and infants, as revealed by contemporary research, have become democratized.

The theory shift from drives to object relations and then to the self is an important factor in bringing the practicing psychotherapist closer to developmental psychology. The change in psychoanalytic perspective from an authoritarian to an egalitarian model for the psychoanalytic situation, and the analogous shift from the undifferentiated, acted-upon baby of Freud to Kohut's baby as an interactive center of initiative was, however, preceded by another analogous shift in the physics of small particles. Kohut (1977, p. 31n) already called attention to the parallelism between the development of physics from the Newtonian theory to the quantum theory, and the development of psychoanalysis from Freudian metapsychology to the psychology of the self. Among the various parallels, Kohut points out that in modern physics, the means of observation and the target of observation constitute a unit that, in certain respects, is in principle, indivisible. Kohut stresses that the counterpart in self psychology is its fundamental claim that the presence of the empathic or introspective observer defines, in fact, the psychological field. In Kohut's posthumous work (1984, pp. 36–38) he again called attention to the analogy between the physics of small particles and self psychology; in particular that, fundamentally, the observing agency is always a part of what is being observed. I cannot escape the observation that the interest in mutual interactions of the most intimate kind, including those that seem to dissolve the boundaries between objects, started not in psychology but in physics. With the object inescapably acting on the observer and the observer inescapably acting on the object, the hierarchical view of reality is put in question. It is intriguing to think that Heisenberg and Bohr (cited in Kohut, 1977, p. 31n) unwittingly may have been prophets of antihierarchical revolutions not only in science, including psychoanalysis and developmental psychology, but also in Russia, China, and Eastern Europe.[1]

NORMALITY AND PATHOLOGY

Let us take another look at psychoanalytic patients and the nature of their illness. What do we mean when we call the patients sick? Hartmann (1939) put it succinctly:

> As is well known, it is never at any time an easy matter to say what we really mean by "health" and "illness" and perhaps the difficulty of differentiating between them is even greater when we are concerned with the so-called "psychological illnesses" than it is with physical maladies. Health is certainly not a purely statistical average . . . [p. 4–5].

I think we may clarify this issue by asking more directly about psychoanalysis: Does it treat illness or does it reorganize disturbed relationships between people? Perhaps psychoanalysis does both, and one's answer to this question is a matter of emphasis. If one conceptualizes in the terms of a one-body psychology, then one probably thinks in terms of health or illness of this one-body object. However, if one thinks about individuals as always existing within a network of relationships, that is, as conceptualized within a two-body psychology, one is more likely to think about the harmony or disharmony of these interactions without needing to conceptualize health or illness. When a therapist by his unresponsiveness creates what most normal people experience as the discomfort of abstinent deprivation, an attempt by the patient to correct or protect the relationship by doing something, for example, being provocative, withdrawing, or whatever, is not pathological or wrong. What is

---

[1]The microbiological theories of Lynn Margulis that see complex organisms as conglomerates of cooperating symbiotic cells held together by billions of microbes seem to me like a template for the organization of societies and cultures evolving out of the symbiotic network of selfobject relationships.

wrong is to label "pathological" the patient's restitutive efforts at restoring a more cohesive self by manipulating relationships.

Kohut was well aware of the need to define normality. He quotes C. Daly King that the "average may be, and very often is abnormal. The normal, on the other hand, is objectively, and properly, to be defined as *that which functions in accordance with its design.*" King's formula allows a fixed point on which to anchor discussions of health and illness if one can agree on what is the design and the functioning of the structure or process under consideration. Protecting the integrity of structure and functioning against noxious influences by invoking a restitutive reaction is clearly functioning in accordance with design as we understand it.

This brings us back to self psychology and Heinz Kohut. Kohut supervised me as a candidate, and during subsequent years I consulted him on numerous occasions. I recall vividly how astonished I was, at first, when I would come in for supervision and to proudly demonstrate my diagnostic detective skills in bringing to light hidden psychopathology, only to have Kohut gently but firmly point out the self-protecting motivations underlying this so-called pathology. Working with Kohut gradually turned my psychoanalytic clinical world upside down. Where I had a tendency, with a sense of physicianly superiority, to confront patients with their sick impulses and obnoxious defenses, Kohut taught me to appreciate the same phenomena as needed for the restoration of health-preserving, selfobject experiences in interaction with others. In a report on his consultations with Kohut, Miller (1985, p. 14) recounted Kohut's emphasis on the naturalness of patient responses. When a patient seemingly overreacted to the analyst's sneeze, Kohut stressed the intrusiveness of the stimulus rather than the sensitivity of the analysand. It would be easy to mention many more revealing examples of Kohut's thinking.

SUMMARY

During the last 200 years, Western society has gradually moved in the direction of an antiauthoritarian and democratizing trend. One might paraphrase Freud by saying: Where there were kings, there shall parliaments be. This liberalizing evolution has not been painless but has been interrupted at intervals by violent reactions in the form of ideologically motivated wars. Similar trends have also been observable in the sciences and the arts. One consequence in philosophy, for instance, has been a loss of the old certainties and the ascent of a relativistic approach to age-old questions of truth and knowledge.

(Galatzer-Levy, 1980). Psychoanalysis has been similarly affected by this trend, which in psychoanalytic science is represented by the shift from the classical, Freudian doctor–patient relationship to the less authoritarian, analyst–analysand relationship characteristic of Kohutian self psychology. This shift is noticeable, not only in clinical attitudes, but also in theoretical conceptualizations that give added emphasis to the subjective centrality of empathy and self rather than to the objective interactions of drives and defenses within a quasimechanical apparatus, the ego. Furthermore, the same shift can also be noticed in changing conceptualizations as well as changing attitudes regarding the mother–infant couple. Seen within this larger context of an historical progression, Kohutian self psychology, together with developmental psychology, are the leading edge of an evolution toward a psychologically less hierarchical, more open, and freer world.

REFERENCES

Beigler, J. S. (1975), A commentary on Freud's treatment of the Rat Man. (Presented to the Chicago Psychoanalytic Society, Chicago, IL. 1974.

Beigler, J. S. (1975), A commentary on Freud's treatment of the Rat Man. The *Annual of Psychoanalysis*, 3:271–285. New York: International Universities Press.

Bettelheim, B. (1983), *Freud and Man's Soul*. London: Chatto & Windus.

Blanton, S. (1971), *Diary of My Analysis With Sigmund Freud*. New York: Hawthorn Books.

Eissler, K. R. (1950), The Chicago Institute of Psychoanalysis and the sixth period of the development of psychoanalytic technique. *J. Gen. Psychol.*, 42:103–157.

Freud, S. (1912), Recommendations to physicians practicing psychoanalysis. *Standard Edition*, 12:111–120. London: Hogarth Press, 1958.

––––––– (1915), Observations on transference love. *Standard Edition*, 12:159–171. London: Hogarth Press, 1958.

––––––– (1926), The Question of lay analysis. *Standard Edition* 20:177–250. London: Hogarth Press, 1959.

––––––– (1927), The future of an illusion. *Standard Edition* 21:5–56. London: Hogarth Press, 1961.

––––––– (1928), Letter to Oskar Pfister of November 11, 1928. In: *Briefe 1909–1939*, Frankfurt: S. Fischer Verlag, 1963, p. 136.

H. D. [Doolittle, H.] (1956), *Tribute to Freud*. New York: Pantheon Books.

Galatzer-Levy, R. (1980), Characterizing our ignorance. *The Annual of Psychoanalysis*, 8:77–82. New York: International Universities Press.

Galatzer-Levy, R. & Cohler, B. (1989), The developmental psychology of the self and the changing worldview of psychoanalysis. *The Annual of Psychoanalysis*, 18:1–43. Hillsdale, NJ: The Analytic Press.

Greenson, R. (1967), *The Technique and Practice of Psychoanalysis*. New York: International Universities Press.

Grunberger, B. (1966), Some reflections on the Rat Man. *Internat. J. Psycho-Analysis*, 47:160–168.

Hartmann, H. (1939), The concept of health. In: *Essays in Psychology*. New York: International Universities Press, 1964.

Kanzer, M. (1952), The transference neurosis of the Rat Man. *Psychoanal. Quart.*, 21:181-189.

Khan, M. M. R. (1973). Mrs. Alix Strachey (Obituary). *Internat. J. Psycho-Anal.*, 54:370.

King, C. D. (1945), The meaning of normal. *Yale J. Biol. and Med.* 17:493-501.

Kohut, H. (1959) In: *The Search for the Self*, Vol. 2, ed. P. Ornstein New York: International Universities Press, 1978, pp. 205-232.

_____ (1977), *The Restoration of the Self*. New York: International Universities Press.

_____ (1984), *How Does Analysis Cure?* ed. A. Goldberg & P. Stepansky. Chicago: University of Chicago Press.

Kris, E. (1951), Ego psychology and interpretation in psychoanalytic therapy. *Psychoanal. Quart.*, 20:15-30.

Lewin, B. D. (1946), Countertransference in the technique of medical practice. *Psychosom. Med.*, 8:195-199.

Lipton, S. (1977) The advantages of Freud's technique as shown in his analysis of the Rat Man. *Internat. J. Psycho-Anal.* 58:255-273.

Mannoni, O. (1971), *Freud*, (trans. R. Bruce). New York: Pantheon Books.

Miller, J. (1985), How Kohut actually worked. In: *Progress in Self Psychology, Vol. 1*, ed. A. Goldberg. New York: Guilford Press, pp. 13-30.

Murphy, L. (1980), Psychoanalytic views of infancy. In: *The Course of Life, Vol. 1.*, eds. S. Greenspan & G. H. Pollock. Washington, DC: US Govt. Print. Off., 313-363.

Prawer, S. S. (1983 July 29), Freud and Man's Soul. *New York Times Literary Supplement*, p. 812.

Ruitenbeek, H. M. (ed.) (1973), *Freud As We Knew Him*. Detroit, MI: Wayne State University Press.

Sherwood, M. (1969), *The Logic of Explanation in Psychoanalysis*. New York: Academic Press.

Stern, D. (1985), *The Interpersonal World of the Infant*. New York: Basic Books.

Stone, L. (1961), *The Psychoanalytic Situation*. New York: International Universities Press.

Tolpin, M. (1986), The self and its selfobjects: A different baby. *In: Progress in Self Psychology, Vol. 2*, ed. A. Goldberg. New York: Guilford Press, pp. 115-128.

Weiner, N. D. (1973), Aposiopesis: a special type of silence. *Bull. Phil. Assn. for Psychoanal.*, 23:281-287.

Wortis, J. (1954), *Fragments of an Analysis With Freud*. New York: Simon & Schuster.

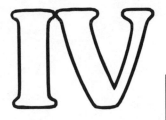

Exhibitionism
in Group
Psychotherapy

Chapter 14

Hamlet: The Self of Despair

Hyman L. Muslin

In its 350-year-old history, Shakespeare's tragedy of Hamlet aroused endless commentary from literary critics (Bradley, 1904; Wilson, 1935; Hawkes, 1959; Knight, 1961), philosophers (Goethe, 1899), and psychoanalysts (Freud, 1900; Jones, 1949; Eissler, 1971). From their respective disciplinary orientations, students of the play have posed and attempted to answer certain basic questions that Wirtz (1966) summarized: Is Hamlet mad? Is Gertrude an adulteress? Does Hamlet vacillate? Why is Hamlet tragic? Why does he doubt the ghost? In this chapter, I comment on these timeless questions by reviewing the tragic history of Hamlet, the record of a self struggling to overcome a pervasive state of weakness and disharmony. In adopting this perspective, I will attempt to illuminate, within the idiom of psycho-analytic self psychology, Goethe's (1899) classic observation that Hamlet's tragedy is that of ". . . a great deed imposed upon a soul unequal to the performance of it" (p. 282).

At the outset of the drama, we confront a Hamlet suffering from the experience of his own futility. In the first of his seven soliloquies, he summarizes the various burdens contributing to this sense of futility. These burdens, which revolve around his uncle Claudius's usurpation of the throne of Denmark and his mother's sin of incest (from the standpoint of Elizabethan ecclesiastical law) with Claudius, are soon compounded by the appearance of his father's ghost, attempting to rouse Hamlet to action. Here are the terms in which

Hamlet introduces us to the malaise centering on his pathologically diminished sense of self:

> O that this too too solid flesh would melt,
> Thaw, and resolve itself into a dew!
> Or that the Everlasting had not fixed
> His canon 'gainst self-slaughter! O God! O God!
> How weary, stale, flat, and unprofitable
> Seem to me all the uses of this world!
> Fie on't! ah, fie! [Act I, Scene II, l. 135–141*]

And then directly after unfolding his pervasive anhedonia, Hamlet goes to the heart of his hurt—his mother, who had been so devoted to his father, had deserted his memory (and him) so soon after he died. He rails on:

> Within a month,
> Ere yet the salt of most unrighteous tears
> Had left the flushing in her galled eyes,
> She married. O, most wicked speed, to post
> With such dexterity to incestuous sheets!
> It is not, nor it cannot come to good.
> But break my heart, for I must hold my tongue!
> [Act I, Scene II, l. 159–165]

The ghost of Hamlet's father appears shortly thereafter, commanding Hamlet to take vengeance on the uncle who has slain him and who now commits incest with Hamlet's mother, Queen Gertrude. But these demands are not sufficient to stir Hamlet to the action of revenge, Hamlet continues to reveal his enervated self. In his second soliloquy, following his confrontation with the ghost, Hamlet cries:

> O all you host of heaven! O earth! What else?
> And shall I couple hell? O fie! Hold, hold, my heart!
> And you, my sinews, grow not instant old,
> But bear me stiffly up.
> [Act I, Scene V, l. 99–103]

Although he is concerned that his "sinews will grow old" he resolves himself to revenge him on his executors:

---

*All quotations from *Hamlet* from *The Folger Library General Reader's Shakespeare*, 1958.

I'll wipe away all trivial fond records,
All saws of books, all forms, all pressures past,
That youth and observation copied there;
And thy commandment all alone shall live
Within the book and volume of my brain,
Unmixed with baser matter. Yes, by heaven!
O most pernicious woman!
O villain, villain, smiling, damned villain!
[Act I, Scene V, l. 107–114]

Significantly, it is not until the "play within the play" and the emergence of Claudius's guilt later in the drama that Hamlet, and the audience as well, become convinced that the ghost he encountered in Act I is really a spirit of the departed father of Hamlet returning from Purgatory on a special mission and not a devil in disguise. On meeting the ghost, therefore, Hamlet's burden does not merely reside in the ghost's challenge that Hamlet be his avenger; the burden further concerns Hamlet's inability to give himself over to the ghost, given his doubts about the ghost's provenance.

In this connection, Wilson (1935) pointed out that the depiction of the ghost in Hamlet as a dramatically convincing humanized spectre was a revolutionary innovation in Shakespeare's time. The four witnesses of the ghost embody the various attitudes of different Elizabethans to such a spectre. The Catholic viewpoint, represented by Marcellus and Bernardo, holds that "ghosts might be departed spirits returning from Purgatory with a special purpose" (Wilson, 1935, p. 12). The Protestant viewpoint, represented by Hamlet himself, questions the existence of Purgatory and deems it more likely that ghosts are devils who, in the guise of departed relatives, may harm those before whom they appear. Last, the skeptic viewpoint, represented by Horatio, prior to his own vision of the ghost, rejects the claim that ghosts are real and can assume a material form.

By the end of Act I, Hamlet's basic uncertainty about the meaning of the ghost compounds the pervasive mood of depression that antedates the ghost's appearance. This depression, to repeat, constitutes a reaction to several related events: (a) the death of his father; (b) the royal council's acceptance of Claudius as successor to King Hamlet; and (c) the marriage of his mother to Claudius shortly after his father's death.

In addition to the fact of his manifest depression, Hamlet's mysterious behavior toward his heretofore trusted comrades stands out in Act I of the play. Hamlet is unwilling to relate to his friends the exchange with the ghost that culminates in the command to kill King Claudius; indeed, he demands that his friends swear an oath never to reveal that they have seen the spirit at all. It is at this juncture in the play, furthermore, that Hamlet decides "To put an antic disposition on" (Act I. Scene V, line 195), that is, to exhibit psychotic behavior. In the famous cellarage scene that follows, we find Hamlet behaving inappropriately, joking and punning with the departing ghost, whose voice seems to come from the ground.

By this point in the play, Shakespeare presented us with material clearly indicating that Hamlet experienced a profound alteration of his self. Prior to the appearance of the ghost-father, Hamlet's enfeebled self effectively paralyzes his resolve. When the ghost-father appears and issues the command to spill blood, Hamlet's initial reactions betoken a unique phenomenon; we see Hamlet's failure to avenge his father as a dramatic characterization of the ineptitude of the self. Nowhere in literature is a picture of diminished self-esteem more finely drawn. Whereas literary critics explain Hamlet's procrastination in executing the ghost's command as "a convenient disguise while he was maturing his plans" (Wilson, 1935, p. 202), [p. 202] (18), and psychoanalytic critics relate Hamlet's difficulties to inhibitions attendant upon his revived oedipal strivings (Jones, 1949; Eissler, 1971), I believe Shakespeare's presentation in Act I points to a more compelling alternative interpretation: Hamlet's failure to act reflects the depleted vigor of a pathologically weakened self.

The content of Acts II and III represents the testing of the ghost's story or, to put it differently, Hamlet's attempts to ascertain the authenticity of the ghost's story by probing the secret guilt of Claudius and Gertrude. Here Hamlet begins to show his characteristic symptoms of "madness," first to his sweetheart Ophelia and subsequently to all the members of the court. His symptoms take the form of loosened associations and inappropriate affect; they are sufficient to gain the attention of the King and the court who construe them as a modal reaction to Ophelia's rejection of Hamlet's lovesuit, albeit throughout the play, Claudius continues to suspect Hamlet's underlying wishes to regain the throne of Denmark. Claudius summons Rosencrantz and Guildenstern, old cronies of Hamlet, to determine the cause of the Prince's "antic disposition," what Claudius calls "Hamlet's transformation" (Act II. Scene II, l. 5). Hamlet unburdens himself to his two former friends in the following way:

> I have of late—but wherefore I know not—lost all my mirth, forgone all custom of exercises; and indeed it goes so heavily with my disposition that this goodly frame, the earth, seems to me a sterile promontory; this most excellent canopy, the air, look you . . . why it appears no other thing to me than a foul and pestilent congregation of vapors. What a

piece of work is a man! how noble in reason! . . . And yet to me what is this quintessence of dust? Man delights not me—no, nor woman neither . . . [Act II, Scene II, l. 309–325].

At this juncture in the drama, a company of players arrive at the castle, and Hamlet seizes on the idea that the troupe should perform a play, *The Murder of Gonzago,* which will prod the King's conscience. It seems that the passing of time has diminished the effect of the ghost's revelation, and we now find Hamlet attempting to reassure himself that he has in fact beheld a ghost and not a devil. But the ensuing soliloquy makes it clear that he continues to experience a paralysis of will. Hamlet now says of himself:

> Now I am alone.
> O, what a rogue and peasant slave am I!
> [Act II, Scene II, l. 555–556]

He goes on to say:

> Yet I,
> a dull and muddy-mettled rascal, peak
> like John-a-dreams, unpregnant of my cause,
> and can say nothing!"
> [Act II, Scene II, l. 573–576].

Hamlet continues:

> Am I a coward?
> Who calls me villain? breaks my pate across?
> plucks off my beard and blows it in my face?
> [Act II, Scene II, l. 577–580].

And once more:

> 'Swounds, I should take it! for it cannot be
> But I am pigeon-livered and lack gall
> To make oppression bitter, or ere this
> I should have fatted all the region kites
> With this slave's offal.
> [Act II, Scene II, l. 583–587]

Through his anguished self-recriminations, Hamlet continues to manifest the self-hatred that derives from his fractured resolve and inability to take action. He now hopes that the device of the play will strengthen his determination to fulfill the vow he has made to the ghost of his father. The same current of inaction and self-abuse appear elsewhere when Hamlet contrasts the attractiveness of death with his fears of the after-life:

> To die—to sleep.
> To sleep—perchance to dream: ay, there's the rub!
> For in that sleep of death what dreams may come
> when we have shuffled off this mortal coil,
> must give us pause.
> [Act III, Scene I, l. 71–75]

Hamlet's rageful dismissal of Ophelia in the famous "Get thee to a nunnery" sequence (Act III. Scene I, l. 130) constitutes yet a further interruption to the definitive uncovering of Claudius's guilt. Ophelia, to be sure, has entered into a conspiracy against Hamlet with her father and her monarch, and Hamlet has in all probability suspected this collusion. But his anger at her has a second source: For Hamlet, Ophelia is clearly identified with the mother who is, in no small way, responsible for Claudius's usurpation of the throne. Although Gertrude was the original agent of disappointment to Hamlet in the play, Ophelia disappoints Hamlet mightily. She rejects his appeals for comfort (Act II. Scene I, l. 82–85) and ultimately conspires against him.

We arrive at the ingenious play within the play that parallels the story of king Hamlet's demise (Gonzago in the play) by poisoning at the hands of the villain Claudius (Lucianus in the play). On viewing the play, Claudius indeed becomes distressed and leaves the performance. Hamlet responds with elation and, ostensibly reassured that the ghost he encountered was not a devil in disguise, goes on to say:

> Now could I drink hot blood
> and do such bitter business as the day
> would quake to look on.
> [Act III, Scene III, l. 397–399]

Having made this powerful declaration, it would seem that Hamlet is finally energized to the point of taking his vengeance and thereby fulfilling his vow to the ghost. No so! Approaching the kneeling Claudius, Hamlet experiences yet another inhibition, this one in the form of an elaborate rationalization. Because Claudius is in the process of purging his soul through prayer, Hamlet reasons, to murder him now would only ensure his swift passage to heaven.

Better to wait and kill Claudius at a more opportune time—during sex, or gaming, or swearing.

Hamlet's confrontation with his mother following *The Murder of Gonzago* is perhaps the most exciting and revealing scene in the entire tragedy. Having once again delayed in his mission to revenge his father by killing Claudius, Hamlet now enters his mother's room. Queen Gertrude, we are informed, has entered into a conspiracy with Polonius in an attempt to stifle Hamlet's "pranks." As Hamlet's demeanor on entering her room is clearly agitated and violent, Gertrude sounds an alarm and calls for help. When Polonius echoes her cries for help from behind the curtain where he is hiding, Hamlet, believing him to be Claudius, stabs blindly through the curtain. Even after discovering that it is Polonius whom he has killed, Hamlet continues to rail at his mother, recounting once more her egregious misdeed of marrying Claudius and thus committing incest. As Hamlet continues in his agitated tirade, Gertrude pleads for mercy:

> O Hamlet, speak no more!
> Thou turn'st mine eyes into my very soul,
> And there I see such black and grained spots
> As will not leave their tinct.
> [Act III, Scene IV, l. 99–102]

Suddenly the ghost enters. Frightened, Hamlet pleads for mercy and direction. The ghost reminds Hamlet of his mission and admonishes him not to tarry in his visit to his mother:

> Hamlet: Do you not come your tardy son to chide,
> That, lapsed in time and passion, lets go by
> The important acting of your dread command? O, say!
> Ghost: Do not forget. This visitation
> Is but to whet thy almost blunted purpose.
> But look, amazement on thy mother sits.
> O, step between her and her fighting soul!
> Conceit in weakest bodies strongest works.
> Speak to her, Hamlet.
> [Act III, Scene IV, l. 121–130]

Gertrude, however, not sharing Hamlet's vision of the ghost, now becomes gentler with her seemingly disturbed son. But Hamlet remains inconsolable and continues to revile against his mother for her crime of incest. Finally, after extracting from Gertrude a promise that she will not be disloyal to him and reveal to Claudius that Hamlet

is "not in madness," Hamlet leaves. His parting words to his mother
are filled with gentleness.

For me, this scene is the crux of the play. We see Hamlet in a state
of disarray so severe that his mother is instantly alarmed. It is
noteworthy that, having unleased his violence on Polonius, Hamlet's
verbal assault on his mother continues unabated:

> O Shame! where is they blush? Rebellious hell
> If thou canst mutiny in a matron's bones,
> To flaming youth let virtue be a wax
> And melt in her own fire.
> [Act III, Scene IV, l. 92–95]

As Hamlet's rage abates, he becomes reconciled with his mother;
his episode of fragmentation has passed. What Shakespeare depicts
for us in this scene is the intrapsychic disarray of a fragmented self
unable to control impulses. In fact, as Hamlet's fierce anger toward
his mother continues throughout the scene, it becomes clear that
Hamlet is not acting aggressively toward a fully differentiated object,
but is immersed in narcissistic rage deriving from the failure of a
maternal selfobject to perform functions necessary to his very sense of
self-cohesion. Gertrude, it should be remembered, is accused
throughout the play—by herself as well as by others—of both an "o'er
hasty marriage" and of depriving Hamlet of the throne. In his angry
tirade of Act III, and throughout the play as well, Hamlet is always
ready to rail at Gertrude for defaming and defiling his father, on the
surface at least paying little or no attention to his own losses as son of
the murdered king and successor to the throne. But his defenses
prove inadequate, and in the crucial scene in question, we finally see
the essential Hamlet, a Hamlet so engulfed in narcissistic rage that he
is on the verge of inflicting Nero-like violence on his mother.
Deflected in Shakespeare's conceit by the introduction of two distrac-
tions—the aged conspirator Polonius and the reappearance of the
ghost of his father who directs Hamlet not to forget his mission of
revenge—Hamlet's narcissistic rage finally subsides and he is able to
reestablish a self–selfobject bond through which Gertrude comforts
him, that is, performs a vitally needed selfobject function.

The remaining portion of the play deals with Hamlet's conquest
over Claudius in several particulars. He succeeds in conspiring
against his conspirators, Rosencrantz and Guildenstern, that is, he
arranges for their death in England, the very fate they had planned
for him. It is, however, only in the final dueling scene in the castle
that Hamlet succeeds in killing King Claudius, even as he and his

mother die practically together from poisoned rapiers and poisoned wine. In the ensuing discussion, we shall return to the outcome of the play as a commentary on the final vicissitude of Hamlet's fluctuating self-states.

DISCUSSION

Freud (1900), Jones (1949), and Eissler (1971), who have provided much of the principal psychoanalytic critiques of *Hamlet*, are all convinced that Hamlet's tragedy is the tragedy of the Oedipus complex. It is Hamlet's identification with his father's killer, they reason, that is at the heart of his tragic inaction. In killing Claudius, Freud (1900) remarked, Hamlet would effectively be killing himself. Jones's more substantial treatment of the play restates Freud's early verdict. Hamlet detests Claudius, Jones (1949) observes:

. . . but it is the jealous detestation of one evil doer towards his successful fellow. Much as he hates him, he can never denounce him with the ardent indignation that boils straight from his blood when he reproaches his mother, for the more vigorously he denounces his uncle, the more powerfully does he stimulate to activity his own unconscious and repressed complexes. (p. 88)

Eissler (1971) approaches the study of Hamlet from the view of Freud's ego psychology. His thesis is as follows:

If a man is to become an adult he must, in his unconscious, kill his father and accept incest. The path is tortuous and painful. Hamlet succeeds in slaying the father and in reducing the good father to a memory of something that he has now outgrown; he loses his horror of incest and commits the oedipal crime, albeit symbolically (p. 129)

Virtually every facet of the tragedy of Hamlet has been explored by the psychoanalytic critic: Hamlet's Oedipus complex, the poison in the ear, the play within the play, the Ghost, Claudius, Gertrude, Queen, Hamlet's antic madness, Ophelia's death, and Osric. Virtually every psychoanalytic school and other nonpsychoanalytic commentary have been represented in the criticism of the play: Classical psychoanalysis [Freud, 1900; Jones, 1949], ego psychology (Eissler, 1971), Eriksonian psychology (Erikson, 1962), Freedman and Jones, (1963), Lacanian psychoanalysis (Lacan, 1977), the object-relations approach (Leverenz, 1980), and authors utilizing psychoanalytic views (Erlich, 1977; Lidz, 1975).

In contrast to these viewpoints, my discussion will derive from the viewpoints of psychoanalytic self psychology, which center on the experiences of the self. Moreover, in my view, the vantage points of self psychology are especially relevant to an understanding of this play because I perceive the central issue in the play to be the depiction of a self so immersed in a feeling of worthlessness that its capacity to act is stymied.

From the standpoint of poetics, Shakespeare's *Hamlet* qualifies as a tragedy because it deals with a hero–protagonist who falls from greatness as a result of a tragic fault, hamartia, or unforseen circumstances. In Hamlet's case, the descent is initiated by a series of massive losses, and the unfolding tragedy revolves around the 30-year-old prince's psychologically comprehensible reaction to these losses. What exactly were Hamlet's losses? Most obviously, there is the loss of his father. Throughout the play, the deceased King Hamlet is equated with Hyperion, the Greek god of the sun. In general, Hamlet speaks of his father as the ideal monarch and ideal husband for whom Claudius can be no match. Of the suffering Hamlet himself has experienced through the loss of his father, we hear nothing.

More psychologically telling than the loss of the father is the loss of the mother, whose abandonment of Hamlet ushers in the self-experience of worthlessness that Shakespeare describes so powerfully. From the outset of the play, we encounter the melancholy Dane, whose deep grief cannot be appreciated, least of all by his mother. Gertrude's first speech to her son begins with this admonition:

> Good Hamlet, cast thy nighted color off,
> And let thine eye look like a friend on Denmark.
> Do not for ever with they vailed lids.
> Seek for thy noble father in the dust.
> Thou know'st 'tis common, all that lives must die,
> Passing through nature to eternity.
> [Act I, Scene II, l. 71–77]

Hamlet, we recall, rejects the implication that he should abruptly terminate his mourning and attempts to clarify for his mother his genuinely depressed emotional state. But Gertrude remains unresponsive to Hamlet's protestations of distress and urges him to remain at court rather than return to Wittenberg. Hamlet accedes to his mother's request, but his exchange with her ushers in the first soliloquy, in which he unmistakably reveals the true depth of his despair.

In contrast to his reverence for his departed father, Hamlet has only criticism for his mother, but it is never criticism that openly focuses on her lack of maternal support for him. Instead, Hamlet is content to berate Gertrude continually for marrying her brother-in-law, and especially for marrying him in such haste. Significantly, in the only point in the drama where Hamlet alludes to his own frustrated wishes for the throne, he implicates only his uncle as the culprit, leaving unmentioned the mother who is equally responsible for the act of usurpation (Act V, Scene II, l. 71).

But Shakespeare provides us with ample hints of the psychological state of affairs that underlies Hamlet's disinclination to castigate his mother on his own behalf. In the first soliloquy, for example, Hamlet not only describes his despair, but reveals the hurt his mother has inflicted on him. Thus, at the same time as he rails about her incestuous union with Claudius, he simultaneously protests her mistreatment of him. From this vantage point, the most telling line comes at the end of the soliloquy:

> But break my heart, for I must hold my tongue!
> [Act I, Scene II, l. 165]

This line encompasses the self-experience of a deserted Hamlet, a Hamlet whose maternally empty world has become "weary, stale, flat and unprofitable" (Act I, Scene II, line 139). Why must Hamlet hold his tongue? It is the second time in the soliloquy that he has attempted to distract himself from ruminations about his mother's actions. Earlier in the soliloquy he remarked:

> Let me not think on't! Frailty, thy name is woman!
> [Act I, Scene II, l. 150].

I believe these two interjections are very significant; they signify Hamlet's attempt to suppress the festering rage that is consequent to his disappointment in his mother.

To summarize our observations to this point: By the end of the first soliloquy, Shakespeare has already provided us with suggestive evidence that Hamlet is suffering from a narcissistic injury. This injury is triggered by a rebuff from Gertrude, who has been shown to be unempathic to his need for understanding and support and singularly incapable of comprehending the appropriateness of his grief reaction following the murder of his father (and the loss of her). Hamlet's self is thereby depleted and his actions become mired in a self-state of worthlessness. He is vulnerable, both to experiences of fragmentation and to archaic narcissistic rage. From the standpoint of contemporary self psychology, we can appreciate Gertrude's value to Hamlet as an archaic mirroring selfobject (Kohut, 1971), perhaps temporarily cast in this role in response to Hamlet's loss of his father and the breakup of the family unit. To wit, Hamlet's intense suffering is based in the main on the unavailability of a mother who had apparently been reinvested with archaic selfobject functions in the aftermath of King Hamlet's murder. Moreover, the attempt at idealizing his lost father to gain self-strength also failed. Finally the experience of Hamlet in relation to the ghost is that the ghost-father is not able to lead Hamlet to the required action of revenge. The ghost fails as an idealized parent selfobject and cannot serve the prince as the messianic leader in regaining the throne. Critics who have viewed Hamlet's procrastination either as the character trait of a sensitive aesthete or the symptom of an inhibited neurotic have been content to focus on Hamlet's inhibited or inconsistent behavior following the ghost's "command" to obtain vengeance, or following the clear demonstration of Claudius' guilt during the play within the play (Goethe, 1899; Jones, 1949; Eissler, 1971). What these critics overlook is the fact that Hamlet's distress antedates these particulars; it is a distress that is present from the beginning of the play and is represented as emanating from the vicissitudes of a disturbed self–selfobject relationship between the prince and his mother, and the failure of his compensatory attempts to gain an infusion of strength from the idealized memories of his father and the resurrected father's ghost.

The next phase in Hamlet's deteriorating self-state finds the prince actually displaying the disposition of the distraught, fragmented madman who frightens Ophelia and induces Claudius to send Rosencrantz and Guildenstern to calm him and, of course, to determine the extent of his wishes to usurp Claudius from his throne. Although Hamlet's mission of revenge is now buried beneath a mask of madness, he continues to reveal to his erstwhile comrades the extent to which his malaise and his inability to act are rooted in a state of melancholy. The entry of the troupe of players momentarily absorbs him in an attempt to determine whether the ghost that accosted him is a true ghost by seeing if the troupe's play can move Claudius' conscience: "The play's the thing wherein I'll catch the conscience of the king" (Act II, Scene II, 1. 612–613). But the weakness of his self-state and resulting inability to act pervade even this gesture. As he reveals in his famous soliloquy:

> To be, or not to be, that is the question:
> Whether 'tis nobler in the mind to suffer

> The slings and arrows of outrageous fortune
> Or to take arms against a sea of troubles,
> And by opposing end them.
> (Act III, Scene I, l. 64–68)

When Ophelia next wishes to return to Hamlet his love letters, the prince, seemingly aware of her collusion with her father and Claudius, experiences a rage reaction in which he reveals his underlying hatred of the woman who disappoints. The referent here, I believe, is clearly his mother:

> Hamlet: If thou dost marry, I'll give thee this plague for thy dowry: be thou as chaste as ice, as pure as snow, thou shalt not escape calumny. Get thee to a nunnery. Go, farewell. Or if thou wilt needs marry, marry a fool; for wise men know well enough what monsters you make of them. To a nunnery, go; and quickly too. Farewell. [Act III, Scene I, l. 145–50]

And then again:

> Hamlet: I have heard of your paintings too, well enough. God hath given you one face, and you make yourselves another. You jig, you amble, and you lisp; you nickname God's creatures and make your wantonness your ignorance. Go to, I'll no more on't! it hath made me mad. I say, we will have no more marriages. Those that are married already—all but one—shall live; the rest shall keep as they are. To a nunnery, go. [Act III, Scene I, l. 152–159]

Thus, behind Hamlet's antic disposition, we see his teeming narcissistic rage at women who "jig and amble and lisp," that is, at the mother who has turned away from the "glass of fashion and mould of form," (which Ophelia has) equated with Hamlet's previous self (Act III, Scene 1, l. 163).

As the players perform the mousetrap play and Claudius reveals his guilt, Hamlet, now exultant, finally appears resolved to fulfill his mission of revenge on Claudius while sparing his mother. Once again, however, he proves unable to execute the act of vengeance in confronting Claudius in the act of prayer.

In the pivotal confrontation with his mother that follows, Hamlet's self is finally revealed in all its complexity. His rage reaction is uncontrollable from the outset of the meeting; he is unable to harness his Nero-like spirit. When Gertrude cries out for help and Polonius answers her from behind the arras, Hamlet's frenzy is at a peak and he kills the man he believes to be Claudius. In this scene, we see the culmination of Hamlet's experience of self-wounding at the hands of Gertrude, as the prince finally reveals the depth of his narcissistic rage that culminate in Hamlet murdering the man he believes to be Gertrude's love object. At this juncture in the play, Hamlet's ordinary sensibilities are diminished and his self is fragmented; Gertrude has reason to be frightened. Indeed, the extent of his rage is such that, having already killed once, he continues in his frenzied state until the hallucination of the ghost appears in the capacity of a calming and soothing agent. Only at this point does Hamlet's violence finally subside.

As Shakespeare depicts it and as it has always been played on the stage, when Hamlet faces Gertrude in her chamber, his manner is so wild that she fears for her safety. As is stated in the Arden Shakespeare's edition (1982), "Evidently the Queen makes as if to depart and is forcibly prevented by Hamlet. The accompanying action is suggested by Q I (First Quarto) at iv.i.8, 'then he throwes and tosses me about' " (p. 319).

Hamlet reveals his manner in the following excerpt:

Hamlet: Come, come, and sit you down, you shall not budge! You go not till I set you up a glass Where you may see the inmost part of you.
Queen: What wilt thou do? Thou wilt not murder me? Help, help, ho.
Polonius: (Behind) What, ho! help, help, help!
Hamlet: (Draws) How how? a rat? Dead for a ducat, dead!
Polonius: (Behind) O, I am slain!
Queen: One, what hast thou done?
Hamlet: Nay, I know, not. Is it the king?
Queen: O, what a rash and bloody deed is this!
Hamlet: A bloody deed, almost as bad, good mother, As kill a king, and marry with his brother. (Act III, Scene IV, 1. 21-35)

This scene is remarkable for its depiction of the reactive self of Hamlet finally unleashing pent-up rage at the disappointing selfobject, the mother, who has abandoned him for another. His wish, not only to preserve the mother but to resurrect her as a source of nurturance, gains expression with the entry of the ghost, able to help contain his Nero-like spirit. The reappearance of the ghost new reveals the ghost performing selfobject functions that do cause an impact on the self of the prince. Clearly Hamlet turns for control to the ghost-father. The ghost-father's responses are in the nature of issuing controlling and calming directives, to which Hamlet responds. Thus, in this scene, the father-ghost is experienced as an idealized parent who gives guidelines for action and who calms and soothes. It will be remembered that previous directions from the ghost were not able to be followed; the prince was previously not able to form a self–selfobject merger with King Hamlet sufficient to fuel his assertiveness and go on and kill Claudius.

The remaining portion of the scene reveals Hamlet and his mother, now in a transformed posture toward each other; she expressing concern over her son's agitated state; he pleading that she remove herself from her new husband:

> Confess yourself to heaven;
> Repent what's past; avoid what is to come;
> And do not spread the compost on the weeds
> To make them ranker. Forgive me this my virtue;
> For in the fatness of these pursy times
> Virtue itself of vice must pardon beg—
> Yea, curb and woo for leave to do him good.
> Queen: O Hamlet, thou hast cleft my heart in twain.
> Hamlet: O, throw away the worser part of it, And live the purer
>   with the other half.
>   Good night—but go not to my uncle's bed.
> [Act III, Scene IV, l. 170–180]

The scene ends with Hamlet still exhibiting self-alterations reflected in his unrestrained speech, as his mother continues to be solicitous of his welfare:

> I'll lug the guts into the neighbor room. —
> Mother, good night. —Indeed, this counsellor
> Is now most still, most secret, and most grave,
> Who was in life a foolish prating knave.
> [Act III, Scene IV, l. 235–238]

What is the aftermath of this emotionally draining scene? Has the confrontation with his mother and guidance from the father-ghost finally steeled Hamlet to do his duty? No! When Claudius orders him to England (where he is to be killed), Hamlet not only obeys, but demonstrates once more his self-paralysis; he rails against himself, vainly trying to inflate himself with a sense of resolve.

It is only at the end of the play, when the dying Gertrude turns only to Hamlet, that Hamlet can finally maim and poison Claudius:

> "O my dear Hamlet!
> The drink, the drink! I am poisoned"   [Dies.]
> [Act V, Scene II, l. 329–330]

Prior to this final farewell, the union between mother and son is seen to be solicitous, from Gertrude's side, and appreciative, from Hamlet's side, as can be seen in the following:

> King: Our son shall win.
> Queen: He's fat and scant of breath. Here, Hamlet, take my napkin, rub thy brows. The Queen carouses to thy fortune, Hamlet
> Hamlet: Good madam! (Act V, Scene II, lines 299–303).

And later:

> Hamlet: I dare not drink, madam; by-and-by.
> Queen: Come, I will wipe thy face. (Act V, Scene II, l. 308–309)

It is the final reestablishment of the self–selfobject bond between mother and son that bolsters Hamlet's self-cohesion to the point of action. Thus Hamlet emerges finally as the prototypical Tragic Man (Kohut, 1977), caught up in his search for self-esteem. His incapacity to act is reflective of his diminished self, which is brought into equilibrium when his self–selfobject bond with Gertrude is restored. From the outset of the tragedy to the final outcome, Shakespeare centered his drama on the melancholy prince preoccupied with his loss of self-worth and his quest to regain his esteem. These are not the preoccupations of Guilty Man, Freud's version of man as the victim of guilt over incestuous wishes (Kohut, 1977).

In conclusion, from the viewpoint of self psychology, the tragic history of Hamlet is that of the mourning prince reacting to an unresponsive environment. His mother will not or cannot empathize with him in his melancholy; she is too absorbed in her romance with her brother-in-law, the new king. The prince turns now to his idealized memories of his deceased father but, here too, he fails to gain the needed supplies to repair his flagging self-esteem. Finally, his reaction to the ghost-father is not effective in instituting a self–selfobject relationship to give him the strength required to perform his mission of vengeance. In connection with this line of thought, Eissler called attention to the special nature of the relationship between Hamlet and the Ghost. As Eissler (1971) stated: "Upon reflection, it will be seen that the Ghost behaves toward Hamlet in a way that must necessarily provoke ambivalence" (p. 67).

Eissler goes on to say:

The conscious memory Hamlet had of his father was of the man who had defeated Fortinbras and slain the Poles, who tenderly loved his wife and was an ideal husband; yet now Hamlet hears that this idealized father had not been able to keep his wife faithful, had been cuckolded, all the while that he himself had lived up to all the restrictions traditionally imposed on man's sexual life. Moreover, the heretofore omnipotent parent is now smarting in purgatory and lamenting his fate. Hamlet is suddenly face to face with a castrated, weak, and defeated father, who treats him harshly, who neither expresses the slightest sign of pity, love, or affection for his son nor mentions the son's claim to the throne, but rather imposes on him a demand that is couched exclusively in terms of the father's own self-interest. [p. 68].

These remarks offer an explanation of Hamlet's inability to act in accord with the commandments uttered by the father-ghost. Thus, from the view of the self of Hamlet, his experience of the ghost did not offer him sufficient strength to execute the necessary acts to revenge his father's death. The ghost for Hamlet was an inadequate selfobject, unable to be idealized sufficiently to serve as an idealized parent imago. Thus, Hamlet is faced with a milieu bereft of appropriate or available selfobjects to bolster his weakened self. Ultimately, Hamlet's mother performs the needed selfobject mirroring function— even as she is dying—and Hamlet's self, now energized, can destroy the father-killer, Claudius. The "Hamlet problem," the complex of the man unable to act, recounts the problem of modern man in search of self-enhancement.

Finally, I submit it is important to offer a rationale for this reinterpretation of the Hamlet tragedy. Just as historical figures are interpreted anew in each generation by critics of history, so too are poets' heroes reinterpreted by the current generation of historians and psychoanalysts. Thus it is hoped that this interpretation of Hamlet from the view of self psychology offers an addition—not correction—to the psychological understandings of the tragedy that have been offered by previous psychoanalytic authors. Whereas their views reflect the psychoanalytic thinking of their generation, this chapter is an attempt to understand Shakespeare's tragedy of Hamlet using one of the psychoanalytic views of this generation.

REFERENCES

Bradley, A. C. (1904), *Shakespearean Tragedy*. London: MacMillan, 1924.

Eissler, K. (1971), *Discourses on Hamlet and Hamlet*. New York: International Universities Press.

Erikson, E. (1962). Youth, fidelity and diversity. *Daedalus*, 91:5–27.

Erlich, A. (1977), *Hamlet's Absent Father*. Princeton, NJ: Princeton University Press.

The Folger Library General Reader's Shakespeare (1958), *The Tragedy of Hamlet, Prince of Denmark*, by William Shakespeare. New York: Washington Square Press.

Freedman, N., & Jones, R. M. (1963), On the mutuality of the Oedipus complex: Notes on the Hamlet case. *American Imago*, 20:107–131.

Freud, S. (1900). Interpretation of dreams. Standard Edition, 465. London: Hogarth Press, 1953.

Goethe, J. W. (1899), *Wilhelm Meister*. London: Chapman & Hall.

Hawkes, T., ed. (1959), *Coleridge's Writings on Shakespeare*. New York: G. P. Putnam's Sons.

Jenkins, H., ed. (1982), *The Arden Shakespeare, Hamlet*. ed. New York: Methuen and Company.

Jones, E. (1949), *Hamlet and Oedipus*. New York: Norton.

Knight, L. C. (1961), *An Approach to Hamlet*. Stanford, CA: Stanford University Press.

Kohut, H. (1971), *Analysis of the Self*. New York: International Universities Press.

——— (1977), *Restoration of the Self*. New York: International Universities Press.

Lacan, J. (1977), Desire and the interpretation of desire in Hamlet. In: *Literature and Psychoanalysis*, ed. S. Felman. Baltimore, MD: Johns Hopkins University Press.

Leverenz, D. (1980), The woman in Hamlet: An interpersonal view. In: *Representing Shakespeare*, ed. M. M. Schwartz & C. Kahn. Baltimore: John Hopkins University Press.

Lidz, T. (1975), *Hamlet's Enemy—Madness and Myth in Hamlet*. New York: Basic Books.

Wilson, J. D. (1935), *What Happens in "Hamlet"?* Cambridge: Cambridge University Press.

Wirtz, M. (1966), *Hamlet and the Philosophy of Literary Criticism*. Cleveland: Median Books.

Chapter 15

Exhibitionism in Group Psychotherapy

Deborah Weinstein

As a self-psychologically oriented psychotherapist, I currently lead a coeducational therapy group for high functioning adults, ages 25 to 50, that has been operating continuously for 15 years. The members of the group usually stay in the group for several years and are either in individual treatment with me concurrently or have terminated individual treatment with me, or are in concurrent individual treatment with a close colleague. I have found self psychological understanding to be invaluable in analyzing what occurs in the group and what appears to be curative. Mirroring, idealizing, and alterego transferences manifest in group therapy as well as individual therapy, and both modalities done concurrently benefit many patients (Weinstein, 1987). I would first like to review briefly a few theoretical premises, and then share an extraordinary event that occurred last year in our group, and to analyze the event from a self psychological perspective, specifically focusing on the grandiose, exhibitionistic line of development.

It is generally held among group therapists writing from a self psychological view, that the increased number of available selfobjects provided in a group setting can offer, for a narcissistically vulnerable patient, an increased opportunity for optimal response, which can lead to increased psychic-structure building. There are many individuals on whom a group patient can transfer his mirroring needs, indeed the experience of having eight sets of empathic eyes focused on one can be experienced as an intense dose of mirroring. Of course,

219

the possibilities of being retraumatized expand in a group setting as well, compared to the relatively safe environment of the individual session. This is where the skill of the group therapist plays an important part in modeling empathy and in intervening if a response within the group seems to be too retraumatizing to an individual. In individual work, a patient can report retraumatizations or injuries from his or her life or from the therapeutic interaction, but in a group, the therapist can see both parties involved in the hurtful interaction and can more clearly assess the intrapsychic contributing factors to the event. I have used the analogy of the difference between hearing from your child about a problem with another child, and actually accompanying your child to the playground to see first hand what goes wrong.

In addition to increased negative and positive mirroring opportunities in a group setting, idealization needs can be fulfilled and examined in interesting ways in a group setting. There are many group members to idealize (or devalue if that is the transferential need), as well as the therapist, as well as the group-as-a-whole, which can become an internalized imago. Meyers (1978) posits that the merger with an idealized group-as-a-whole offers a patient a kind of safety that allows temporary suspension of his or her mirroring vulnerabilities and encourages risk in an environment where risk taking is the valued behavior. I can also report from individual sessions with members of my group that the group-as-a-whole can function as a parental idealized imago, present when a patient needs to conjure up courage to take risks outside of the group. Knowing that the group-as-a-whole awaits the retelling of a certain event can be experienced as a soothing safety net. Of course, anticipating the censure of the group can lead as well to all manner of acting out (such as no-shows, etc.).

The thwarted alterego needs of individual patients can perhaps best of all be met in a group setting. In individual sessions, the patient may feel inhibited by the unspoken limits on the therapist's self-disclosure, whereas in group the patient can indulge his or her need to find out if he or she is similar to others in the group by asking directly about the group members themselves. Yalom (1970) called this universal group need "welcome to the human race." Kohut (1984) saw this line of narcissistic development as crucial to developing skills and tools for life and, more profoundly, for feeling a part of humanity. Including new members in the circle, creating subgroup cliques, and fear of being different can all be examined and elucidated with an understanding of the alterego needs of group members. Likewise, the interpersonal skills of communication and empathy are the skills and tools learned in group, and are always being taught by negative or positive example, with or without the intervention of the therapist.

With this brief review of some of the basic applications of self psychological selfobject transferences in a group setting, I want to report now on an unusual and profound experience that took place in our group and from which I believe we can learn a great deal. Namely, that if we follow the lead of our patients and empathically attune ourselves to their needs in a group setting, much as we would in an individual session, no matter how out of the ordinary these needs might seem, we can allow the unfolding of the pathognomonic transferences that the group members need to make in order to continue their development that has been derailed. We can allow the group-self to solidify, that is, the group as an organism with its own boundaries, and its own self-cohesion-fragmentation spectrum. We can help individual group members heal their psychic wounds.

One night during a group meeting, a member named Ruth complained that our group was getting dull for her, that she envied other groups she had heard of, which were more activity oriented, where they would go on camping trips together and get to know each other in another setting, or bring in parts of their lives for each other to see, like their hobbies or avocational interests. A giggle went through the room, an excited, uncomfortable ripple of energy. I was silent but smiling and affected by the excitement. Ruth saw the reaction she was getting and was delighted. She was characteristically shy in group and from a family whose parents absolutely never asked for, or listened to, her ideas or opinions. "Yes, I think we should have a hobby night," she declared. General laughter followed, then silence, and then animated agreement with this idea. Several members spoke at once, but the general notion was, yes, we all talk about our avocations, but we never really *see* them. I was fascinated that this suggestion came from Ruth, whose parents disapproved strongly of her serious pursuit of piano and dance. (They felt she should be working full time at a corporate job where she could gain security, benefits, and "a future.") Also, Ruth's struggle within group focused almost exclusively on her mirroring issues, that is, learning to tolerate group attention without experiencing her exposure of affect as humiliating, or the group's recognition as overstimulating. She had been pouring more and more time and money into music and dance lessons, and had kept this as a painful secret from her parents.

A more Freudian or classically oriented psychotherapist would have tended to see this excited suggestion as having exhibitionistic and voyeuristic meanings. He or she probably would have focused on what stages of psychosexual development the fantasies represented, what was really being seen or what the patient wanted to see, and which defenses were being used in response to these impulses. The psychotherapist probably would have assumed that to actually have a "hobby night" in group would be "acting in," and would prevent a more mature analysis and sublimation of the impulses that created the idea in the first place. Rather than conceptualizing her suggestion and the group's response as a regressive wish to exhibit, that is, as an undesirable or immature representation of infantile longings, the clinical stance I took was self psychologically informed. I did not focus on the sexual implications behind the wish to exhibit or the possible rivalrous meanings in her suggesting that "siblings" exhibit to each other in "mother's" presence.

Instead, I chose to hear the need Ruth was expressing and the immediate enthusiasm of the group for her idea as a multifaceted, whole-group longing for attunement to grandiose exhibitionistic needs. To allow the transference to unfold and not to interpret the suggestion as resistance was the avenue to more insights. As I discovered later, there were infinitely complex reasons for, reactions to, and repercussions from the "hobby night" idea. But rather than discourage the idea, I treated it the way I would have if a patient had brought in a painting or a poem to show me in an individual session. Here is a piece of important transferential material; let's understand together the needs that this represents. Rather than my focus being on avoiding the gratification of the patient's exhibitionism (so as not to ruin the analysis of the wish), and perhaps in the process of withholding this gratification, retraumatizing the patient or perhaps recreating a shameful response for wanting mirroring in the first place, I would find out all I could about the desired response, and the meanings, and I would assume that a need to be mirrored in the present, within the transference, was driving the patient to expose his vulnerable product to me. Appreciation of artistic efforts, rather than thwarting analytic insight, can often be experienced as optimal responsiveness or attunement to deeply held feelings, allowing the therapeutic environment to feel safer for further expressions of deep affect. In an accepting environment where preoedipal grandiosity can be exhibited in the transference, the original unmet needs can be explored, understood and responded to optimally (Bacal, 1984).

The remainder of that group session was spent in enlivened planning of the evenings, where each member could exhibit his or her own beloved hobby. We decided we would spend our next two sessions processing any feelings about the anticipation of hobby night and allowing members preparation time of several weeks. Then three would share during one, two-hour group and three more would share the following week. Some fears emerged immediately and everyone talked about what he or she would exhibit to the group. Inadvertently, I assumed that one member, Ruth, would be sharing her piano playing, and made some reference to that.

The next week brought a slew of feelings to discuss. Some group members were still excited by the idea, others were apprehensive. Ruth seemed closed off and slightly hostile. When I asked how she was feeling, she was pouty and said she felt resentful that I had assumed she would be sharing her music. The group responded quickly and pointed out how automatically Ruth assumed she would have to meet my expectations, no matter what her preference was. Even though her idea to have hobby night was being actualized by the group and she was obviously having an impact, Ruth found it difficult to avoid feeling the old constrained experience of her family life, where she was always expected to do as her parents wished, regardless of her own preferences. The empathic break caused by my erroneous assumption led to archaic retrenching into a piqued, sullen stance, which was the pervasive mood of her childhood. Once I verbalized this and called my assumption presumptuous, Ruth asserted vehemently "That's right!" She would share her dancing and clearly this choice was an important autonomy statement for her.

As each person spoke that night, anxieties emerged. Each had considered a few options during the week. Common themes surfaced: Would others really appreciate my hobby? Would I flub my presentation? Would I be better than everybody else? Who would Deborah think was best? Toni said that she had never felt so competitive in her whole life as she had felt in the past week, anticipating hobby night. Toni was the newest member in group and had been in intensive therapy with me for three years before joining group. Her mirroring transference had progressed from a merger transference—where she could never have tolerated the notion that I existed in another setting outside of the office, no less that I was also the therapist for other people—to a more mature mirroring transference. This fluctuated from a preoedipal emphasis on overstimulation of her grandiosity, to a more oedipally tinged emphasis on sibling rivalry and competition. For her, this opportunity to exhibit to the group her talent as a composer and singer evoked her already strong anxieties regarding being overstimulated. Given that Toni never even played her piano when her neighbors were home for fear they would hear her, I was surprised and intrigued at her willingness, even eagerness, to exhibit to the group, and at her articulate and revealing declaration of competitive strivings. The group ended the evening with discussions about borrowing various equipment from each other, as well as jokes about how much material this event had already given the group to discuss.

The next group meeting was concerned with more urgent matters in several group members' lives, with about 45 minutes devoted to discussing and anticipating "hobby night." Everyone anticipated it enthusiastically, as well as with other more ambivalent feelings, mostly performance anxiety. The plan was that next week, Ruth was to show a videotape of her dancing in a city competition, Adam would bring an audiotape of his synthesizer music, and Kathy would share her macrame and selections from her collection of quotes. The following week, Tim would bring examples of his prize-winning begonias and provide a horticultural minilecture, Toni would bring an audiotape of a song she had arranged, accompanying herself on piano, and Diane would share what she could of her dance career, past and present.

What was not immediately apparent to me was that, unconsciously, each person would bring to the group an unintegrated, split-off, devalued, or disavowed aspect of his or her self, represented by the hobby each chose to share. The urge and need to reveal the parts of their selves that were most vulnerable and most needing attunement and validation was unerring, often unconscious, and without exception, touching. Each member was hoping, consciously or unconsciously, to receive optimum mirroring for an unintegrated aspect of the self in an effort to knit together an affect-laden and split-off part of the self. In bringing a visible piece of their outside life into group, each individual was attempting to bring more of what was inside out, to the light, to the scrutiny of the group. The group-as-a-whole was hoping, I believe, to do three things: most importantly, to receive mirroring and attunement for their grandiose exhibitionistic selves; second, to benefit from idealizing one another as talented and thus merging with a bigger-than-life, idealized group-imago; and lastly, to create an experience of sameness among themselves, thus further solidifying the group.

At last, hobby night arrived and I was eager for group to start that evening at 6:30. However, very unusually, a curt message from Ruth appeared on my phone machine tape late that afternoon, an hour before group. "I won't be able to make group tonight. I'm not feeling well. Bye." Well, I thought, Adam and Kathy will have the whole two hours tonight. An hour later, just before I was leaving my office to go to the group, Adam called. He was not coming to group tonight, the all-stars game was on, he was going to watch it with his sons, and anyway, he wasn't prepared. I didn't linger on the phone with him as

I thought it best to deal with whatever was being acted out later in group, not separately with Adam on the phone.

When I came to group, three of the four members were eager to proceed without the two missing performers. But Kathy (the macrame artist) was disheartened at the two no-shows. She did not want to perform alone. Part of her pleasure in anticipating hobby night had been in imagining the sense of belonging she would have as a threesome of nervous "performers." As she said this, she choked back tears and then revealed her pain at being deserted by the others. Living alone, finding friendships hard to create, aloneness was a painful topic for Kathy, and somehow this scenario of anticipating camaraderie only to be followed by disappointment was an all too common experience for her.

The other three group members responded with punitive fantasies toward the two truant members, then seemed sobered by our predicament. Had we as a group bitten off more than we could chew? Was everyone's performance anxiety stronger than we were willing to admit? Would we ever actually have hobby night or were we doomed to discuss it forever in some kind of self-created purgatory? Why were we presently discussing these issues, when it was obvious that the acting-out absent parties needed to discuss these issues, not us? Should we spend the next session discussing Ruth and Adam's absences or should we allow them to present their hobbies? Would we be too angry and unreceptive to them to enjoy their offerings? Already, submerged themes of shame at feeling let down or disappointed in their attempts to be mirrored were being acted out by the disgruntled members. The extra "charge" or readiness to feel fooled or shamed was obvious. The vulnerability of the group after taking on such an assignment was clear. We left group with more questions than answers and decided to just see what happened the next week.

When all six members appeared bright and early for group the next week, laden with audiovisual aids, there was a palpable excitement in the group and the mood was festive and forgiving. I suggested that we talk about the absences last week and Ruth volunteered first to discuss hers. She had given it some thought, and honestly didn't know whether her sudden illness last week was a somatization of her anxiety or whether she really did have the flu. Her guess was that she was very nervous in anticipating a lot of exposure. I remarked that she didn't seem very nervous tonight. Yes, she agreed—she was more eager than nervous. Could her delay in presenting have anything to do with that? I asked. Ruth looked a little sheepish and said, "You know I do think I needed some more control." When asked about this, she associated to childhood. "We moved eight times and each time I got half-a-day's notice. Maybe just slowing all this down one week was something I needed." I also thought, but did not interpret to her, that perhaps seeing her own idea to have hobby night actualized was overstimulating to her. The group members remarked on how they had felt "left high and dry" last week, and then turned to Adam to include him in the admonishment. "I'll deal with my part in this when I present—OK?" he said. Yes, the group was eager to see Ruth's presentation and they seemed to feel satisfied with her explanation of her motives for not showing up last week.

What followed was a very exposing, five-minute videotape of Ruth dancing with her dance partner who also is her boyfriend. The group knew she had a boyfriend but Ruth had had a hard time sharing much about their relationship with the group. What the group did know was that her parents didn't know she was sexually involved with him, though they had been living together for a year. The reason this was kept secret was that Ruth is Caucasian and her boyfriend is Black. After the spirited tape was shown, the group applauded. Ruth beamed. "I had no idea you were so talented!" "Your boyfriend's cute!" "How can you remember all those steps?" "Aren't you nervous when the judges are watching?" The first level of comments were exclamatory and Ruth clearly enjoyed the attention. When the room settled I wondered aloud whether anyone learned anything new about Ruth by watching the video.

Several group members offered similar observations: Inside the shy, easily blushing woman they knew in group, was a sexy, lively woman who, in the realm of dance, could celebrate her sexuality and her desire to shine and to be applauded. It was clear to me that the tape was doubly exposing—here is my body-self expressing joy, sexuality, grandiosity. And here is my Black boyfriend for all of you to see—an openly rebellious act, kept quite secret from her southern army officer father and conservative mother.

One person remarked on how, by sitting on pillows and staying on our own seats all night in group, we never really get to see how each other moves. "We sort of don't have legs," someone said, "or groins," someone else quickly added, accompanied by group laughter. I asked if the sexiness of Ruth's dancing referred to by another group member created any feelings. The men laughed and the one gay man shouted "not in me," and again the mood was festive and light. The most important part of Ruth's work was her willingness to risk exhibiting the joyous, body-self to the group, and to take in their appreciation of her. The enormity of the risk was apparent to me, first revealed by her absence the week before, evident in her blushing during the showing of the tape, and by the visibly expanded self I could see during the applause. In front of judges, it was easier to reveal this, but here, where there were transferences at work, the risk was higher. Coming from a repressive family where sexuality was ignored and/or shame laden, Ruth was using the group to mirror her womanhood, to see and accept her boyfriend, to help her integrate her own conflicted feelings about her sexuality, her choice of avocation, and her rebellion against her family's values.

The next presenter was Kathy, whose childhood was marked by social isolation. She recalls that her parents had no friends. She cannot recall one time in her entire childhood when anyone outside of her family came to dinner. As an adult, Kathy is a 35-year-old virgin, totally isolated socially when she first came to group two years ago, who is slowly attempting to reach out to others, and to melt down her insulation of obesity. She did not often show her crafts to others, and took her quilt and macrame out of their bags with a careful reverence that spoke volumes about how these art pieces represented a precious part of her self. As she told the story behind her artistic choices, she got teary and admitted how crucial it was to her to be doing this with the other two performers, to feel a part of a group. She then shared a few favorite quotes she had collected and told us about her years of quote collecting. At this point, a group member remarked that each of her three hobbies was a solitary activity. It was clear that this opportunity to exhibit her hobby was an invitation to her to be less solitary with her creativity, to experience it not only as an outlet and a solace in her solitude, but as a bridge with which to connect to others. The slow, slightly hesitant way in which she unwrapped her pieces to show them to the group represented to me her difficulty in unwrapping her most prized parts of herself for public scrutiny.

Intrapsychically in her individual sessions, she was working through her inhibitions about exhibiting herself (her best parts) to others. She was working through her fear of retraumatization, her fear of not being appreciated. In Kathy's individual and group work, she was attempting to make herself more available to men, to reach out more for contact, to make friends of both sexes. Showing what is "precious" about her to others metaphorically and literally in this exercise was crucial to her development. Her intrapsychic work involved acknowledging her own strengths and internalizing positive mirroring from her therapy so that she could begin to value herself. "Was showing us your art work difficult for you?" I asked. A soft "yes, very" followed. It was indeed one more hard-won step for Kathy toward a life with people, one that I could see was self-esteem enhancing.

Finally, it was Adam's turn to present his synthesizer music. Instead of this, Adam surprised the group with his opening statement. "I didn't bring anything. I'm embarrassed but I didn't have any time." The group was agitated and someone said "bullshit." "Now I realize how pissed off I am at everyone," Adam declared. "I feel like no one knows what it's like to run your own business, manage a marriage, raise two kids. I don't have time to keep up my hobby. I said I play the synthesizer just to fit in, but I haven't in years, really, not in any concentrated way. None of you have families and I feel all this censure about not coming last week, and not having anything prepared this week, and I was sure no one would buy that either." There was silence, a softer one than I think he had anticipated.

We were hearing his pain under the anger. He must have felt this silent empathic response because his next comments were less defensive and even more exposing. "I feel like a has-been. I never have time to do anything anymore that feels creative. I spend all my time maintaining my life and trying to raise my boys and spend some time with them, like my father never did with me." "And you call that *not* creative?" I asked. "It seems to me you're having to create your relationship with your boys out of nothing—no models from your own childhood." As if on cue, Adam smiled and said he had thrown a videotape of his boys in the car when he was leaving for group "just in case he felt like showing it" and he'd like to show it now. The group encouraged him, and what followed was an eight-minute talent show of silly jokes and antics by his 6- and 8-year-old boys, with Adam's voice from behind the camera interacting with the boys on the video. There was banter, "knock-knock" jokes, and obvious fun in the tape; we were getting a first-hand view of Adam's fathering style and his rapport with his boys. His history with his own father had been explored several times in his year in group and was characterized by humiliation, discomfort and estrangement. The easy hilarity in this tape showed a marked contrast to his own history and surprised the group.

During the discussion after the tape, group members pointed out how often Adam told of the problems with his boys and of his faults as a father and how little emphasis he gave to his accomplishments as a parent. Adam expanded on this to say he often devalued his own accomplishments and the ways in which he spent his time, and failed to see the value in his own efforts at maintaining a family. His stance in group this night had been belligerent and defensive at first, then vulnerable enough to offer a glimpse of what he wanted help in valuing in his own life and self. Months after this night in group, Adam still carried with him more appreciation of his devotion to his children; he was allowing himself to idealize himself as a parent. His self-esteem continued to grow as he internalized more mirroring experiences in the group.

The next week's group began with anticipatory excitement but without some of the nervousness of the first hobby night. We had broken some ice and exhibiting accomplishments to each other was a little less taboo by now.

Tim had planned to show us his prize-winning flowers and to focus on his interest in horticulture. But because of the delays in doing hobby night, our group happened to fall on the night before Tim was due to get back his results on his AIDS test, which he and his lover had taken three weeks prior. As the only gay man in group and the longest member of the group, Tim had always played the role of the "group historian." He was often teased about this, and often appreciated for his ability and need to put into chronological order the sequence of events, the comings and goings in group, and to offer his group-as-a-whole viewpoint when the group was confused or shaky, or when no one else was able to see the whole picture. I always felt that Tim felt pressure to do this, as a way of keeping his own self cohesive. Tonight, Tim had decided spontaneously not to bring his flowers, but to share his "attic trunk" with us. He began to reveal a collection of memorabilia of his life that was remarkable in its personal, historical significance. Here were newspaper headlines with momentous events of the Bay of Pigs, Kennedy's assassination, and the moon landing saved for his children. He poignantly remarked on the fact that he didn't understand at that time that he was gay and would have no children. Here were high school letters, pictures, baby teeth, a favorite cat's tail, a box of report cards.

In Tim's exhibiting his past to us in such a concrete way, I was reminded of Kohut's (1977) case of Mr. W, (p. 167) who describes the contents of his pockets in such detail to his analyst that Kohut interprets this to himself as an archaic need for mirroring, like a little boy emptying his pockets, wanting the parent to be fascinated with each collected and treasured item.

Tim's offering of his past and his collections revealed that being an historian was a role he had played his whole life and probably helped him to compensate for his distracted mother's faulty mirroring and to keep his own sense of self-cohesion over time. I think there was an additional, poignant, unconscious motivation for his last-minute change in plans in bringing his attic trunk to us—and that was his own need to review his life, and to be affirmed in his own appreciation of his life. He needed a validation of his self-worth on the eve of the day he might find out that his life would end prematurely. Given the shame-laden connotation accompanying the diagnosis of AIDS, the need for bolstering his sense of self-esteem was urgent and the vulnerability of exhibiting his personal history in an effort to cement his sense of self-cohesion was touching.

The group tone went back and forth, from amused to reverent, depending on what Tim pulled out of his attic chest. No one made the connection between his impending test results and his choice for hobby night. When I asked why he had chosen to do this, his answer was flippant—"I had to clean out my attic sometime." I chose not to pursue it.

The next presenter was Diane. She began by saying she was going to "start with what she could do now," and that is teach dance. And then she would show us her scrapbook of her past career, a subject she almost never even alluded to in group. "Everyone up," she said. For the next five minutes Diane led us in a dancer's "warm up." For a few group members, it was their first experience with any dance class. There was some nervous giggling and I noticed, being next to Diane, that she was shaking. Several members commented on how she kept the beat exactly, and how she seemed confident. "Well, you can't admit when you're performing that you're nervous, but I can as a teacher. I'm nervous," she declared. When we sat down, she pulled out her scrapbook of her ballet career and what we saw was a much younger Diane, in full performance costume and beautiful ballerina poses. The group was duly impressed, oohing and ahing at her classical beauty, asking questions about the performance world. Diane's affect was sad, not at all the kind of happy exhibitionism one might imagine resulting from the positive mirroring.

I remarked on the difference in her mood and ours. Almost immediate tears followed. Diane closed the book and told us the story of why she had left dance for the corporate world, and had only recently started teaching at a local high school in her free time. After four years of constant work in her late adolescence, Diane had auditioned for a job in a ballet company and had been turned down. What made it even more painful was that the head teacher and auditioner was a close friend of her mother's. "I wonder if she had known how little I got from my mom, would she have favored the other girls in class or been so aloof with me." There were tears in her voice, and she concluded with "I might look good in these photos, but I wasn't good enough." The room was sobered, silent. Tim ventured reassurance. It fell flat. Ruth offered praise for how Diane taught us. That seemed to help her reconstitute a bit. "Yeah, I do enjoy that. You know the truth is, I never really *enjoyed* performing, I mean, it made me nervous and you couldn't see the audience." She was starting to enlist us in valuing her real abilities. After exhibiting the picture perfect grandiosity of the photographs, the modified grandiosity of her teaching abilities could begin to be psychologically integrated as she brought her real abilities to the group, which represented the reality ego. The shame-laden defeat, the conflictual feelings about being a performer, the attempt at a more realistic expression of her abilities as a teacher were brought to the group in an effort to integrate the difficult affect and to value her abilities and temper her grandiosity through optimal mirroring.

The last presenter was Toni. I was most apprehensive about her performance. In individual sessions, I knew she was struggling with overstimulating grandiose fantasies of being the best in the group. She seemed to wish this and fear this intensely. As a child, she was all but ignored in her family, except when she would be exuberant and then stern admonishment would follow. Her mother cared almost exclusively about how Toni looked, buying her clothes and constantly criticizing her dress and hair. Clearly, Toni had rebelled unconsciously by identifying with her father—and by getting quite obese in adolescence. Now she was a slim adult, but her mannerisms and language were extremely masculinized. After three years of intensive two-times-a-week psychotherapy, Toni was just becoming able to admit that much of her depression was related to longing for a boyfriend, and to admit that a mate and children were deeply desired. Before, any tenderness, femininity, or experience of being womanly was disavowed and pushed away in our sessions.

Toni presented an audiotape of her arrangement of a popular song, accompanying herself on the piano. If I didn't trust her morals completely, I honestly could have imagined that Toni had bought a tape of a professional blues singer to substitute for her own efforts. We all sat amazed while Toni, in her characteristic tomboy attire and stance, smiled shyly. Here was a full-throated, steamy, passionate, tender, and womanly voice, full of longing and depth. Her abilities were remarkable, but more psychologically significant was the split off, compartmentalized aspect of her feminine identity. Unable to admit to any of these feelings for years in our therapy and actually disdainful of them, they were being expressed in her art, in a very powerful, if disowned, way. Clearly, her choice for hobby night was a "coming out" for her. In watching our faces intently, Toni was, I believe, looking for permission to have these feelings, to be proud of them, to integrate her adult sexuality and her femininity into her self-concept.

The sessions wherein group members presented their hobbies provided a forum in which all members of the group could expose the grandiose self in the hopes of being optimally responded to. For Toni, for instance, this meant risking exposure to reality, instead of keeping her grandiose, exhibitionistic self cloistered away from the reality ego (represented by the group) in the hopes of maintaining equilibrium with a private grandiose fantasy. For others, the hope was for validation for an undervalued aspect of the self, or for help in solidifying the body-self positive concept, or in firming up the sense of cohesion over the time line of life. In a group effort to modify the grandiose self to a "mature form," all of the participants risked vulnerable exposure. Unconsciously, each brought in some shame-laden mirroring issue in the hopes of getting healed through optimal mirroring.

I believe this event in our group was important for many of the participants in different ways. There was carry-over in their outside lives. Toni began to examine more openly her relationship to her sexuality and her "feminine side" and to more directly pursue contact with men. Ruth began her own dance club and used the interpersonal skills she learned in group to create her new environment. Kathy became more assertive in her pursuit of friendships, both with men and women, and joined a few social groups for that purpose. Tim's AIDS test was negative, but he became much more active in the gay community and even started his own leaderless, gay men's group after he terminated with our group. It seemed to me that the opportunity to explore so directly their grandiose exhibitionistic wishes, defenses and fears in our group was an important confidence-building step for many participants. Psychologically, it seemed to provide a launching pad into more social involvement, leadership, and ambition in their outside lives.

There was something more innocent and raw in the group presentations than in comparable transference material in individual sessions. The channeling of the grandiose, exhibitionistic wishes into creative pursuits is one thing to report about in an individual session. It is quite another to exhibit your cherished representation of your valued self in a group setting. The stakes seemed at once higher—in that each participant was risking "real life" feedback about their accomplishments—and also safer, because each group member knew that others were risking too. This put the patients on more of an equal footing than any patient would have been in an individual session, where the therapist would not be equally vulnerable or exposed.

The group-as-a-whole became more bonded through the alterego experience of belonging and of creating an event together. Individually, the members became more idealizable to each other, as talented and multifaceted, as well as more trusted in responding to each other's risky exposures. As a leader, I was most impressed with the reminder that the patient will unerringly lead us to the wounded self and the derailed development, if we only have the wisdom to follow.

REFERENCES

Bacal, H. (1984), Optimal responsiveness and the therapeutic process. In: *Progress in Self Psychology*, Vol. 1, ed. A. Goldberg. New York: Guilford Press.

Kohut, H. (1984), *How Does Analysis Cure?* ed. A. Goldberg & P. Stepansky. Chicago: University of Chicago Press.

Meyers, S. (1978), The disorders of the self: developmental and clinical considerations. *Group*, 2:131–140.

Weinstein, D. (1987), Self psychology and group therapy. *Group*, 11/3:144–154.

Yalom, I. (1970), *The Theory and Practice of Group Psychotherapy*. New York: Basic Books.

Author Index

Subject Index

239